Herodotus

The tale of the great Persian war from the histories of Herodotus

Herodotus

The tale of the great Persian war from the histories of Herodotus

ISBN/EAN: 9783741162961

Manufactured in Europe, USA, Canada, Australia, Japa

Cover: Foto ©ninafisch / pixelio.de

Manufactured and distributed by brebook publishing software (www.brebook.com)

Herodotus

The tale of the great Persian war from the histories of Herodotus

THE GREAT PERSIAN WAR

LONDON
PRINTED BY SPOTTISWOODE AND CO.
NEW-STREET SQUARE

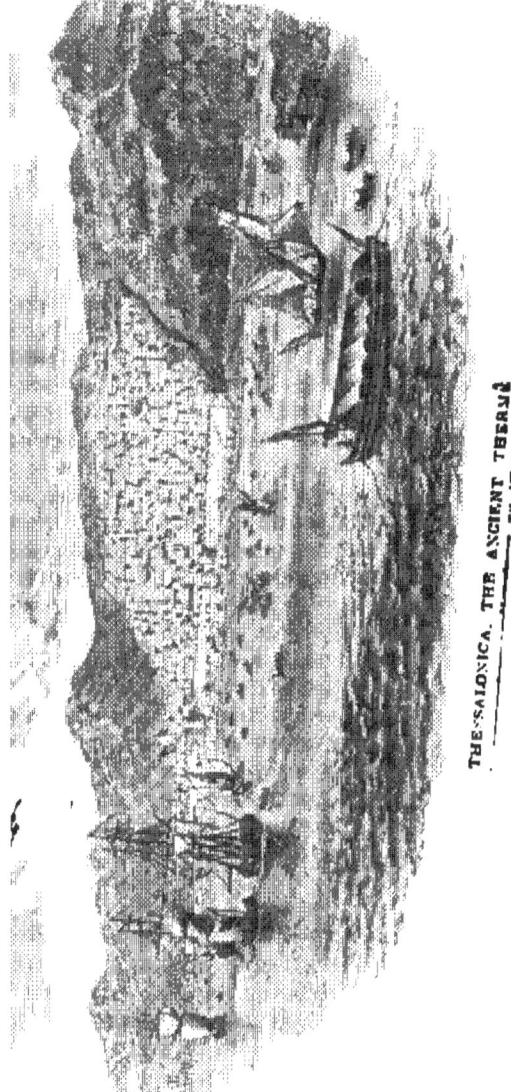

THESSALONICA, THE ANCIENT THERMA

THE TALE

OF

THE GREAT PERSIAN WAR

FROM THE HISTORIES OF HERODOTUS

BY THE REV. GEORGE W. COX, M.A.
Late Scholar of Trinity College, Oxford

GRAECIA BARBARIAE LENTO COLLISA DUELLO

LONDON
LONGMAN, GREEN, LONGMAN, AND ROBERTS
1861

TO

EDWARD A. FREEMAN, M.A.

Late Fellow of Trinity College, Oxford

THIS VOLUME

IS AFFECTIONATELY INSCRIBED

IN GRATEFUL ACKNOWLEDGMENT OF A LONG AND TRIED
FRIENDSHIP

PREFACE.

THERE are few, perhaps, who, even in the first reading, have failed to perceive something of the beauty which pervades the histories of Herodotus, —few who have not felt the deep religious sentiment, the sympathy for unmerited suffering, the keen appreciation of all pure and lofty motives, the strict impartiality towards friend or foe, which pre-eminently characterise his writings. But there are probably still fewer in whom the first perusal has not left an impression of strange incoherence and incongruity. The mention of each fresh king, or city, or people leads into long and apparently arbitrary digressions; and a narrative of the struggle between Greece and Persia is introduced by an account of all the wars and battles of the world. His work assumes the appearance of history within history, of legend within legend, until the existence of any connecting principle seems doubtful or impossible. Soon, however, the reader begins to perceive, first, that a distinct religious conviction underlies each personal history, and then that the same moral sentiment is found in every episode of personal adventure. The jealousy of the gods who will not suffer pride to go too long unchecked, or wealth and happiness too long unbroken,—the inevitable course of a destiny which bears sway over the majesty of Zeus himself,— the influence, sometimes kindly, sometimes malignant, which the gods exercise over men,— the retributive justice which visits the sins of the forefathers on their guiltless or devout posterity,— the reverent caution which refuses to call any man during this life happy,—all make up a body of religious belief which supplies not only a theological creed, but also a system of moral philosophy. And presently he will see that this religious sentiment is not confined to personal history. The national fortunes of Greeks and Lydians, Persians and Egyptians, exhibit the working of the same laws and teach the same religious lessons. If after this he cares to follow the track which opens before him, he will see that this moral or theological conviction has imparted to his history a strictly epical unity : he will see that from the beginning to the end there is a chain of cause and effect, quite distinct from that sequence of human and political motive which we are wont to regard as the mainspring of history. He will learn to trace the working of this moral power from the legends of Io or Europa, through the tale of Troy and of the Lydian dynasties, to the punishment which Persian arrogance brought upon itself at Delphi and Salamis and Mycalê. And, last of all, he may perceive that such a conviction, so wide yet so penetrating, so comprehensive in its general survey, yet so careful of minute detail, can never have originated in the historian himself; that, to whatever extent the strength of his genius and the purity of his mind may have heightened his moral and religious sentiment, yet the impulse must have come from without; and that, in all essential features, the historian is but the representative of the age in which he lived.

He will thus see that the historical conception of the age (if it deserves the name) was pre-eminently religious; that it sought less for the truth of actual facts than for evidence of its theological convictions; and that a narrative which met this test underwent in other respects no careful and rigorous scrutiny. The tale which proved the living jealousy of the gods, which spoke of vengeance taken on fraud or violence or overmuch prosperity, which asserted the visible interference of heavenly beings among the children of men, satisfied every condition of credibility. The story was believed if it told of marvellous sights and preternatural sounds on the earth or in the heavens: it was disbelieved if it gave no further explanation of personal or national fortunes than that which may be furnished by motives of human appetite or passion. Things beyond nature presented to that age nothing startling or strange; the absence of prodigies and wonders alone precluded the hearty acceptance of a story.

But the region of signs and portents and heavenly manifestations is also the region of poetry. The mingling of gods and men, of those men, at least, whose soul was in some way raised above the mere appetite of food and drink and sleep, is the groundwork of all epical poems, and in a special degree of the great epics of the Greek heroic ages. The mythical belief of those ages surrounded the people with an atmosphere of poetry. The bard may have surpassed his hearers in the strength of his sensations and his power of expressing them; the statesman and the general may have had a keener appreciation of their grandeur and their loveliness: but, from the greatest to the meanest, the same religious faith, the same moral convictions, appealed to the deepest feelings of their heart, and guided at once their judgment and their actions.

At no time, perhaps, has there existed a condition of thought which could with greater truth receive the name of public opinion. It was a universal belief, not as enforced by some despotic power, but as the spontaneous expression of an all-pervading faith. It was a belief which needed neither proof nor argument, for no one was conscious of a single thought which questioned or denied it; and when the course of time gradually brought into life a new power, and men became conscious of another principle of causation than that which alone they had hitherto recognised, it was long before it was felt that the new principle had in it anything antagonistic to the former. The idea of a natural order, which was impressed on them by the interchange of times and seasons, suggested no thought of a similar order in the world of men. And even when the regulated operation of physical causes had conveyed to their minds some notions of probability or impossibility, the influence of this new knowledge was very uncertain, and its application very capricious. Men could believe that Apollo quenched the fire that rose around his devout worshipper, while they would not believe that doves had spoken with human voices. They could affirm that deified heroes came back to mingle in human strife, when they would not believe that Heracles in his mortal state had slain thousands at a single blow.

It is this middle ground of unquestioning faith and an incipient historical criticism which is occupied by the great work of Herodotus. The exquisite beauty of the narrative may be his own; the poetical conception and religious sentiment he shared with the whole Hellenic family. This sentiment has moulded every part of his history, has guided him in the choice of his materials, has supplied the connecting link through the twisted chain of episodes and digressions. It has imparted a character to his language of which the peculiarity never breaks the charm, and in which a certain monotony never destroys the freshness. Such a history, it would seem, can scarcely be divested of its original form without weakening or destroying its vigour and beauty; and if presented in any other shape, it may to a greater or less degree satisfy the requirements of modern criticism, but it will not be the same history as it rose before the mind of Herodotus. We may possibly arrive at the truth of facts by a careful analysis of its materials and sifting of its evidence; but it will no longer be the narrative whose beauty is said to have extorted the applause of thousands at the great Olympic games.

This narrative, whose exquisite beauty cannot be altogether veiled in the critical histories of our own time, has perhaps not yet been presented to English readers. There are many translations of Herodotus, but no translation can be free from some at least of the many defects which seem inseparable from the work of expressing literally in one language the thoughts and feelings of another. Phrases not without force and beauty in the original become heavy and cumbrous in the translation, while natural and expressive idioms pass into unmeaning and disagreeable verbiage. And if the long episodes and complicated digressions so interrupt the march of the narrative for the reader who studies it in the original language, there can, it would seem, be no necessity to introduce the same interruptions in another. The omission of those portions of the tale which do not belong immediately to the main subject of the history, will probably give a far more faithful and vivid idea of the original narrative.

It is not a question for historical criticism. Unquestionably, the statements of the work are either credible or incredible, and we may reasonably attempt to determine the bounds and degrees of that credibility; but no analysis of its contents and no examination of its evidence can lay before the reader the palpable form which has undergone this necessary dissection. The story, as conceived by Herodotus, can be told in no other way than his own. We may criticise and compare and draw inferences from the mythical legends of Greece or Rome or Scandinavia, but to realise them fully we must also read and tell them as they are. And, while we read such narratives, we must remember that the poetical conception which they exhibit is not confined to the writer, and that all terms of praise or dispraise grounded on his poetical, or fanciful, or credulous tendencies, or his love of exaggeration and contrast, are equally erroneous. He cannot be accused of personal credulity, if his faith is but the reflection of the universal belief of his age; he cannot be charged with equivocation or falsehood, if he only remains true to the ordinary convictions of his countrymen.

This narrative, certainly one of the most beautiful that mortal hand has written down, has been examined with admirable power and judgment by the great critical historians of the present century. The religious sentiment, the human and supernatural sequence of events, with every episode and every incident, has been minutely analysed; but even in the pages of writers whom it would be presumptuous to praise, the reader will fail to find the history of Herodotus as it appears in his own pages. It is impossible that he should so find it; and the want may furnish some justification for the present attempt to clothe in an English dress, and without the restraints imposed on a professed translation, a narrative rich with all the wealth of Homeric imagery and never perhaps surpassed in the majesty of epical conception.

But the narrative of Herodotus is also, to whatever extent, a chronicle of facts. If it does not relate in the strictest sense to a wholly historical age, it speaks of a time so near to it as to leave for much of the story no reasonable doubt of its truth. In the chapters appended to the Tale of the War, this narrative has been examined, not in any vain effort to rival or depreciate the invaluable histories of Dr. Thirlwall and Mr. Grote, yet in the hope that it may tend to settle some points which they have left uncertain, and to present in a different light some facts to which they would seem to have given an unduly harsh interpretation. More perhaps than any other writer, Mr Grote has deserved the gratitude of his own and coming generations for making them feel that the history of Greece is the history of living men, and that the political and national struggles of Athens were not less real than our own, and perhaps not very different. More than any others he has made us think of Pericles and Cleon, of Nikias and of Brasidas, as we think of Harold and Stephen Langton, of Strafford and of Hampden. He will not, perhaps, regret if a less severe judgment can, consistently with historical truth, be passed on a greater man even than Pericles, though neither so pure nor so fortunate, and if at least a plea of unproven guilt can be urged for the illustrious name of Themistocles.

Some of the illustrations employed in this work have been taken, by permission, from "The Life and Epistles of St. Paul, by the Rev. W. J. Conybeare, M.A., and the Rev. J. S. Howson, M.A."

NOTE

ON THE

ORTHOGRAPHY OF GREEK NAMES.

If the right way of giving Greek names in English must be admitted to be to some extent an open question, it is still very difficult to see why for the names of Greek gods and heroes should be substituted certain Latin names with which, for the most part, they have no connection either of sound or of idea. The practice of continental scholars is more consistent than our own; but although we may be still perplexed to determine what in all cases should be the equivalents of Greek vowels and consonants, it yet seems a strange thing to introduce into Greek narrative names which can but be associated with Latin notions. The system of adhering to the Greek names of deities had been long since adopted by Dr. Thirlwall and other writers, when Mr. Grote endeavoured in his History of Greece to bring the English spelling of all Greek names into a more strict agreement with the original. In his work on Homer and the Homeric Age, Mr. Gladstone retained not merely the Latin forms for ordinary names, but once more placed Jupiter, Mars, and Minerva on the thrones of Zeus, Arês, and Athêna. Of the reasons which led him to this determination Mr. Gladstone said nothing; but Mr. Rawlinson, who in his recent work on Herodotus has followed his example, thinks that "in a work intended for general reading, unfamiliar forms were to be eschewed, and that accuracy in such matters, although perhaps more scholarlike, would be dearly purchased at the expense of harshness and repulsiveness."

It is not easy to determine with any precision what may be familiar or unfamiliar forms in the world of letters. They must necessarily vary in successive generations, or perhaps during the same generation. Yet, probably, the use of the Greek forms in translating the great epic and tragic poets is as familiar now to the boys of our public schools, as was the practice of calling Hêra Juno, and Dêmêtêr Ceres, some twenty or five-and-twenty years ago. At the least, it is a use which every year is becoming more general and more familiar; and when once the scholar has accustomed himself to adopt the Greek forms in English translation, nothing will more grate upon his ear than to hear Poseidon called Neptune, or more offend his eye than to see "Diana" written where he looks to find "Artemis." It may safely be maintained that to the readers of Homer or Herodotus generally the Greek forms are nearly if not quite as familiar as the Latin, and that the objections which may here and there be raised are fast growing weaker and will soon be abandoned.

"Harshness" and "repulsiveness," again, are qualities

which in some measure are matters of taste; yet we might be tempted to think that the terms apply far more forcibly to the Latin nomenclature than to the Greek. The former is undoubtedly good in its place; but by the side of the euphonious names of Hellas those of some at least among Latin gods and heroes may well be thought harsh and ugly, and it needs a very long practice to make their sound agreeable, although it may be familiar.

But a more serious objection to the use of the Latin forms is the confusion of ideas which it must cause in any subjects closely connected with Greek mythology. It is of less consequence to talk of Mars, Ceres, or Bacchus in Thucydides, for Arês, Dêmêtêr, and Dionysus do not much figure in his pages; but the system as applied to Homer not only introduces innumerable blemishes to offend the eye, but places side by side words which convey notions entirely contradictory. The same page will contain the names of Mars and Ascalaphus, Ialmenus and Vesta, Podaleirius and Mercury, names of which the one may be said to belong wholly to Latin, the other wholly to Greek mythology.

The question of precise English equivalents for Greek sounds is more difficult and perplexing. Yet the difficulty may perhaps appear greater than it is, although we may admit that a thoroughly consistent practice has not as yet been attained. It is not easy to overthrow Mr. Grote's arguments for using the English K even where our C will yield the same sound: for the latter, when followed by *e*, *i*, *œ*, *æ*, and *y*, is in fact another letter; and to retain C where it chances to represent K is perhaps nothing more than a weakness which may yet be pardoned. Still there are some names in which it would seem that our C must for a while be retained even where the sound yielded is wrong. The names of Cyrus, Cyprus, and Lacedæmon, are familiar sounds to the English ear; and to substitute Kyprus and Lakedæmon is perhaps unnecessarily to offend it. In such names, again, as Cyrus or Cambyses, nothing is gained by the change. The Greek forms are themselves changes, and generally corruptions, of foreign words.

In vowel equivalents, however, Mr. Grote's practice is not altogether consistent. To write Corcyra for Κέρκυρα is wrong; to write Korkyra is not right. Kerkyra would probably give the precise sound of the original to a Greek ear. The use of æ for ai may be defended as regards euphony; and the forms "Kithæron" and "Kelænæ" may more truly represent Κιθαιρών and Κελαιναί, and would, if pronounced by a German or Italian, produce the same sound.

The diphthong ei has been retained in such names as Peneius, Rheneia; but æ has been used as the equivalent for οι, in Trœzen, &c., as this form must more nearly give the sound of the original than if it were written Troizen.

As a practical rule, we may surely be permitted to adhere to the true Greek form, except in the comparatively few instances where its use might sound strange and possibly disagreeable to an English ear. In the following pages I have endeavoured to carry out this rule, without presuming to think that my practice is in all points consistent, or that it is by any means the best that may be devised. Some little time, perhaps, must yet pass before a real uniformity may be attained; but, whatever uncertainty there may be in these questions of very minor moment, there can be none in restoring Dêmêtêr to her Eleusinian home and banishing Minerva from the Alcan chapel beneath the Delphian hill.

CONTENTS.

PART I.

CHAPTER I.

The Beginnings of the Strife.—The Tales of Crœsus and Cambyses.—The Athenians regain their Freedom . Page 3

CHAPTER II.

The Fall of Polycrates.—Demokedes at Susa and at Croton 21

CHAPTER III.

The Inroad of the Persians into Scythia.—The Tale of Aristagoras and Histiæus.—Miltiades and Marathon . 34

CHAPTER IV.

The Council of Xerxes.—His Dream and its Issue.—The Tale of Pythius, his Riches and his Children.—The March of the Army, and the Passage of the Hellespont . . 56

CHAPTER V.

The Oracles of Delphi, and the Counsels of Themistocles.—The Embassies to Argos and to Syracuse.—Leonidas and Thermopylæ 87

CHAPTER VI.

The Strife of Ships and Storms at Artemisium.—The Sight-seeing at Thermopylæ.—The Persians at Delphi . Page 117

CHAPTER VII.

The Greeks at Salamis.—The Fight and Victory.—The Counsel of Mardonius.—The Flight to Sardes. . . . 129

CHAPTER VIII.

The Greatness of Themistocles and the Athenians.—Mardonius at Athens.—The Feast of Attaginus 163

CHAPTER IX.

The Gathering at Platææ.—Mardonius atones for the Death of Leonidas.—The Storming of the Persian Camp.—The Flight and Trick of Artabazus 182

CHAPTER X.

The Fight at Mycalè.—The Marvel of the Herald's Staff.—The Loves of King Xerxes at Sardes and at Susa.—The Vengeance of Protesilaüs 222

PART II.

CHAPTER I.

ON THE HISTORICAL CONCEPTION AND METHOD OF HERODOTUS.

	Page
The Object and Scope of his History	239
Mingling of Divine and Human Causes and Agency .	242
Prominence given to the Divine Element . . .	243

	Page
This Religious Sentiment imparts an Epical Unity to his History	244
Connection of Mythical and Historical Causes	246
Epical Contrasts and Coincidences	253
Epical Distribution of Merit	254

CHAPTER II.

ON THE EPICAL UNITY IN THE HISTORY OF HERODOTUS.

In the Historical Conception of Herodotus, the Sequence of Events is chiefly Ethical or Religious	255
Growth of an Historical Sense	257
Contrast between Herodotus and Thucydides	257
Intellectual Condition of the Age of Herodotus contrasted with that of Thucydides	263
Its Influence on the Credibility of his History	265
His Treatment of the old Mythical Tales	266
The Nature and Extent of his Scepticism	268
Results of the Application of Modern Critical Tests to the History of Herodotus	268
Introduction of Greek Forms of Thought into the Descriptions of Oriental Society	270

CHAPTER III.

ON THE SOURCES OF INFORMATION ACCESSIBLE TO HERODOTUS.

Distinction between History and Fiction	272
The Impartiality of Herodotus is a strong Argument for his Credibility	273
Causes which tend to modify Oral Tradition	274
Advantages of the Poetical Form for the Perpetuation of Tradition	275
Comparison of Greek and Mahometan Tradition with the Traditions of Mediæval Christendom	278
Birth and Lifetime of Herodotus	281

xxviii   CONTENTS.

	Page
Herodotus not a contemporary Historian	282
Circumstances which favour the Permanence of Oral Tradition	283
Limits to the Credibility of Herodotus	283
Authority of Public Monuments	284
Nature and Value of Greek Genealogies	286
No written Records existed contemporary with the earlier Greek Monuments	287
Evidence furnished by Works of Art	288
Value of Egyptian or Assyrian Monuments	290
Extent of their Authority and of the Evidence furnished by them	291
Limited Range of Assyrian and Persian Inscriptions	292

CHAPTER IV.

ON THE SUPERNATURAL MACHINERY IN THE HISTORY OF HERODOTUS.

Difficulties connected with the Oracular Responses	295
Amount of Evidence necessary to prove the Fact that they were delivered in the Form which has been handed down	296
Manifold Character of the Greek Oracles	298
Classification of the Oracular Responses	300
I. Enigmatical Answers	300
II. Ambiguous Answers	301
III. Answers dictated by a Calculation of Probabilities	302
IV. Answers extorted by Political and Personal Influences	303
V. Answers which enforce a Moral Principle	304
VI. Predictions made up after the Event	305
The Oracles of little Use as Historical Documents	306
Oracles relating to the last Dynasty of Lydian Kings	308
Oracles relating to the Taking of Athens by Xerxes	309
These Answers do not affect the Conduct of Themistocles	310

	Page
Poetical Literature of the Greeks before the Historical Age	313

CHAPTER V.

ON THE CAUSES AND INCIDENTS OF THE PERSIAN WAR.

Authority of Herodotus in Greek and Barbarian History respectively	314
Historical Value of recent Assyrian Discoveries	315
Character of the Historical Information obtained from them	317
Its Bearing upon the History of Herodotus	317
Historical Residuum in the Legends of Cyrus	320
The Reign of Cambyses and the Magian Usurpation	321
The Conspiracy of the Seven Persians	322
Difficulty of ascertaining Facts in all Eastern History	323
Plausible Tales of Persian Intrigue	323
Utter Uncertainty in the Details of Persian Narratives	324
The Story of Demokedes	325
The Scythian Expedition of Darius	327
The Removal of the Pæonians	330
The Story of Histiæus	330
The Complicity of Histiæus in the Schemes of Aristagoras	331
The Expedition to Naxos	333
The Ionian Revolt	335
The Taking of Miletus	336
The Treatment of the Persian Envoys at Athens and Sparta	336
The Battle of Marathon	337
The Motives of the Athenian Generals in bringing on the Battle	340
Charge of Treachery against the Alcmæonidæ	341
Change in the Character of the Narrative after the Battle of Marathon	342
The March of Xerxes to the Hellespont	345
The Numbers and Quality of his Forces	346

CONTENTS.

	Page
The Bridge across the Hellespont and the Canal of Mount Athos	348
The March of the Persians through Thrace and Macedonia	349
The Counsels of Demaratus	350
The Motives and Conduct of the Greek States and their Leaders	352
The Story of Thermopylæ	353
The Conduct of the Thebans at Thermopylæ	356
Personal Anecdotes connected with the Battle	357
Merit of Leonidas as a General	358
The Migration of the Athenians to Salamis and Trœzen	358
The Attack on Delphi	359
The Battle of Salamis	361
Ethical and Poetical Features of the Narrative	362
The History of Artemisia	364
The Counsel of Mnesiphilus	364
The Mention of Keos and Kynosûra	366
The Defeat and Flight of Xerxes	366
The Story of his Retreat	368
Policy and Motives of the Greek States	371
The Feast of Attaginus and the Story of Thersander	373
The Battle of Platææ	376
Anecdotes of Pausanias	377
Coincident Battles of Platææ and Mycalê	377
The Phêmê, or Rumour, at Mycalê	378
The Incident of the Herald's Staff	379
The Story of Xerxes and Amêstris	380

CHAPTER VI.

ON THE CHARACTER OF THE GREAT ATHENIAN LEADERS IN THE PERSIAN WAR.

Nature of the Difficulties involved in the History of Miltiades and Themistocles	384
The Athenians charged with Ingratitude towards Miltiades	385

CONTENTS.

	Page
The Charge of Ingratitude untenable	386
Their Fault lay in a Disposition to shrink from Public Responsibility	387
Element of Fiction in the History of Themistocles	391
Exaggeration in the Contrast between the Character of Themistocles and that of Aristeides	392
Uniform Policy of Themistocles	392
Mixed Character of Themistocles	395
Prejudice of Herodotus in the Case of Themistocles	396
Judgment of Thucydides on the Guilt of Themistocles and Pausanias	397
Statements of later Writers	400
General Assumption of his Guilt	401
The Case of Pausanias furnishes no Parallel to that of Themistocles	403
Reasons for the Welcome given by Artaxerxes to Themistocles	405
Ostracism of Aristeides	406
Compact of the Euboeans with Themistocles after the Battle of Thermopylæ	407
The First Message of Themistocles to Xerxes	408
Revocation of the Ostracism of Aristeides	410
The Second Message of Themistocles to Xerxes	410
The Ostracism of Themistocles	412
The Compact between Themistocles and Artaxerxes	414
Probable Nature of his Relations with the Persian King	415
The Guilt of Themistocles was heightened by the Want of strictly Contemporary Historians	416

LIST OF ILLUSTRATIONS.

Thessalonica, the ancient Thermê.—Herodotus vii. 121, &c.	*Frontispiece*
Cyrus, from a Pillar at Pasargada	*To face page* 5
Crœsus on the Funeral Pile	,, 12
Plain and Tumulus of Marathon	,, 53
Plain of Troy	,, 75
The Nine Roads (the site of Amphipolis)	,, 84
Syracuse	,, 93
The Acropolis of Athens, from the Areiopagus	,, 132
Eleusis	,, 138
Corinth	,, 150
Sparta	,, 177
Tombs at Platææ	,, 219

PART I.

THE TALE

OF

THE GREAT PERSIAN WAR

CHAPTER I.

THE BEGINNINGS OF THE STRIFE.—THE TALES OF CRŒSUS AND CAMBYSES.—THE ATHENIANS REGAIN THEIR FREEDOM.

> Those far renowned brides of ancient song
> Peopled the hollow dark, like burning stars;
> And I heard sounds of insult, shame, and wrong,
> And trumpets blown for wars.
> TENNYSON.

For many ages there was enmity between the Persians and the Greeks; and many tales were told on both sides to show how it began. So Herodotus of Halicarnassus sought diligently to learn the truth, by asking questions of those who knew; and he wrote a book to keep alive the memory of the great things which had been done, as well by the barbarians as by the Greeks.

The Persian tale-tellers lay the beginning of the quarrel to the charge of the Phœnicians, and say that these, as they sailed about the wide sea, came to Argos, which was then the greatest place in all Hellas, and there began to sell their wares. A few days afterwards, Iô, the daughter of Inachus the king, came with other maidens into the ship;

and as they stood near the stern, buying the things for which they had need, the Phœnicians fell upon them, and carried away Iô, with those of her maidens who were not able to escape. In requital of this, some Greeks, they say, went to Tyre, the great city of the Phœnicians, and stole away the king's daughter Europa. Thus far both sides were equal. But after this the Greeks opened up the strife afresh, when they sailed to Aia, in the Colchian land, and to the river Phasis, and thence brought away by force Medeia, the daughter of the king, who sent a herald after them to Hellas to ask for the maiden and to demand a recompense. But the Greeks said that they would give none, because they had received none when Iô was taken away from Argos. In the second generation after this, Alexander, the son of Priam, heard the tale, and determined to steal a wife from Hellas and give no recompense for her. So he went and stole Helen; and when the Greeks asked them to give her up and to make an atonement, the men of Troy told the Greeks that they had made no requital for Medeia, and now they would make none for Helen. Thus far, there were but single thefts on either side; but henceforth the Persians lay much guilt to the charge of the Greeks; for if it be unjust to steal women, still (they said) it was folly to seek to avenge them, and wisdom to take no heed to what was

CYRUS. FROM A PILLAR AT PASARGADA

done, seeing that women were never stolen against
their will. Instead of doing thus, the Greeks
gathered together a great army, and, going into
Asia, destroyed the kingdom of Priam: and therefore was there hatred between the Persians and
the Greeks,—for the Persians claim all the nations that dwell in Asia as their own, and a
wrong done to any of them they hold to be done
to themselves.

Such are the tales which are told of the former
days; but in after times there came other causes
of quarrel.

Crœsus, the son of Alyattes, ruled over the
children of the Lydians, and over all the nations
who live within the river Halys, westward; and
he made many of the Greeks pay him tribute,
when up to his time they had all been free; but
the Lacedæmonians he won over to be his friends.
In his days the power of the Persians began to
grow very great, and Crœsus thought how he
might break it down before it should become too
strong; for Cyrus, the son of Cambyses, had put
down his grandfather Astyages from being king
of the Medians; and even before his day, Kyaxares, the father of Astyages, had taken Nineveh,
and conquered the kingdom of Assyria. And
therefore Crœsus was the more afraid, because
Cyrus was the master of the Medes and Assyrians, and of the Persians, who were the bravest

of all; and the thought of these things turned aside the grief which he had for the death of Adrastus his son whom Atys the Phrygian had unwittingly slain, so that he resolved to make trial of all the oracles to see which of them spake truly, before he asked them whether he should prosper in the war. He sent, therefore, to Ammon in Libya, to Amphiaraus and Trophonius and the Milesian Branchidæ, to Delphi also, and Abæ of the Phokians, and Dodona, charging the men to count one hundred days from the time of leaving Sardes, and then to ask all the oracles at once what Crœsus, the king of Lydia, might then be doing. What the other oracles answered, there are none to tell us; but at Delphi, when the Lydians had asked as Crœsus bade them, the priestess answered and said:

"I know the number of the sand and the measure of the sea;

"I understand the dumb man, and hear him who speaks not;

"And there comes to me now the savour of a hard-shelled tortoise,

"Which is seething in a brazen vessel with the flesh of a ram.

"And brass there is beneath it and brass above it."[1]

[1] I have not attempted to put the oracular responses into the form of hexameters, for it can scarcely be said with truth that

These words the Lydians wrote down and carried back to the king; and when all had returned to Sardes from the other oracles, Crœsus took the answers and unfolded them. But none of them pleased him until he came to the words of the Delphian god, for he alone knew that on the hundredth day Crœsus went into a secret place where none might see him, and boiled a tortoise and a ram in a brazen vessel over which he placed a brazen cover. This oracle alone, with that of Amphiaraus, he held to have spoken truly. Therefore with mighty sacrifices he sought to win the favour of the god at Delphi. He offered up three thousand cattle, and he set on fire a great pile of couches broidered in silver and gold, with golden goblets and purple robes. He sent him also many talents of fine gold and silver, which he wrought out into the shape of bricks, with the figure of a lion made of gold, ten talents in weight, which now stands in the treasure chamber of the Corinthians at Delphi. Many other gifts also he sent, goblets and jars and vessels for sprinkling, all notable for their beauty and their richness. Others

---

any such metre exists in English. The hexameter is eminently a measure for a language guided wholly by quantity, while the English is governed altogether by accent: and any attempt to reproduce the Greek metre in an English dress serves only to place the latter language under restraints which are utterly alien to its character and spirit.

1. 53 also he sent to the temple of Amphiaraus; and he charged his messengers to go to both these oracles and ask if he should march against the Persians, and if he should ask any others to help him in the war. And both gave the same answer that if he went against the Persians he would destroy a great kingdom; and counselled him to find out the mightiest among the Greeks and make 54 them his friends. Then was Crœsus still more pleased, feeling sure now that he would throw down the kingdom of Cyrus; and he sent money for all the Delphians, two pieces for each man; in return for which the Delphians gave great honours to Crœsus and all the Lydians.

55 After this Crœsus questioned the god for the third time; for when he found that he might trust him, he loaded him with questions. And now, when he asked if his empire should last a long time, the priestess answered,

"When a mule shall be king of the Medes,

"Then, O tender-footed Lydian, flee by the banks of the pebbly Hermus,

"Flee and tarry not, neither care to hide thy fear."

Then Crœsus was more than ever pleased, for he thought that a mule would never rule over the Medes, and so his own power should last for ever.

56 After this he sought to learn who were the

mightiest among the Greeks, and he found that the
Athenians were at the head of the Ionic race
and the Lacedæmonians of the Dorian; but the
Athenians were at this time hard pressed under
the rule of their tyrant Peisistratus the son of
Hippocrates; while the Lacedæmonians had risen
to great power and were well ordered by the laws
which they had received from Lycurgus. To these
therefore he sent a herald, and made a covenant
with them that they should help him in the war;
and so he made ready to march against the
Persians, neither would he listen to the words of
Sandanis, who counselled him well, saying, "O
king, thou art going against men whose raiment
is of leather, and who eat not what they like but
what they can get in a rough and barren country,
who have neither wine nor figs nor anything else
that is good. If then thou shouldest conquer them,
what canst thou take away from men who have
nothing? If thou art conquered, think what thou
wilt lose. When they have once tasted of our
good things, they will not cease to pour in upon
us: and therefore I thank the gods who have not
put it into the mind of the Persians to come forth
against the Lydians."

Thus he despised all counsel, and marched to
the Halys, where the army crossed over on the
bridges which were there before; or, as some say,
Thales of Miletus made a new channel for the

river, so that, when some part of the water was taken off, the men were able to cross it easily.

76 Then Crœsus went on to Pteria, and took many cities, and ravaged their lands, until Cyrus came up with his armies. And first he tried to draw off the Ionians from Crœsus, but they would not hearken to him; and afterwards a great battle was fought, in which neither side had the victory,
77 for the night came on and parted them. On the next day, when Cyrus came not again to the attack, Crœsus drew off his army to Sardes, for he liked not the scantiness of their numbers: and he was minded during the winter to gather to his aid the Egyptians and Babylonians, with the men of Lacedæmon, and so in the spring to march out once more against the Persians. So when he reached Sardes, he sent away all the army which he had with him, for he thought not that the Persians were even now coming against him.
79 For when Cyrus knew that Crœsus was gone to Sardes after the battle in Pteria and was about to scatter his army, he determined to march against him before his allies could come together, and himself to bring the news of his coming. Then was Crœsus in a great strait, but still he led forth his Lydians, who were at this time the bravest of the nations in Asia and fought on
80 horseback with long spears; and he drew them up on the large plain which lies before the city of

Sardes. These horsemen Cyrus greatly feared; and at the counsel of Harpagus, a Mede, he placed riders on all the camels, and drew them up in front of his army. And so when the battle began, and the horses of the Lydians smelt the camels and saw them, they turned and fled, and the hopes of King Crœsus perished. But still the Lydians fought on bravely until many were killed, and at last they were driven into the city and shut up there. Then Crœsus sent in haste to his allies, and bade them come at once to his aid; for, before, he had charged them to be ready at the end of the fourth month.

So fourteen days passed away; and then Cyrus promised to reward richly the man who first should climb the walls. But the men tried in vain to climb them, until a Mardian, named Hyrœades, found a part where no guards had been placed, because the hill was steep and the Lydians thought that no one would ever attempt to climb up by that way. But Hyrœades had seen some one go down there and fetch up his helmet, which had rolled from the wall; and by the same path he went up himself, and other Persians with him: and so was Sardes taken, and all the city plundered.

Thus Crœsus was made prisoner, when he had reigned for fourteen years and had been besieged for fourteen days, and when, as the oracle had foretold, he had destroyed his own great power. And the men who took him led him to Cyrus, who raised a great pile of wood and placed Crœsus on it, bound in chains, with fourteen of the Lydians, either because he wished to offer them up as the firstfruits of his victory, or to see if any of the gods would deliver Crœsus who (as he had learnt) was one who greatly honoured them. Then to Crœsus in his great agony came back the words which Solon had spoken to him, that no living man was happy; and as he thought on this, he sighed, and after a long silence thrice called out the name of Solon. And Cyrus, hearing this, bade the interpreters ask him whom he called; but for a long time he would not answer them. At last, when they pressed him greatly, he told them that long ago Solon the Athenian came to see him and thought nothing of all his wealth; and how the words had come to pass which Solon spake, not thinking of him more than of any others who fancy that they are happy. While Crœsus thus spake, the edge of the pile was already kindled. And Cyrus, when he heard the tale, remembered that he too was but a man, and that he was now giving alive to the flames one who had been not less wealthy than himself; and when he thought also how man abideth not ever in one stay, he charged them to put out the fire and bring Crœsus and the

CRŒSUS ON THE FUNERAL PILE
From an ancient Vase

other Lydians down from the pile. But the
flame was too strong; and when Crœsus saw that
the mind of Cyrus was changed but that the
men were not able to quench the fire, he prayed
to Apollo to come and save him, if ever he had
done aught to please him in the days that were
past. And suddenly the wind rose, and clouds
gathered where none had been before, and there
burst from the heaven a great storm of rain,
which put out the blazing fire. Then Cyrus
knew that Crœsus was a good man and that the
gods loved him; and when he came down from
the pile, he said, "O Crœsus, who persuaded
thee to march against my land, and to become
my enemy rather than my friend?" And Crœsus
answered, "It is the god of the Greeks, O king,
who urged me on; for no man is so senseless as
to choose war rather than peace, in which the
children bury their fathers, while in war the
fathers bury their children: but so it pleased the
gods that thus it should be."

Then Cyrus unloosed his chains and kept him
by his side, and Crœsus gave him good counsel
touching the plunder of the city, so that Cyrus
bade him ask as a gift whatever he should most
desire to have. And Crœsus said, "O king, let
me send these fetters to the god of the Greeks,
and ask him if it be his wont to deceive those
who have done him good." Then Cyrus asked

14. him what he meant; and when Crœsus had told him all the tale, he laughed, and said, "This thou shalt have, O Crœsus, and whatsoever else thou mayest wish for." So he sent men to Delphi to show the chains, and to ask if it was the wont of the Hellenic gods that they should be ungrateful.

91. When the Lydians came into the temple, the priestess said, "Not even a god can escape from the lot which is prepared for him; and Crœsus, in the fifth generation, has suffered for the sin of him who, at the bidding of a woman, slew his lord and seized his power. Much did the god labour that the evil might fall in the days of his children and not of Crœsus himself, but he could not turn the fates aside. Still, what he could he obtained for him. For three years he put off the taking of Sardes; and he came to his aid when the flame had grown fierce on the blazing pile. And, yet more, he is wrong in blaming the god for the answer, that if he went against the Persians he would destroy a great power; for he should then have asked if the god meant his own power or that of Cyrus : and, therefore, is he the cause of his own sorrow. Neither, again, would he understand what the god spake about the mule; for Cyrus himself was this mule, being the son of a Median woman, the daughter of Astyages, and of a man born of the meaner race

of the Persians." This answer the Lydians brought to Sardes; and Crœsus knew that the god was guiltless, and that the fault was all his own. So was Crœsus taken, and so was Ionia first subdued.

But soon the Ionians rebelled against the Persians and sent to ask aid from the Lacedæmonians, who refused to help them but yet sent men in a ship of fifty oars to charge Cyrus not to hurt any city of the Greeks, for the Spartans would not overlook it. But Cyrus asked of the bystanders who the Spartans might be; and when he heard, he answered, "I never yet feared men who have a place in the midst of their city where they take oaths and cheat one another. If I live and prosper, these men shall have sorrows of their own to talk about instead of the woes of the Ionians." So Harpagus, the Median, was sent against the Ionians; and soon he conquered them, and Ionia was a second time brought into slavery.

Then the power of King Cyrus grew stronger, and he went against Babylon and took it, and put down Labynetus from being king: and after this, he purposed to march against the Massagetæ, a great and strong nation, who dwell beyond the river Araxes and who at this time were ruled by a queen named Tomyris, whose husband was dead. So Cyrus asked her to become his wife; but Tomyris knew that he sought not herself but her

1. kingdom, and forbade him to approach her. And
Cyrus, seeing that craft availed not, marched openly
206 to the Araxes and built bridges by which his army
might cross over. But as he was thus busied,
Tomyris sent a herald, and said, "King of the
Medes, cease from thy toil, for thou canst not
know the end of thy labour. Rule over thine own
people, and leave me to rule over mine. But
if thou wilt not do thus, come, let us make a
covenant together. Either we will go three days'
journey from the river, so that thou mayest cross
over into my land; or, do thou depart in like manner from the river and let us pass into thy country."
Then Cyrus called together the first men of the
207 Persians, who all besought him to let Tomyris pass
over into their land; but Crœsus liked not their
counsel, and he said, "O king, I promised at the
first, when Zeus gave me into thy hands, to do all
that I could in thy service. My sorrows have been
my teachers; but there will be no use in my
words, if thou thinkest thyself immortal and that
thou art leading an army of men who will never
die. But if thou knowest that thou art a man and
rulest also over men, then learn this, that there is
a cycle in human fortunes, which, as it turns round
in its course, suffers not the same men to be always
prosperous. Now if we receive the enemy into our
land, there is this danger, that if defeated thou wilt
ruin all thy kingdom, for the Massagetæ will not

care to return to their own country; and if thou gainest the victory, it will avail thee more to gain it where we may follow them as they flee; and, besides this, it is not to be borne that Cyrus, the son of Cambyses, should yield ground at the bidding of a woman. Cross the river then, and leave in the camp the weakest men in our army with plenty of food and wine; and the Massagetæ, who have but rough and poor fare, will turn greedily to the feast made ready for them, and leave thee to win glory elsewhere."

This counsel Cyrus followed, and went on a day's journey from the banks of the Araxes. There he left the sick and weak of his army; and the Massagetæ came upon them and took them, and when they had so filled themselves with food and wine that they fell asleep, the Persians came back, and, slaying many, took many more alive, and among these the son of Queen Tomyris who was their general. But Tomyris, when she heard it, sent a herald and said, "O Cyrus, who canst not quench thy thirst for blood, be not proud and lifted up because thou hast taken my son, not in open fight, but by the fruit of the vine with which ye so fill and madden yourselves that, as the wine goes down into the body, vile words rush up to your lips. And now hearken unto me. Give me back my son and depart scatheless from my land; for, if thou wilt not do this, I swear by the Sun who is the lord of the Massagetæ, that I will make even thee drink thy fill of blood." But Cyrus cared not for her words, and Tomyris gathered all her people together and fought with him in a very fierce battle, in which, when their arrows were all spent, they smote each other with spears and daggers. At last the Persians were beaten, and Cyrus himself was killed. Then Tomyris filled a skin with human blood, and when she had found the body of Cyrus among the dead, she thrust his head into the skin; and thus was fulfilled the word which she had spoken to him.

Cyrus had been king for twenty and nine years; and when he died, his son Cambyses ruled in his stead, and made war on Amasis, king of Egypt, because, when he asked for his daughter in marriage, Amasis had sent him not his own child but the daughter of Apries, who had been king before him, and whom he had himself slain. So Cambyses marched against the Egyptians and fought in Pelusium with Psammenitus the king (for Amasis, his father, was now dead), and conquered him in the battle. Then going to Saïs, he charged his people to bring before him the body of Amasis, and scourge it and pluck off the hair; and when they were not able to do this because it had been embalmed, Cambyses ordered it to be burnt, which both Persians and Egyptians hold to be an unholy thing; for the Persians think it wrong to give the body of a man to the god Fire, and the Egyptians give not their dead to that which they hold to be a wild beast, which eats up all that it can seize and dies when its feast is ended.

After this, Cambyses purposed to go against many nations; but his armies prospered not, and he did continually things more and more strange and horrible. He put to death many of the Egyptians because they rejoiced at the birth of the calf-god Apis. And at last, sending for the priests and the calf, he smote the calf with a dagger, and said to them, "Poor fools, these then are your gods, with flesh and blood, and which may be wounded by men. Truly the god well matches his worshippers; but ye shall smart for your insult." So he scourged the priests, and the feast was broken up, and the calf died in the temple where it had been smitten.

For this cause the Egyptians say that Cambyses was struck with madness; while others hold that his body had been always unsound, and that the disease of his mind was caused by the sickness of his body. But, however this may be, he slew his brother Smerdis, and his sister, and then he shot the son of Prexaspes to the heart, to show that he was not mad. At last the Magians arose, and one of them, who pretended to be Smerdis, the king's brother, seized the kingdom, and shared it with his brother Patizeithes. But

III. 65 Cambyses was not able to march against him, for he died childless at Ecbatana in the Syrian land.

70 Then the Magians reigned at Susa, and the power went over to the Medes, until seven men of the noblest of the Persians conspired against 88 the Magians and slew them, and set up Darius, the son of Hystaspes, on the throne of Cyrus the Persian.

Not many years after these things, it came to pass that the Athenians also rose up against their v. 55 tyrants, the children of Peisistratus; for when Hipparchus had been slain by Harmodius and Aristogeiton, his brother Hippias began cruelly 65 to oppress them, so that the people obtained help from Sparta and drove away Hippias, who went to dwell at Sigeium on the banks of the river 66 Scamander. And, as soon as they were free, the Athenians became great and strong, and conquered many people and took their land. And v. 78 not only in this, but in every way, we see how good a thing is freedom, since even the Athenians were in nowise better than their neighbours until they had put down their tyrants: for up to that time they were faint of heart, because they were toiling for a master; but when they were free, every man knew that he was working for himself.

CHAP. II.

THE FALL OF POLYCRATES.—DEMOCEDES AT SUSA AND AT CROTON.

> I see thy glory like a shooting star
> Fall to the base earth from the firmament.
> Thy sun sets weeping in the lowly west,
> Witnessing storms to come.
> **SHAKESPEARE.**

Now in the time of Cambyses, king of Persia, there ruled over the island of Samos a tyrant named Polycrates, the son of Æakês. This man had taken the city by force; and at the first he divided it into three parts, and gave two parts to his brothers Pantagnôtus and Sylosôn. But afterwards he slew the one and drove away the other, and so he gained all Samos for himself. And when he had gained it, he made an alliance with Amasis, king of Egypt, both sending him gifts and receiving gifts from him. In a little while Polycrates became very great, and his fame was noised abroad throughout Ionia and the rest of Hellas; for, whithersoever he went, all prospered

Herodotus III. 39

III. to his hand. And he had one hundred ships of fifty oars each, and a thousand bowmen. He robbed and plundered all, neither did he respect any; for he said that he should make his friend more glad by giving back that which he had taken from him, than if he had never taken it away from him at all. He conquered also many of the islands and many of the cities on the mainland; and in a sea fight he beat the Lesbians and took them, when they came forth with all their strength to the help of the people of Miletus; and he made them dig in chains the great moat around the wall in Samos.

40 Now Amasis, king of Egypt, had heard of the well-doing of Polycrates, and it was a grief of mind to him. And when he prospered yet more exceedingly, Amasis wrote a letter and sent it to Samos, saying, "Thus saith Amasis to Polycrates. It is pleasant to hear of the well-doing of a man who is a friend: but thy great success pleases me not, for I know that the Deity is jealous. So, for myself and for those whom I love, I wish that in some things we may prosper and in others fail, and thus pass our days with changes from good to evil, rather than that we should do well in all things. For never yet have I by hearsay or tale known one so prospering in everything, who has not perished miserably at the last. Heed thou then what I say, and do thus for thy great glory.

Seek out that thing for the loss of which thy soul would most be grieved, and cast it away, so that it may never come to mortal hand. And if hereafter thy good fortune be not mixed with pain, remedy it in the manner which I have set before thee."

So the words of Amasis seemed good to Polycrates, and he sought amongst his treasures for that which was most precious to him; and he found a seal-ring of emerald stone, set in gold, the work of Theodorus, the son of Têlecêlês of Samos. Then he filled with men a ship of fifty oars, and bade them row out into the sea; and when they were far away from the island, he took the ring from off his finger in the sight of all the men and cast it into the sea, and went home in great sorrow.

Now, on the fifth or sixth day after these things, there came to the door of his house a fisherman with a large and beautiful fish, and asked to see Polycrates. And when he was come into his presence, he said, "O king, though I live by the work of my hands, I would not carry to the market this fish which I have caught, for it seemed to me a gift fit for thee; and therefore I have brought it." And Polycrates was pleased and said to him, "Thou hast done well, and I thank thee for thy words and for thy gift, and I bid thee to sup with me." So the fisherman went home rejoicing; but

III. the servants, as they made ready the fish, found within it the seal-ring of Polycrates, and they were very glad and took it to him, and told him how they had found it. Then it seemed to him a marvellous thing; and he wrote in a letter all that he had done and all that had happened unto him, and sent it to Amasis to Egypt.

43 When Amasis had read the letter which came from Polycrates, he knew that no man could deliver another from that which was to come upon him; and that, for all his well-doing, Polycrates would come to no good end, seeing that he found even those things which he threw away. So he sent a herald to Samos, and broke off the alliance; and for this reason he brake it, that when some evil fate overtook Polycrates, his own heart might not be grieved as for a friend.

120 Now Cyrus, the king of Persia, had set up a ruler over Sardes, who was called Orœtes. This man was set on doing an evil deed, for although he had suffered no wrong in word or in act from Polycrates and had not even seen him, yet he sought to slay him, as the more part say, for some such cause as this. It chanced that as Orœtes sat before the doors of the king's palace and talked with another Persian, named Mitrobates, who ruled the province in Daskyleium, they strove with each other to know which was

the braver. And Mitrobates made it a reproach to Orœtes, and said, "What! dost thou count thyself to be a man, seeing thou hast not gained for the king the island of Samos which is close to thy province, so easy too for any one to seize, since one of the men of the island has taken it with fifteen heavy-armed soldiers, and now is tyrant therein?" When Orœtes heard these words, they say that he was grieved at the rebuke, and sought not so much to requite him who had said these things, as, by any means, to slay Polycrates, through whom he was evil spoken of.

So, when Orœtes abode in Magnesia which is on the banks of the river Mæander, he sent a messenger to Samos, to learn the mind of Polycrates; and he came and spake these words: "Thus saith Orœtes to Polycrates. I hear that thou art set on great things, but that thou hast not money according to thy designs. Thus then do thou, and thou shalt both stablish thyself and save me, for King Cambyses seeks to slay me; and this is told me of a surety. Therefore come and take me away and my money, and keep part of it for thyself, and part of it let me have. So if thou thinkest for money, thou shalt be ruler over all Hellas. And if thou believest not about my wealth, send the trustiest of thy servants, and to him will I show it." When Polycrates heard this, he was glad and resolved to send one, for he greatly desired to have money. So he sent a man named Mæandrius, who was his scribe, to see it. And when Orœtes heard that the Samian was at hand, he filled eight vessels with stones, all but a little about the brim; and on the stones he placed gold, and fastened the vessels and kept them ready.

So Mæandrius came and saw them, and told it to Polycrates who made ready to go, although the soothsayers forbade him much, and so did his friends. And his daughter also sought to stay him, because she had seen a vision which betokened evil to him; but he would not hear. Thus he despised all counsel and sailed to Orœtes, taking with him many of his comrades, and amongst them Demokedes, the son of Calliphon of Crotôn, a physician famed beyond all others of his time in the practice of his art. And when Polycrates came to Magnesia, he perished miserably, with an end befitting neither himself nor his great designs; for, saving those who were tyrants of Syracuse, no one of the Greek tyrants deserved to be compared for greatness to Polycrates. And Orœtes sent away those of his followers who were Samians, bidding them to be thankful to him for their freedom; but those amongst them who were strangers or slaves, he kept as prisoners taken in war. So ended the

good fortune of Polycrates in the way which III.
Amasis, king of Egypt, had foretold; but, no 126
long time after, the vengeance of Polycrates
overtook Orœtes. For, when Cambyses was dead
and the Magians were reigning, he did no good
in Sardes to the Persians whose power had been
taken away by the Medes, but killed Mitrobates
who ruled in Daskyleium, and his son Cranaspes,
men of note amongst the Persians; and waxed
wanton altogether, so that he slew a messenger
who came to him from Darius, because he brought
a message which did not please him.

So Darius sought to punish Orœtes for all his 127
evil deeds, and chiefly because he had killed
Mitrobates. But he did not think fit to make war
upon him openly, because his own power was not
yet firm, and because he heard that Orœtes was a
very mighty man and that he was guarded by a
thousand Persians and ruled in the provinces of
Phrygia, Lydia, and Ionia. So he called together
the chief men of the Persians and said unto them,
"O Persians, which of you will do my bidding,
and slay Orœtes or bring him to me alive, for he
has done the Persians no good, but only great evil?
He has killed Mitrobates and his son, and slain the
messengers whom I sent unto him." Then there 128
rose up thirty men, who were each ready to do his
will; and as they strove which of them should
do it, Darius ordered them to draw lots, and the

lot fell on Bagæus, the son of Artontes. And Bagæus wrote many letters and sealed them all with the king's seal, and went with them to Sardes, and gave the letters one by one to the scribe that he might read them. When he saw that they gave great reverence to the letters and to what was read from them, he gave to the scribe one in which were written these words, "O Persians, King Darius forbids you to guard Orœtes." And when they heard this, they lowered their spears, and Bagæus knew that they would obey the command of the king. So he took courage and gave the last letter to the scribe, wherein was written, "King Darius charges the Persians who are in Sardes to slay Orœtes." As soon as the guards heard this, they drew their swords and slew him: and so the vengeance for Polycrates overtook Orœtes the Persian.

Then all that belonged to Orœtes was taken to Susa: and it came to pass in a little while that King Darius in a hunt leaped from his horse and twisted his foot; and it was a very great strain, for the ankle bone was moved from its socket. Now, as he was wont to have about him Egyptians who had great fame for their skill in medicine, he sent for these first; but they forced the foot and worked still greater evil. For seven days and seven nights Darius had no sleep by reason of the pain; and on the eighth day, as he lay in misery,

one who by chance had heard in Sardes of the art 131
of Demokedes of Croton, told it to the king; and
he commanded forthwith to bring the man before
him. And when they had found him lying un-
cared for somewhere among the slaves of Orœtes,
they led him forth into the midst, dragging his
chains and clothed with rags.

Then King Darius asked him if he knew the 130
art; and he denied, for he feared that, if he
showed his skill, he should never see his own land
again. But Darius saw that he was dealing
craftily, and commanded those who had led him
in to bring forth scourges and goads; and then he
confessed that he knew the art but poorly, having
lived for a while with a physician. Then, at the
bidding of the king, he used the remedies of the
Greeks, and, applying gentle means after strong
ones, caused him to sleep, and in a little while
made him well again when he never hoped to be
firm of foot for the time to come.

Then Demokedes, having healed Darius, had a 132
very great house in Susa, and ate at the same table
with the king: and, save that he might not go to
Hellas, all things were granted to him; for, when
the Egyptians were going to be impaled because
they were beaten by a Greek, he begged them
from the king and saved them alive. He also
ransomed a soothsayer from Elis who had followed
Polycrates and lay neglected amongst the slaves.

III. So Demokedes was in very great favour with the king.

133 And it came to pass, not long after these things, that there grew a swelling upon the breast of Atossa, the daughter of Cyrus and wife of Darius; and it burst and spread wide. So long as it was small, she concealed it from shame, and told it to none: but when the evil was now great, she sent for Demokedes and showed it to him, and he said that he would make her well; but he caused her to swear that she would grant him in return that 134 which he should desire of her. So he healed her; and Atossa, being taught by Demokedes, spake thus unto Darius, "O king, thou sittest still with all thy great power, and gainest no nations or kingdoms for the Persians; but a man who is young and lord of great kingdoms should do some great thing, that the Persians may know that it is a man who rules over them. Therefore now rouse thyself, whilst thou art young in years, for, as the body grows old, the mind grows along with it, and is dulled for all action." Then the king answered and said, "Thou hast told me even that which I purpose to do, for I have resolved to make a bridge and cross over from this continent against the Scythians; and this shall be done shortly." Then said Atossa, "See now, go not against the Scythians first, for thou mayest march against these whenever it pleaseth thee; but go, I pray

THE COUNSEL OF ATOSSA. 31

thee, against Hellas: for I have heard the report of them, and I desire to have Laconian maidens, and Argive, and Athenian, and Corinthian, to be my servants; and thou hast one who above all men is fitted to show and tell thee all about Hellas—I mean him who has healed thy foot." And Darius answered, "Since thou willest that we first make trial against Hellas, it seems to me best to send along with this man spies of the Persians who shall see and learn all about them and show it unto me."

Then Darius charged fifteen chosen men of the Persians to follow Demokedes and go through the coast of Hellas, and to see that he did not escape, but by all means to bring him back again. Then he called Demokedes himself, and commanded him to return to Susa when he should have guided the Persians over all Hellas; and he bade him take, as gifts for his father and his brethren, all the movable goods that were in his house, saying that he would give him much more when he came back again. He promised also to send with him a vessel laden with all good things. But Demokedes feared that this might be a trap to catch him; so he said that he would leave his own goods in the land, that he might have them on his return, but that he would take the ship, that he might have whence to give to his friends.

So they went down to Sidon, a city of Phœnicia,

III. and manned two triremes, and with them a merchant vessel laden with good things; and when they were ready, they sailed along the coasts of Hellas and wrote in a book all the wonderful things that they saw, until they came to Tarentum in Italy. There Aristophilides, the king of the Tarentines, who was a friend of Demokedes, took off the rudders of the Persian ships, and shut up the Persians themselves in prison, because he said that they were spies; and while they were in this plight, Demokedes fled away to Croton. So now, when he had come to his own city, Aristophilides let the Persians go, and gave back what he had taken from them; and they followed after Demokedes, and came to Croton and found him in the market-place. But when they laid hands on him, the men of Croton beat them with clubs and took Demokedes away and also the giftvessel which Darius had sent with him. So the Persians sailed back to Asia, and sought not to go any more over Hellas, because they had lost their guide. But, as they were now going, Demokedes charged them to tell Darius that he had married the daughter of Milo the wrestler. Now the name of Milo was very great with the king; and Demokedes, I think, hastened the marriage, that he might appear to King Darius to be a notable man in his own country also. But the Persians, as they went back, were wrecked on the Iapygian

shore and made slaves: but a man named Gillus, III.
who had been driven away from Tarentum, ransomed them and took them to King Darius, who promised to give him whatsoever he should ask. So Gillus told him how he had been banished, and besought the king to restore him to his own city; but, fearing to disturb all Hellas, if a great army should sail to Italy for his sake, he said that the people of Cnidus, who were friends of the Tarentines, could restore him. So Darius charged the people of Cnidus to take Gillus to his own country, and they went with him to Tarentum; but they could not persuade the men of that city to receive him, and they were not able to compel them by force.

Even so did these things come to pass; and these were the first Persians who came to Hellas from Asia.

CHAP. III.

THE INROAD OF THE PERSIANS INTO SCYTHIA.—THE TALE OF ARISTAGORAS AND HISTIÆUS.—MILTIADES AND MARATHON.

> Preserves alike its bounds and boundless fame
> The battle-field, where Persia's victim horde
> First bowed beneath the brunt of Hellas' sword,
> As on the morn to distant glory dear,
> When Marathon became a magic word.
>
> BYRON.

<small>Herodotus IV. 1</small> THEN King Darius led forth his armies against the Scythians, as he was before minded; and they crossed over into Europe at the Thracian <small>87</small> Bosporus, where a bridge had been built by Mandrocles the Samian. At the first the king thought to have the bridge unloosed, as soon as all should <small>9</small> have gone over; but Coës, a man of Mitylene, besought him to let it remain, lest there should be no way to escape if any evil befell them in the war. So Darius charged the Ionians to keep the bridge for sixty days, and then he marched away against the Scythians. But he fared not well in the war, for the people dwelt in desert regions,

and it was hard to track them out. And Darius
and his host were in sore distress, when there came
a man from the Scythians, bringing with him a
bird and a mouse, a frog and five arrows. But
when the Persians asked him what these gifts
might mean, the man said that he had received
no charge but to give them and to return. Then
the Persians took counsel; and the king thought
that by these gifts the Scythians yielded up themselves, their land and their water, because the
mouse lives on the land and the frog in the water,
and the bird signified the horses of warriors, and
the arrows showed that they yielded up their
power. But Gobryas, one of the seven who slew
the Magians, spake and said, " O Persians, unless
ye become birds and fly up into heaven, or go
down like mice beneath the earth, or, becoming
frogs, leap into the lake, ye will not escape being
shot to death by these arrows."

Then the king feared greatly, and at last he
commanded to bind all the sick of the army and
the beasts of burden, and to leave them in the
camp. So they lit fires and left the sick, and then
hastened away to reach the bridge. But when the
Scythians heard the cries of the men who had
been left behind, they knew that the host of the
Persians had fled away; and they made haste to
reach the bridge first. And when they were come
thither, they called out to the Ionians who were

iv.   in the ships to loosen all the bridge and to go
     away.
137   Now among the Ionians there was an Athenian
     named Miltiades, who was tyrant of the Chersone-
     sus; and he gave counsel to do as the Scythians
     bade them, and to set their country free from the
     Persians. But Histiæus, the tyrant of Miletus,
     besought them to guard the bridge until the king
     should come, and he said, "O ye tyrants, be sure
     of this, that, if we leave the Persians to perish,
     the men of our cities will rise up against us,
     because it is the king who strengthens us in our
     power; and if he die, neither shall I be able to
     rule in Miletus, nor you in those cities of which
138 ye are the tyrants." Then all gave judgment to
     wait for the coming of the king, and to cheat the
     Scythians by pretending to unloose the bridge. So
140 the Scythians were deceived and went to look for
     the Persians, who came by another way. It was
     night when they reached the bridge; and when
     they found that the boats were unloosed, they
     feared greatly that the Ionians had left them to
     perish. But Darius commanded an Egyptian in
     his army, who had a very loud voice, to call His-
     tiæus of Miletus; and Histiæus heard the cry, and
     the bridge was made fast again, for the Persians
     to cross over.
v. 11 Now, when Darius reached Sardes, he remem-
     bered the good deed of Histiæus, and he promised

to give him whatsoever he should ask. So he asked for Myrkinus in the Edonian land, because he wished to build a city there; and he went thither and began to make the place strong. But while he was so doing, Megabazus, the general of Darius, heard it; and as soon as he came to Sardes, he spake thus unto the king: "O king, what hast thou done? Thou hast given to a Greek, who is wise and crafty, to have a city in Thrace, where there is much timber for building ships, and blades for oars, and mines of silver; and round it there are many people, both Greek and barbarian, who will take him for a chief and do his will by night and by day. See then that he make not war against thee in time to come."

So King Darius sent a messenger to Histiæus, to Myrkinus, and said, "O Histiæus, thus saith King Darius. I have pondered it well, and I find none who is better minded to me and to my kingdom than thou art. This I know, for I have learnt it not by words, but in deed. And now I purpose to do great things. Come therefore to me in anywise, that I may intrust them to thee." So Histiæus went to Sardes, for he was proud that he was to be the king's counsellor. And Darius said to him, "O Histiæus, there is nothing more precious than a wise and kind friend; and I know that this thou art to me. So now thou must leave Miletus and thy Thracian city, and

come with me to Susa. There thou shalt sit at my table, and all that I have shall be thine." So
29 Darius left his own brother Artaphernes to be
30 ruler over Sardes, and went with Histiæus to Susa. And Aristagoras, who was brother-in-law and cousin to Histiæus, was left to rule in Miletus.

Now about this time the people of the isle of Naxos rose up and drove out some of the nobles, who came to ask help from Aristagoras. But he said, "I am not able to conquer the Naxians by myself; but Artaphernes, who rules in Sardes, is my friend, and he is the brother of the king. This man, I think, will do what we desire." So
31 he went to Artaphernes, and promised him much money and great gifts if he would let him have one hundred ships to go against Naxos. And Artaphernes promised to give him two hundred, if it should please the king. When Darius heard
32 it, he was glad; and Artaphernes charged Mega-
33 bates to go with the ships to Naxos. So he took Aristagoras and the Naxians up from Miletus, and sailed to Chios, that he might cross over from thence to Naxos. But it happened that there was no watch kept that night in a Myndian vessel: and Megabates was wroth, and made them place the captain of the ship in one of the large oar-holes, so that his head hung over the side of the ship. Then Aristagoras went and prayed Mega-

bates to let the Myndian go; but he would not. So Aristagoras set him free himself. Then Megabates was yet more angry, but Aristagoras came forth and said, "What hast thou to do with these things? Hath not Artaphernes sent thee to obey me, and to go whithersoever I may bid thee?" Then Megabates sent secretly to the Naxians, and warned them; and they brought much food into their city, and made the walls strong, so that the Persians were unable to take it. Presently the money which Megabates brought with him was all spent, and the money of Aristagoras was also gone; and yet the Naxians were not subdued. So Aristagoras could not fulfil the promise which he made to Artaphernes, and he was greatly troubled, for he knew not how he should be able to pay the men; and he feared that Megabates was slandering him, that he might not rule any more in Miletus. Wherefore he thought to rebel against the king; and just at this time there came from Susa a messenger from Histiæus with marks upon his head, telling him to revolt from the king; for Histiæus knew not how to tell him safely in any other way, because the roads were guarded. So he shaved the head of the trustiest of his slaves, and marked letters thereon, and waited till the hair was grown; and then he sent him to Miletus, bidding him only tell Aristagoras to shave off his hair and look at his head. This did Histiæus because he was wearied at being so long kept in Susa, and he hoped that, if Aristagoras rebelled, he should be sent down to the sea, but if Miletus revolted not, he never thought to see it again.

Then Aristagoras rebelled openly against the king, and he said that he would no more be tyrant in his own city. He put down the tyrants in the other cities also, and made them all free, that they might help him more cheerfully against the king. And when he had done this, he went in a trireme to Lacedæmon, for he needed some great help in this war.

Now at this time Cleomenes, the son of Anaxandridas, was king in Sparta; and Aristagoras came to him, and besought him to help the Ionians, who were men of the same blood. He told him also how easy it was to conquer the Persians, and how they might go to Susa and plunder the treasures of the great king, and become as rich as Zeus himself. Then Cleomenes said, "In three days we will give our answer;" and on the third day Cleomenes asked how long time it would take to go to Susa from the sea; and Aristagoras said, "Three months." Then the king said hastily, "O stranger of Miletus, depart from Sparta before the sun goes down; thou art no friend to the Lacedæmonians, when thou seekest to lead them three months' journey

from the sea." But Aristagoras took an olive- v. 51
branch in his hand, and went into the house of
Cleomenes; and when he saw him, he prayed
him to send away his little daughter Gorgo, who
was standing by: but Cleomenes bade him think
not of the child. Then Aristagoras began to urge
him with gifts, beginning with ten talents; and
when Cleomenes refused, he went on to more,
till he promised him fifty talents, and the child
cried out, "Father, the stranger will corrupt you,
unless you rise up and go." Then Cleomenes
went away, and Aristagoras could tell him no
more of the journey to the great king.

So he left Sparta and went to Athens, which
was now free, for the Athenians had risen up
against the sons of Peisistratus, and Hippias had 55
fled with his children away to Sigeium, which is
on the banks of the river Scamander; and there
he sought if by any means he might bring Athens 96
under the power of Artaphernes and Darius.

Then Aristagoras besought aid from the Athe- 97
nians, and he urged them so, that at length
they promised to send twenty ships, and appointed Melanthius to be the admiral; and these
ships were the beginning of evils, both to the
Greeks' and to the barbarians. So Aristagoras 98
sailed back to Asia; and when he came to Miletus,
he remained there himself, but he sent his brother
Charopinus to lead the Ionians against Sardes.

v. 100 And when they reached Ephesus, they left their ships in Coressus, and went up thence with a great host, having the Ephesians for their guides. So they went along the banks of the Caÿster, and took all Sardes, except the Acropolis which Artaphernes himself held with no small number of
101 men. But the Ionians did not plunder the city when they had taken it. For most of the houses in Sardes were made of reeds, and even those that were built of brick had roofs of reeds: one of these a soldier happened to set on fire, and the flame went from house to house, until it spread over the whole city. Then the Persians and the Lydians ran down to the market-place, which is by the river Pactôlus; and when the Ionians saw this, they were afraid, and retreated fast to the mountain which is called Tmolus; and then, as the night came on, they went away to their ships.
102 So Sardes was burnt, and in it a temple of Kybêbê, the goddess of the country; and the Persians always spake of this burning, when they burnt afterwards the temples of the Greeks. Then the Persians followed after the Ionians, and overtook them in Ephesus, and beat them in a battle with great slaughter; and those who escaped from the fight were scattered among the cities.
103 After this, the Athenians altogether forsook

the Ionians, and would listen no more to the
prayers of Aristagoras. But the Ionians went on
no less to make war against the king, and subdued Byzantium, and made alliance with the men
of Caunus. And all the Cyprians joined them,
except the people of Amathus, who were besieged
by Onesilus, the son of Gorgus, because they
would not rebel against the king.

And when it was told to Darius that Sardes
had been taken and burnt by the Athenians and
Ionians, and that the man who had guided them
and woven these things together was the Milesian
Aristagoras, they say that he took no heed to the
Ionians, because he well knew that they should
not escape for their rebellion, but he asked only
who the Athenians were. And when he was
told, he called for a bow, and fitted an arrow to
it; and as he shot it into the air, he said, "O
Zeus, suffer me to avenge myself on the Athenians." Then he charged one of his servants to
say to him thrice during every meal, "O king,
remember the Athenians." After this, he summoned Histiæus the Milesian, whom he had now
so long kept at Susa, and said to him, "O
Histiæus, I hear that the man to whom thou hast
given thy city has been doing strange things.
He has brought over men from Europe to help
the Ionians, whom I shall punish; and by their
aid he has deprived me of Sardes. How can all

v. this seem good to thee? and without thy counsels how could such a thing have been done? See that thou bring not thyself into blame afresh." Then answered Histiæus, "O king, what hast thou said—that I have devised anything from which harm may come to thee? Why should I do thus, and of what do I stand in need? That which thou hast, I have also; and I am thought worthy to listen to thy counsels. But if Aristagoras is thus doing, be sure that he is doing it of himself. Still, I do not believe the tale at all. Only, if it be true, see what thou hast done by taking me away from the sea; for, when I am out of sight, the Ionians may well do that which they have long wished to do. Had I been there, not one city would have stirred itself. Send me, then, quickly to Ionia, and I will put all things right again, and give Aristagoras into thy hands. Yea, I swear by the gods whom the king worshippeth, that I will not put off the tunic in which I shall go down to Ionia, before I bring under thy power the mighty island of Sardinia." Then Darius let him go, having charged him to come back again to Susa when all this should be done.

113
116 So the war went on; but at length the Cyprians were beaten in a great battle, and having been free for one year, were then made slaves again. Then the Persians took many cities on the

THE FLIGHT OF HISTIÆUS. 45

Hellespont, and defeated the Carians in two v.
battles, so that Aristagoras was afraid, because he 124
had disturbed Ionia and was not able to carry out
his great counsels. So he gave Miletus in charge 126
to Pythagoras, a man of great repute among the
citizens; and, taking with him every one who
wished to go, he sailed to Thrace, and seized on
a part of the country. But as he was going out
from it, he was attacked by the Thracians; and
Aristagoras was destroyed, and all his army.

Now, when Histiæus reached Sardes from vi. 1
Susa, Artaphernes asked him why the Ionians had
rebelled against the king; and Histiæus said that
he could not tell, and that he marvelled at all the
things which had happened. But Artaphernes
knew the reason well, and saw that he was dealing craftily; so he said, " O Histiæus, thou hast
thus much to do with these matters. Thou didst
sew this sandal, and Aristagoras hath put it
on." Then Histiæus was afraid, and when the 2
night came he ran away to the sea, and fled to
Chios. But when he desired to go to Miletus, the 5
people would not receive him: so he went to
Mitylene and got some ships, and sailed away to
Byzantium.

But the Ionians would not agree together; and 11
when there was a battle between them and the
Persians on the sea before Miletus, the Samians
fled away treacherously, and the Lesbians followed 14

them. So the Persians conquered in the fight, and took Miletus in the sixth year after the rebellion of Aristagoras; and the people were made slaves.

After this Histiæus went to Thasos, and besieged the town in that island. But when his men wanted food, he crossed over one day to Atarneus in the Mysian land; and Harpagus, the Persian general, took him alive after he had landed, and slew almost all his army. Now, if Histiæus had been sent away alive to King Darius, he would not, I think, have suffered any harm, but his trespass would have been forgiven him; but now, for fear of this, and lest he should again become great with the king, Artaphernes and Harpagus put him to death at Sardes, and sent his head to Susa. And when Darius heard it, he rebuked them because they had not brought Histiæus alive; and he charged them to wash the head and adorn it well, and to bury it as the head of one who had done much good to himself and to the Persians.

Thus were the Ionians made slaves for the third time. And after this King Darius made trial of the Greeks, to see whether they were minded to make war against him or to yield themselves up. So he sent heralds all over Hellas to ask earth and water for the king; and others he sent to his own cities which were on the sea-coast, charging them to make ready long ships and vessels to carry horses.

But before this, strange things had happened at Sparta, for the two kings were not friendly towards each other, and one of them, who was named Demaratus, was put away from being king; and he fled away from Sparta to the Medes.

So time went on; and the Persian was accomplishing his own work, for every day his servant bade him remember the Athenians, and the children of Peisistratus were ever at hand to slander them. And Darius named two generals to go to Athens and Eretria,— Datis, a Mede, and Artaphernes, his own brother's son; and he charged them to make the men of Athens and Eretria slaves, and to bring them all before him. So these generals set out, and when they came to the Aleïan plain of the Cilician land, they were joined by all the ships which Darius had ordered his subject cities to make ready. And when they had put all the men and horses on board, they sailed with six hundred triremes to Ionia; but after that, they did not go along the mainland towards the Hellespont and Thrace, but sailed from Samos through the islands, for they feared the voyage round Mount Athos, because, in the year before, Mardonius had lost there about three hundred ships and more than twenty thousand men. And they wished also to take Naxos,

VI. because they had not been able to take it with
95 Aristagoras; but as they came near, the Naxians
fled from their city, and the Persians made slaves
of all that they found in it, and burnt the temples
and the town; and then they sailed against the
other islands also.

97 Now the Delians had fled away to Tenos, and
Datis would not suffer his ships to anchor at the
island, but kept them opposite in Rheneia. And
he asked where the men of Delos were, and sent a
herald to them, saying, "O holy men, why have
ye thus fled away? for thus hath it been commanded me of the king, and so is my mind, to
hurt not the land in which the two gods were born,
neither the country nor any that dwell in it." So
he offered three hundred talents of incense upon
98 the altar, and sailed away with his army to Eretria,
taking with him the Ionians and Æolians. And
immediately after this, as the Delians said, the
island was shaken for the first time; nor has it
ever been shaken since. But this was assuredly a
sign from the gods of all the evils that were coming
on the earth.

100 But the Eretrians had heard that the Persians
were coming; and they sent to Athens to ask for
help, and the Athenians gave them four thousand
men. But the men of Eretria were divided in their
counsels, and some wished to fly to the mountains,
and others sought to betray their city to the

Persians, hoping each for his reward. And when
Æschines the son of Nothon, who was chief among
the Eretrians, heard this, he prayed the Athenians
to depart to their own land, that they might not
perish also; and so they crossed over to Oropus.
Then the Persians came and moored their ships at
Tamynæ, and Chœreæ, and Ægilia, and made ready
to attack the enemy; but the Eretrians sought only
to defend their wall. So the onset began, and for
six days there fell many on both sides; and on
the seventh, Euphorbus and Philagrus, men of repute amongst the citizens, betrayed the city to the
Persians: and they entered it and plundered the
temples and burnt them, in vengeance for the
temples which had been burnt in Sardes; and they
made the people slaves according to the command
of King Darius.

After a few days, the Persians sailed onwards to
Attica, thinking that they would do to the Athenians as they had done to the men of Eretria;
and Hippias, the son of Peisistratus, guided them
to Marathon, because that was the best place in
Attica to encamp with horses. When the Athenians
heard this, they also hastened to Marathon; and
they had ten generals, of whom the tenth was
Miltiades, the son of Kimon, who had lately come
from Chersonesus.

But before they left the city, the generals had
sent to Sparta a herald named Pheidippides, who,

VI.   as he told the Athenians, met the god Pan upon his
106 journey, when he had come near to Tegea. And
on the day after he left Athens, Pheidippides
reached Sparta and went to the rulers and said,
"O Lacedæmonians, the Athenians pray you to
help them, and not to suffer a most ancient city
of the Greeks to be enslaved by barbarians; for
Eretria has been already taken, and Hellas is
made weaker by a notable city." Then the Spartans
wished to aid the Athenians, but they could not
do so at once without breaking the law, for it was
the ninth day of the month, and they could not go
out while the moon was not yet full.

107   Thus the Spartans waited till the moon should
be full, while Hippias, the son of Peisistratus,
108 guided the barbarians to Marathon. And when
the Athenians were drawn out in the sacred ground
of Heracles, the Platæans came to their help with
all their strength; for the Platæans had given
themselves up to the Athenians, and had received
much help from them against the Thebans.

109   But the minds of the generals were divided, and
some of them were not willing to fight, for they
feared the numbers of the Medes. So Miltiades
hastened to the polemarch, Callimachus of Aphidnæ, (for the polemarchs in old time voted even as
did the generals), and said to him, "It depends on
thee, Callimachus, either to bring Athens into slavery, or to deliver it and leave behind a memorial

for all time such as has been left not even by Harmodius and Aristogeiton; for now are the Athenians in such peril as they have never been in from the time that they were a people; and if they yield to the Medes, we know what they will suffer at the hands of Hippias; but if our city gain the victory, it will become the first of all the cities of Hellas. Now, of our generals one half are not willing to fight; and if we fight not, I fear that the Athenians may follow evil counsels and take the side of the Medes; but if we fight at once, then, with the equal aid of the gods, I think that we shall be conquerors in the battle. All this depends on thee. If thy mind is as mine is, then is our country free, and our city the first of all in Hellas; but if not, then shall befall us the contrary evils to those good things which I have set before thee."

Thus Miltiades gained over Callimachus, and it was decreed that they should fight, and each general, as his day of command came, gave it over to Miltiades; but he chose not to attack them until his own day came. And on that day he drew out the Athenians in battle array; and the polemarch Callimachus (for such was then the law of the Athenians) led the right wing. Then came the tribes in their order; and the Plataeans were drawn up last upon the left wing. And from this it is that, whenever the Athenians offer solemn sacrifice, the herald prays for all blessings on the Athenians

VI. and Platæans together. Now when the army was drawn up, so as to face all the host of the Medes, the middle part of it was only a few men deep and was very weak; but both the wings were strong.

112 So, when the victims gave good omen, the Athenians began the onset, and went running towards the barbarians. Now the space between the two armies was not less than eight furlongs; and the Persians, when they saw them coming, made ready to receive them; but they thought the Athenians mad because, being so few in number, they came on furiously without either bows or horses. Then the Athenians, when they fell upon the barbarians, fought well; for they were the first Greeks, that I know of, who charged the enemy running and endured the sight of the Median dress, for up to this time the Greeks had dreaded even to hear their name.

113 Long time they fought in Marathon; and in the middle the barbarians were victorious, where the Persians and the Sakæ were drawn up. These broke the centre of the Athenians, and drove them back on the plain; but the Athenians and Platæans had the best on both the wings. Still they would not follow the barbarians who were running away, but they closed on the enemy who had broken their centre, and fought until·they overcame them. Then they went after the Persians as they fled, and slaughtered them until they

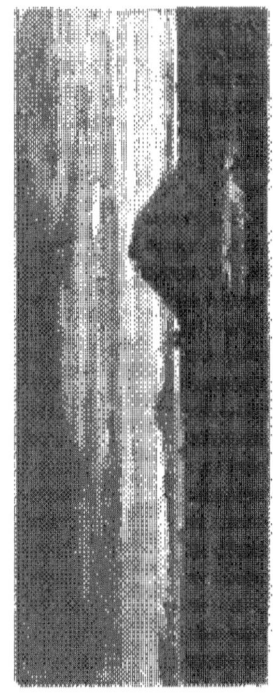

PLAIN AND TUMULUS OF MARATHON.

reached the sea; and then they tried to set the ships of the Persians on fire. In this struggle the polemarch Callimachus fell fighting bravely, and there died also Stesilaus, one of the generals, and Kynegeirus, the son of Euphorion, whose hand was cut off by an axe when he had seized the stern-ornament of one of the ships. In this way the Athenians took seven ships; with the rest the barbarians beat out to sea, and, taking up the Eretrian slaves, sailed round Sunium, wishing to reach the city before the Athenians could return thither. But the Athenians ran with all speed, and, reaching the city first, encamped in the Heracleium which is in Kynosarges, as they had encamped in the Heracleium at Marathon. And the barbarians lay for a while with their ships off Phalerum, which was at that time the port of the Athenians, and then sailed back to Asia.

In this battle at Marathon there died of the barbarians about six thousand four hundred men, and of the Athenians one hundred and ninety-two. And in the battle there happened a marvellous thing. As Epizelus, an Athenian, was fighting bravely, he was struck blind without hurt or wound in all his body, and remained blind ever after; and I have heard him tell how in the battle there stood before him a tall hoplite, whose beard overshadowed all his shield, and that this phantom passed by himself, but slew his comrade.

VI. 119 So Datis and Artaphernes sailed away to Asia, and led the Eretrians, whom they had made slaves, up to Susa. Now King Darius had been very wroth with the men of Eretria, because they had begun the wrong; but when he saw them brought before him as slaves, he did them no harm, but made them to dwell in the Kissian land in his own region which is called Ardericca: and there they were living up to my time, speaking still their old language.

120 Now when the moon was full, the Lacedæmonians set out in haste, and they reached Attica on the third day after they left Sparta. But although they were too late for the battle, still they wished to look upon the Medes. So they went on to Marathon, and saw them; and they praised the Athenians for all that they had done, and went away again to their own home.

VII. 1 So the tale of the battle of Marathon was told to King Darius the son of Hystaspes. And, though he had been very bitter against the Athenians because they had taken Sardes, yet now he was much more wroth, and desired yet more eagerly to go against Hellas. And straightway he sent heralds to all the cities, and bade them make ready an army, and to furnish much more than they had done before, both ships and horses and corn. And while the heralds were going round, all Asia was shaken for three years; but

in the fourth year the Egyptians, who had been
made slaves by Cambyses, rebelled against the
Persians, and then the king sought only the more
vehemently to go both against the Egyptians and
against the Greeks. So he named Xerxes his son
to be king over the Persians after himself, and
made ready for the march: but in the year after
the revolt of Egypt, Darius himself died, having
reigned in all six-and-thirty years; nor was he
suffered to punish the Athenians, or the Egyptians
who had rebelled against him.

CHAP. IV.

THE COUNCIL OF XERXES.— HIS DREAM AND ITS ISSUE.— THE TALE OF PYTHIUS, HIS RICHES, AND CHILDREN.— THE MARCH OF THE ARMY AND THE PASSAGE OF THE HELLESPONT.

χρυσογόνου γενεᾶς ἰσόθεος φώς,
κυανοῦν δ' ὄμμασι λεύσσων φονίου δέργμα δράκοντος,
πολύχειρ καὶ πολυναύτης Σύριόν θ' ἅρμα διώκων,
ἐπάγει δουρικλύτοις ἀνδράσι τοξόδαμνον Ἄρη.

ÆSCHYLUS.

Herodotus VII. 5 — WHEN Xerxes became king in the stead of Darius his father, he sought not at all to go against the Athenians first, and he made ready his army for Egypt. But there was with him a Persian whom he had in great honour, Mardonius the son of Gobryas, who was cousin to Xerxes and son of the sister of Darius. And he came to the king and said: "O king, it is not seemly that the Athenians, who have done much wrong to the Persians, should not suffer for their evil doing. Still do now that which thou hast in hand; and when thou hast subdued Egypt, then go against Athens, that men may speak well of thee, and that none

may dare henceforth to come against thy land." VII.
Thus he urged the king, and he added also that
Europe was a very fair country, rich in trees and
fruits, and that no man ought to possess it but the
great king.

But Mardonius spoke thus chiefly because he 6
desired a new order of things and wished to be
himself the ruler of Hellas. And in time he prevailed on Xerxes to do this, for other things happened which worked together for this end. There
came heralds from the Aleuadæ, who were princes
of Thessaly, inviting the king; and the children
of Peisistratus came to Susa, bringing with them
an Athenian soothsayer named Onomacritus, who
urged him on with oracles from Musæus. This
man said nothing of any oracles which spoke of
hurt to the barbarian, but told him only that a
Persian was destined to make a bridge over the
Hellespont, and how he should march against
Hellas.

So, in the second year after the death of Darius, 7
Xerxes marched with his army against Egypt; and
when he had subdued the whole land and made
its slavery worse than it had been under his
father, he gave it to his brother Achæmenes to
rule over, whom afterwards Inaros, the son of
Psammitichus the Libyan, slew. After this, before 8
he gathered his armies to go against Athens,
Xerxes called together the chiefest of the Persians,

VII. that he might learn their judgments and tell them his will. And when they were assembled, Xerxes said: "O Persians, I am not going to bring before you any new custom, but I only adopt that which I have received; for, as I learn from our elders, we have never been at rest from the time that we took the chief power from the Medes, when Cyrus dethroned Astyages. So the god leads us on, and good fortune ever attends us. But of those nations which Cyrus and Cambyses and my father Darius subdued, I need not speak, for ye know them well. And since I received the throne, I have striven not to fall behind them in this honour nor to acquire less power for the Persians. Nor do I think that I have failed. Wherefore I have now called you together, that I may tell you of the things which I am minded to do. I purpose to make a bridge over the Hellespont and to march with my army through Europe against Hellas, to punish the Athenians for all the evils that they have done to me and to my father. Now ye know that my father was making ready to go against these men. But he is dead, neither was he permitted to punish them; and therefore, on his behalf and on that of the Persians, I will never cease before I take and burn Athens, because they began the wrong. First they came to Sardes with Aristagoras the Milesian, my slave, and burnt the temples and the groves; and what wrongs they did to those whom Datis and Artaphernes led against them to Marathon, ye all know. Therefore am I determined to march against them; and I think that we shall gain much by going, for if we conquer these men and their neighbours who dwell in the land of Pelops the Phrygian, we shall give to the power of the Persians the wide bounds of heaven. The sun shall look upon no border-lands to ours, but I will make all nations to be one country for you, when I have passed through the whole of Europe. For I believe that no city and no nation will dare to face us in battle, as soon as these men have been put out of the way; and so the innocent and the guilty shall bear our yoke alike. And now if ye do thus, ye will please me well. Come, all of you, readily and quickly, when I name the day for meeting; and the man who comes with the best equipments, I will repay with the most honourable gifts. But, that I may not appear to follow my own counsels, I place the matter before you, that all, who will, may give their judgment."

Then Mardonius answered: "O king, not only art thou the best of all Persians that have lived, but of all that ever shall be; for thou hast given the best and truest counsel, and wilt not suffer the Ionians who dwell in Europe to mock us. Strange indeed would it be if, when from mere lust of power we have made slaves of the Sakæ and the Indians,

VII. the Ethiopians and Assyrians and other nations who never did us wrong, we should fail to punish the Athenians who have begun the quarrel. For what do we fear? Is it their number? is it their wealth or their power? We know their way of fighting, we know their weakness, and we have conquered their kinsfolk, who dwell in our land and are called Ionians and Æolians and Dorians. Yea, even I myself marched against these men at thy father's bidding; and though I came as far as Macedonia and so was but a little way from Athens, not one of them came out against me to battle. Yet these Greeks, I hear, are wont to make wars utterly without counsel, — so mad and so blind are they, — for, when they have declared war, they choose out the richest and the fairest spot, and thither they go and fight, so that the conquerors gain only evil. Of the conquered I speak not: they are utterly destroyed. Now these men, as speaking the same language, ought to settle their quarrels by words and messengers, and in any way rather than by fighting; but if fight they must, they should choose out those spots to fight in where it may be hardest to reach each other. And so, because they are thus mad, they never came out to meet me, though I went as far as Macedonia. And now will any one dare to face thee, O king, with thy great army from Asia and all thy ships? Sure I am that the Greeks are not so desperate.

But if I am wrong, and in their rash folly they
come out to battle, they will find that of all men
we are the bravest. Still we must leave nothing
untried, for things come not of their own accord,
but follow always the efforts of men."

So Mardonius, having ended his flattery, sat
down; and all the Persians kept silence, nor did
any dare to give another judgment, until Artabanus, the son of Hystaspes, the uncle of Xerxes,
rose up and said: "O king, none can choose the
better judgment, unless two have been set forth;
even as we cannot distinguish pure gold by itself,
but when we place it with other gold, then we
see which is the better. Now I urged my brother
Darius, thy father, not to march against the
Scythians, who have no city in all their land.
But he thought that he could conquer these
wandering tribes, and would not listen to me.
So he went, and lost many brave men, and came
home again. But thou, O king, art going against
men much better than the Scythians,—men who
are said to be most brave and strong both by sea
and land. And it is right that I should say why
we ought to fear them. Thou sayest that thou
wilt make a bridge over the Hellespont, and
carry thy army through Europe against Hellas:
and so may we be beaten either by land or by
sea, or even on both; for the men are said to
be strong, and it would seem that they are, if

VII. by themselves alone the Athenians destroyed the great host that landed with Datis and Artaphernes at Marathon. Yet in that fight they conquered only by land; but if they beat us by sea also, and sail to the Hellespont and break up the bridge, then it becomes terrible indeed. Yet it is no wisdom of my own that teaches me this, but the thought of that mishap which all but overtook us when thy father made a bridge over the Thracian Bosporus and the river Ister, and went against the Scythians: for with all their might the Scythians prayed the Ionians, who were guarding the bridge, to unloose it; and if Histiæus, the tyrant of Miletus, had followed then the counsel of the other tyrants, the Persians would have been utterly destroyed. Still it is fearful even to hear that the fate of the king was in one man's hand. Rush not then into so great a danger, when there is no need; but heed my words. Send away this assembly, and when thou hast thought over these matters again, then proclaim thy judgment. To take good counsel is indeed a gain; for even if anything goes against it, none the less was the good counsel taken, but it hath been overborne by chance. But the man who has counselled ill, if he prosper, receives a godsend; yet none the less was his counsel evil. Thou seest how the deity smites those creatures which hold themselves high, but

the little ones do not trouble him at all; and
how the lightning falls on the highest houses and
the tallest trees, for the haughty things are ever
made to bow down. So may a great army be
destroyed by a little one, for when fear enters
their heart, they perish shamefully; for the deity
will suffer none to have proud thoughts but
himself. So, then, to urge on matters will bring
mishaps, and from these great hurt may follow;
but in delay there is good, which time will
discover, even if we may not be able to see it
now. Such is my counsel to thee, O king. But
thou, Mardonius, son of Gobryas, speak no more
vain words about the Greeks, who deserve not
to be evil spoken of; for by thy slanders thou
movest the king yet more to go against them —
and this, I think, is the very reason of thy
counsel. Let it not be so any more, for slander
is a terrible thing. In it there are two who do
wrong, and one who suffers it; for the slanderer
injures an absent man by his words, and he who
listens does wrong if he is persuaded without
clear knowledge; and the absent man receives a
double wrong, in being slandered by one man,
and in being thought evil of by another. But if
an army *must* go against these men, come —
let the king remain in the land of the Persians,
and let us both put our children to the venture.
Then go thou with thy chosen men, and take as

vii. great an army as it may please thee to have. And if the issue be what thou hast said, then let my children be slain, and let me die also; but if it turn out as I have said, then let thy children be killed, and thyself also if thou return. And if thou likest not this but still in any case wilt lead an army against Hellas, then some of those who remain behind will hear some day that Mardonius, after great mischief done to the Persians, and torn to pieces by dogs and birds in the land of the Athenians or Lacedæmonians, if not before by the way, found out against what sort of men he besought the king to march."

11. Then was Xerxes very wroth, and said: "O Artabanus, thou art my father's brother. This shall save thee from the meet reward of thy vain words. And yet this shame do I put upon thee for thy meanness and faintness of heart, that thou shalt not go with me against Hellas, but remain at home with the women. I can do all that I have said without thee; for may I not be sprung from Darius, the son of Hystaspes, the son of Arsames, the son of Ariaramnes, the son of Teïspes, the son of Cyrus, the son of Cambyses, the son of Teïspes, the son of Achæmenes, if I take not vengeance upon the Athenians. Sure I am that if we be still, yet will not they, but will the rather come against our land, if we may judge from what they have already done. They

have burnt Sardes and marched into Asia. It is not possible, therefore, that either should draw back; but there is a struggle before both, to do and to suffer,—that all our lands may be under the Greeks, or all their country under the Persians; for there is no middle path in our enmity. It is good, therefore, that we, who have suffered beforehand, should punish them; and that so I may learn what that evil is which I shall suffer when I march against these men, whom even Pelops the Phrygian, the slave of my father, so subdued, that their land and all that dwell in it are called still by his name."

So the council was ended; and the night came on, and the words of Artabanus troubled Xerxes. And as he listened to the voice of the night [1], he learnt that he ought in no wise to march against Hellas; and when he had thus fixed his mind, he fell asleep. Then in his sleep he saw a vision, as the Persians say; and he thought that there stood over him a man fair and tall, who said, "Dost thou repent, O Persian, from leading an army against Hellas, when thou hast charged thy

---

[1] I should not wish this expression to be taken as a translation of the somewhat unusual phrase νυκτὶ βουλὴν διδούς — although a meaning not unlike it has been assigned to the phrase by some interpreters. (See the note of Bähr on the passage.) Here, however, as elsewhere, it is not my object to furnish an exact translation, or to be fettered by the conditions which must of necessity be imposed upon all translations.

vii. people to gather their hosts together? Thou doest not well in thy change of counsel, neither is there any who will forgive thee. Go thou on the road in the which thou didst purpose to walk on the day that is past." And when he had said this,
13 he vanished away. But when the day dawned, Xerxes took no heed of the dream; but he called the Persians together again, and said, "Forgive me, O Persians, that my counsel is changed. When I heard the judgment of Artabanus, my spirit grew hot within me, as in youth it is wont to do; and I spake unseemly words towards an aged man. Now, therefore, I shall follow his mind; and be ye all still, for I purpose no longer to go against Hellas." When the Persians heard
14 this, they rejoiced and did obeisance. But when it was night, again the same vision stood over Xerxes as he slept, and said, "So now, son of Darius, thou hast changed thy purpose in the sight of the Persians, and hast put aside my words as though they had never been spoken. But be thou sure that if thou set not out forthwith, as thou hast become great and mighty in a little while, so in a little while shalt thou be made low."
15 And Xerxes rose in fear and sprang from his couch, and sent a messenger to call Artabanus; and when he was come, he said, "O Artabanus, I spoke rash and vain words to thee at the first in return for thy good counsel; but in a little while

I knew that I ought to do that which thou didst
desire. And yet I cannot do so, although I wish
it; for a vision comes to me in my sleep, and
will not suffer me thus to act. Even now has it
threatened me and departed. Now if it be a god
who sends it, and if it must be that an army go
against Hellas, then the same vision will come to
thee and give thee the like charge. Therefore
put thou on all my dress, and sit first upon my
throne, and afterwards sleep upon my couch."
But Artabanus would not at the first, because he
did not think himself worthy to sit on the king's
throne, but at length he said, "To be wise, O
king, and to obey the man who gives good counsel, seems to me the same thing. Thou hast both
these virtues, but thou hast been deceived by the
conversation of wicked men, — as the sea, they
say, which is most useful to men, is not suffered
to show its own nature by the winds that fall
upon it. Nor did it so much grieve me to be
evil spoken of by thee, as that thou shouldest
choose the worse opinion when two were laid
before the Persians, seeing that the one puffed up
pride and the other taught that man should not
be ever greedy after more than has been given to
him. But now that thou art turned to the safer
judgment, and hast renounced the journey to
Hellas, thou sayest that there comes to thee a
vision from heaven, which suffers thee not to

VII. change thy purpose. Yet can this scarcely be, my son. The dreams which in their wanderings come to men, are such as I shall show thee who am many years thine elder. In sleep there come to us for the most part the visions of those things on which we have thought most during the day; and we for many days have been much intent upon this expedition. But if it be not as I suppose, but rather something divine, then thy words are rightly spoken. So let it appear to me, and give me the same charge. Yet if it must come, it ought to come to me no more if I put on thy dress than if I wear my own, and if I rest on thy couch than if I sleep on my own. For that which comes to thee in thy sleep, whatever it be, is surely not so silly as to think, on seeing me, that it looks upon thee, judging by thy vesture. If then, refusing to appear to me, it shall return to thee many times, I should say that it was sent from heaven. But if thy purpose is fixed that I must sleep on thy couch, so let it come even to me. In the meanwhile I shall remain in my present mind."

17. So spake Artabanus, for he hoped to show that the vision was nought; and he put on the king's robe and sat down on his throne, and thence went unto his couch. And the Dream of Xerxes came and stood over him, saying, "Art thou he that movest Xerxes from going against Hellas, as though thou carest for him? But neither now

nor hereafter shalt thou go unscathed, if thou seekest to turn aside that which must be; and what Xerxes must suffer if he obey not, has been already shown to him." Then the Dream appeared as though it were about to sear out his eyes with hot irons; and Artabanus cried aloud and leapt up, and told Xerxes of the vision, saying moreover, "O king, as a man who has seen many great and mighty things yield to that which is mean, I was not willing that thou shouldest in all things follow the temper of thine age, for I knew that greediness is an evil thing, and I remembered how Cyrus fared when he went against the Massagetæ, and the march of Cambyses against the Æthiopians, and how I followed Darius against the Scythians; and I thought that, if thou couldst but remain at rest, thy lot would be held blessed by all mankind. But thou art urged on by a dream from heaven, and destruction is prepared for the Greeks. Therefore is my own mind changed within me. Show then to the Persians what hath come to thee from heaven, and charge them to do as thou didst bid them at the first. See also that on thy part there may be nothing wanting." So in the morning the king told all this with gladness to the Persians, and Artabanus now urged on the things which he had spoken against before.

And yet another vision came to Xerxes, from

VII which the Magians judged that all the earth should be subdued before the king. Xerxes dreamed that he was crowned with an olive wreath, and from the olive sprang forth branches overshadowing all the earth; and presently the wreath that was around his head withered away. Then every man of the princes of the Persians went unto his own land, and made haste to gather all his men together, if so he might win the prize which the
20 king had promised. And so was the armament brought together in such sort that all that went before it were as nothing in comparison,—even the armies that had marched against the Scythians, or the hosts which the sons of Atreus led against
21 Troy. For what of all the nations of Asia did not the king lead against Hellas? and what streams failed not, as his army drank of them, save only the great rivers?

Now, because the ships that went with Mardonius the son of Gobryas had suffered much hurt when they tried to sail round Mount Athos, they worked in that part for three years beforehand, and dug a great canal across the isthmus which joins Mount Athos to the mainland; and the people
24 worked under the lash. This canal the king commanded to be made, to show his greatness and to leave a memorial behind him; for when without trouble they might have drawn the ships over the isthmus, he charged them to dig a canal so wide

that they might row two triremes abreast through it. And they who dug the canal were commanded also to make a bridge over the river Strymon.

So all things were made ready, and stores of food were laid up at all places where it was needful to place it, and chiefly at the White Shore of the Thracian land, at Tyrodiza, at Doriscus, and at Eïon, which is on the river Strymon. And in the meanwhile all the foot soldiers marched with the king to Sardes, having set out from Critalla in Cappadocia; for there it had been ordered that all the army should come to meet the king. But which of the princes furnished the best armament, I cannot tell, nor do I know whether they came to any trial in the matter.

Then they crossed the river Halys and came to Kelænæ, where are the sources of the Mæander and the Catarractes. And in this city a Lydian named Pythius, the son of Atys, received the king and all his army with much feasting, and desired to furnish money for the war. Then Xerxes asked who this man was that he should do thus, and they said, "This is he, O king, who gave to thy father Darius the golden plane-tree and the vine, and who after thee is the richest of all men." At this Xerxes marvelled, and asked Pythius what his wealth might be; and Pythius said, "I will tell thee the truth, O king. When I heard that thy army was coming, I wished to give money for

VII. the war, and I counted up my riches, and found that I had two thousand talents of silver and four hundred myriads of golden statêrs lacking seven thousand. All this I give to thee, for I can live
29 by my slaves and by my land." Then was Xerxes greatly pleased, and said that he had found none so well-minded to himself before. Wherefore he made Pythius his friend, and would take no money from him, but gave him seven thousand pieces of gold that he might have the full tale of four hundred myriads.

30 So the king went on his way, and passing by the city of Anaua he came to Colossæ, a great city of Phrygia; and when they were near Callatêbus, Xerxes saw a plane-tree which seemed to him so fair that he gave to it a golden wreath and left a man to take care of it, and then he went on to
32 Sardes. And from Sardes he sent heralds into Hellas to ask for earth and water and to bid them make ready to receive the king. Only to Athens and Lacedæmon he sent not. But to the others he sent, because he thought that all would give it now who had not given it to Darius his father.

33 Now his servants had made a bridge across the Hellespont, between Sestos and Madytos, near
34 Abydos; but a great storm came and broke it to
35 pieces and scattered it. Then was Xerxes very wroth, and commanded to scourge the Hellespont with three hundred lashes and to cast a pair of

fetters into the sea. He sent branders also, as some say, to brand the Hellespont; and he charged them to rebuke the water and cry unto it, "O bitter water, thus doth the king punish thee, because without wrong from him thou hast done him harm. But Xerxes the king will pass over thee, whether thou wilt or whether thou wilt not; and surely thou deservest no sacrifice, for thou art a false and briny river." Thus he charged them to smite the sea, and to cut off the heads of the men who had been over the work. So they who received this charge performed their thankless task, while others made a new bridge with much labour and toil, and placed earth all over it, and raised a hedge on either side, that the horses and cattle might not be frightened by seeing the sea as they passed over it.

So when all things were ready and the spring was now come, the army left Sardes to go to Abydos; and as they were going, the sun left its place in the heaven, and, although there were no clouds, it became night instead of day. And as Xerxes saw this, he was troubled and asked the Magians what this sign might mean; and they said that it foretold to the Greeks the fall of their cities, because the sun gave warnings to the Greeks, but the moon to the Persians.

Then Xerxes went on his way exulting; but Pythius the Lydian was frightened by the sign of

VII. the sun, and he said to the king, "O king, grant me that which I shall ask, for it is but a little thing for thee to give." And Xerxes bade him say on; and he answered, "O king, I have five sons, and they are all in thy army. But I am an old man; wherefore pity me, and leave the oldest of my children that he may take care of me and of my
39 riches." Then was Xerxes angry, and said, "O wretched man, I am going against Hellas, taking with me my children and servants and friends; and dost thou who art my slave, and oughtest to follow me with all thy house, dare to speak of thy son? Yet will I do to thee less than what thou dost deserve." Then he commanded that they should take the oldest of the sons of Pythius and cut his body in two pieces, and place half on either side of the road; and so the army marched between them, a very great multitude, with ser-
40 vants and cattle. When half had passed there was a space left; and behind it there came a thousand chosen horsemen of the Persians, and a thousand chosen spear-bearers with their lances turned towards the ground, and then ten sacred Nisæan horses with beautiful trappings. Behind these came the sacred chariot of Zeus, drawn by eight white horses, and their driver walked behind them holding the reins, for no man may go up upon this chariot. Then came the king himself
41 on a chariot drawn by Nisæan horses, and there

PLAIN OF TROY

followed him a thousand of the noblest of the VII.
Persians bearing spears, and a numberless host
came after them of spearmen and archers and
horsemen; and all that followed the army were
mingled in the rear.

So they went on, and tarried for a night under 42
Mount Ida, where a storm of thunder and lightning slew a great multitude. And when they 43
reached the Scamander, of which the stream failed
as the army drank of it, Xerxes desired to see the
Pergamus of Priam; and he went up and offered
to Athena a thousand cows, and the Magians
poured libations to the heroes; and because they
did this at night, the army who saw it afar off
were sore afraid.

But when they reached Abydos, Xerxes desired 44
to see all his army: and he sat upon a seat of
white stone which had been made ready for him;
and he beheld the army on the shore, and the
ships, and as he looked he desired to see a
battle among the ships. So it was done, and
the Phœnicians of Sidon conquered. Then was
the king pleased with the fight and with the army,
and as he saw the Hellespont hidden by the ships 45
and all the shore and the plains of Abydos full
of men, Xerxes called himself a happy man, and
after that he wept. But when his uncle Artabanus, 46
who had besought him at the first not to go
against Hellas, saw this, he marvelled and said,

VII. "O king, thou doest strange things; even now thou didst call thyself happy, and then thou weepest." And the king answered, "Thought came upon me and sorrow for the shortness of the life of man, because, after a hundred years, of all this great host not one shall remain alive." But Artabanus said, "There are other things more woful than this, for there is no man so happy but what he will often wish to die rather than to live. The sorrows that come upon us, and the diseases that trouble us, make our life which is short appear long, and therefore from so much wretchedness death becomes the best refuge; and heaven, if it gives us a taste of happiness, yet is 47 found to be but a jealous giver." And Xerxes said to Artabanus, "Let us speak no more of mortal life, which is even as thou sayest; nor let us bring evil things to mind, when we have a good work in our hands. But tell me this: if thou hadst not seen the vision clearly, wouldst thou have kept thine old counsel, or wouldst thou have changed? Tell me the truth." Then said Artabanus, "May the dream be accomplished as we both desire, yet am I still full of care and anxious, because I see that two very mighty 48 things are most hostile to thee." And the king asked, "What may these things be? Will the army of the Greeks be more in number than mine, or will our ships be fewer than theirs? for if it be so, we will quickly bring yet another host together." And he answered, "O king, no one who has sense could find fault either with thy army or with thy ships; and if more be gathered together, the two things become yet more hostile, and these are the land and the sea. The sea has no harbour which, if a storm come, can shelter so many ships. And yet there is need not merely of one haven, but of many along the whole coast where we must sail. Chance rules men, and men cannot control chance. The land too is hostile, and if nothing resists thee it becomes yet more hurtful the further that we may go; for men are never satisfied with good fortune, and so the length of the journey must at last bring about a famine. Now that man is bravest who is timid in counsel and bold in action." And Xerxes answered, "Thou speakest well, Artabanus. Yet of what use is it to count up all these things? for if we were always to be weighing every chance, we should never do anything at all. It is better to be bold and suffer half the evil, than, by fearing all things, to escape all suffering. And how can a man find certainty in counsel? Surely advantage follows action; and good fortune comes not to those who will make no venture. See how great is the power of the Persians. If the kings who have gone before me had followed counsellors like thee, it would never have been as it is now.

VII. But they faced the danger and gained this dominion, for great things must be compassed by great risks. We then, like them, go forth at the fairest season of the year, and when we have subdued all Europe we will return home, having been vexed neither by famine nor by any other evil. We carry great store of food with us, and we will take the corn of the lands through which we shall pass; for we march not against wandering tribes, but against men who live by tillage."

51 Then said Artabanus, "Though thou fearest nothing, O king, yet receive my counsel; for weighty matters need many words. Cyrus, the son of Cambyses, brought all Ionia, save only Athens, to pay tribute to the Persians. Send not then these men in any way against their fathers, for even without them we shall be able to conquer. If they go, they must either be most unjust in enslaving the land from which they spring, or most just by setting it free. If they are unjust, our gain is but little; but if they are just, they can do us great harm. Think then on the old saying, that the end of a work is not always clear at the 52 beginning." But the king answered, "O Artabanus, in this thou art most of all deceived; for thou and all who went with Darius against the Scythians know that it lay with these Ionians to save or destroy the whole army of the Persians. But they were faithful and did us no harm; and

besides this, their wives, their children, and their substance are all with us. Wherefore be of good courage, and guard for me my house and my empire, for to thee alone do I commit my sceptre." So Xerxes sent Artabanus away to Susa, and called together the chief of the Persians, and said to them, "Be strong, O Persians, and of great courage, and shame not the deeds of your fathers. We are marching against brave men, and if we conquer these, there are none on the face of the earth who will be able to stand against us. Now then let us cross over, when we have prayed to the gods who guard the Persian land."

So that day they made ready to cross; and on the day after, they waited till the sun was risen, and offered up all kinds of perfumes on the bridge and strewed myrtle branches along the road. And when the sun rose, Xerxes poured wine from a golden cup into the sea, and prayed to the Sun that no harm might happen unto him which might prevent him from conquering all Europe. Then he threw the cup into the Hellespont with a golden goblet and a Persian dagger. But whether he offered these to the sun, or whether he gave them to the sea, because it repented him that he had scourged it, I cannot tell.

So they crossed over, first a thousand Persians with crowns upon their heads, and then the mingled throng of all the nations. These went on the first

vii. day, and on the second day the horsemen and the spear-bearers with their lances turned towards the ground; and these also had crowns upon their heads. And after them came the sacred horses and chariot, and the king himself with his spearmen and the thousand horsemen; and the rest of the army followed. So Xerxes saw his host cross under the lash of those who drove them, and they were seven days and seven nights in passing over; and when they had crossed, a man of the Hellespont said, "O Zeus, why wilt thou, in the likeness of a Persian and calling thyself by the name of Xerxes, uproot all Hellas, leading against it all the race of man? for even without these thou mightest do this."

And while the army passed, the ships also crossed over, and they all met at Doriscus in Thrace; and there the army was numbered, and all the host was one hundred and seventy myriads of men. All the nations of the earth were there, and every fashion of raiment was to be seen, and all kinds of weapons, — Persians and Medes and Kissians, Bactrians, Sakæ, and Hyrcanians, and the peoples of Assyria, of India and Arabia, the Parthians and Chorasmians, and many others. And some went on foot, and some on horses, and each fought after the fashion of his own people. And there were twelve hundred ships of the Phœnicians and Egyptians, and from the Lycians and Cilicians, from the Dorians and Ionians, and from the islands. And in all the ships there were soldiers of the Persians and Sakæ and Medes.

When the hosts were numbered, the king went through them upon a chariot, nation by nation, and asked their names, and his scribes wrote them down, until he came to the end. After this he went into a ship of Sidon, and sailed in front of all the ships, and their names and numbers he caused to be written down also.

Then the king sent for Demaratus, the son of Ariston, who went with him against Hellas, and said to him, "Demaratus, thou art a Greek, and, as I hear, of no mean city. Now therefore tell me, will the Greeks lift up their hands against me? for it seems to me that if they were gathered together with all the dwellers of the West, they would not be able to fight with me, because they agree not one with the other. Still I would hear what thou hast to say about them." Then said Demaratus, "O king, shall I speak the truth, or only that which is pleasant?" And the king charged him to say truly, for that he should be not less dear than he was before. Then Demaratus answered, "Know then, O king (since thou wishest me to speak that which is no lie), that poverty always dwells with the Greeks; but courage they have won from wisdom and the strength of law, by which they keep off both poverty and tyranny. But, though all the Greeks are worthy of praise, yet now I speak of the Lacedæmonians only. Be sure that these will never receive thy words which bring slavery to Hellas, and that they will come out against thee to battle, even though all the rest should take thy side; neither ask thou what their numbers are that they should dare to do this, for if a thousand set out, these will fight with thee, be they more or be they less." And Xerxes laughed and said, "O Demaratus, sayest thou that a thousand men will fight with my great army? Tell me now—thou wast once their king—wilt thou fight straightway with ten men? Yet if each of them will match ten men of mine, thou, their king, shouldest match twenty. And so might thy words be true. But if in size they are like all other Greeks whom I have seen, see that thy speech be not vain boasting. Come and let us reason upon it. How could a thousand or a myriad or five myriads, who are all free and not ruled by one man, withstand so great a host? Nay, we are even more than a thousand to one, even if they be five thousand. If, according to our custom, they were ruled by one, then, through fear of this one, they would become brave beyond their own nature, and being driven by the scourge would go against a larger host than their own. But now, left to their own freedom,

they will do none of these things. Still, I think
that, even if their numbers were equal, they could
not withstand the Persians alone. But I too have
what thou speakest of, though it be but rare; for
among my spear-bearers are men who will fight
with three Greeks at once. Wherefore in thine
ignorance thou speakest foolishly." But Demaratus said, "I knew at the first, O king, that
the truth would not please thee. But since thou
hast compelled me, I have spoken of the Spartans
as I ought to speak. What love I bear to them,
thou knowest well. They have robbed me of my
power and of my honours, and driven me to
a strange land; and thy father received me and
gave me a house and food. Is it likely then that
I should put aside the kindness which he showed
to me? I say not indeed that I am able to fight
with ten men or with two, nor willingly would I
fight with one; but if I must fight, and if the stake
were great, then would I choose to fight with one
of those whom thou thinkest equal to three Greeks.
So, too, the Lacedæmonians one by one are as
strong as other men, but, taken together, they are
strongest of all, for, though they are free, yet are
they not without a lord. Law is their master,
whom they fear much more than thy people fear
thee. So they do whatsoever it commands: and
it commands always the same thing, charging them
never to fly from any enemy, how strong soever he

be, but remain in their ranks and conquer or die. If now I seem to speak foolishly, let me keep silence for the time to come, for I have spoken only at thy bidding. Yet may all things go as thou desirest." Then Xerxes laughed again and was not at all angry, but sent him away kindly.

So the army went onwards, and all those whom they met they compelled to go with them; and when they came to the river Strymon, the Magians offered to it white horses in sacrifice; and at the place called the Nine Roads, they buried alive nine youths and maidens, children of the people of the land. This they did after the fashion of the Persians, even as Amestris, the wife of Xerxes, when she grew old, buried alive fourteen youths, sons of chief men among the Persians, to do honour to the god who dwells beneath the earth.

Now wherever the king and the army came, they ate up all the wealth of the land, and left nothing behind them. And when they were come into Mygdonia, lions fell upon the camels who carried the corn. These came down by night, and touched neither man nor beast, but the camels only. And the king abode many days in Pieria, until the heralds who had been sent into Hellas came back—some empty, and some bearing earth and water.

Now many of the Greeks had given earth to

THE NINE ROADS (the site of Amphipolis)

the king, and among them were the people of Thessaly and Phthiotis, the Locrians and Magnesians, and all the Bœotians, except only the men of Thespiæ and Platæœ; and against these the other Greeks swore with an oath that they would be avenged on them when the war should be over. But to Athens and Sparta the king sent no heralds, because, when heralds came to them from Darius his father, they threw some of them into a dungeon and others into a ditch, and bade them thence to bear earth and water to the king.

So they who gave earth were of good courage; and they who gave not, feared greatly, because of the treachery of the others, and because they had not ships enough to go out against the fleet of the Persians.

And so it was that, if the Athenians had feared the coming danger and left their country, or, even without leaving it, had yielded themselves up to Xerxes, none else would have dared to withstand the king by sea. And on the land this would have been the issue: even if many walls had been raised across the Isthmus, the Lacedæmonians would have been forsaken by their allies, as they yielded one by one to the Persians in their ships. And so, after doing brave deeds, they might have died nobly; or else, seeing all the others yielding to the Mede, would have done

VII. likewise: and so in both ways Hèllas would have come under the rule of the Persians, for I cannot see how the Isthmian walls would have helped them, when the king had the power by sea. But now may we rightly call the Athenians the saviours of Hellas, for with them was the scale of things to turn. And they chose that Hellas should continue free, and raised up and cheered all those who yielded not to the barbarian. Thus, next after the gods, they drove away the king, because they feared not the oracles from Delphi, neither were they scared by the great perils which were coming upon their country.

CHAP. V.

THE ORACLES OF DELPHI, AND THE COUNSELS OF THEMISTOCLES. — THE EMBASSIES TO ARGOS AND TO SYRACUSE. — LEONIDAS AT THERMOPYLÆ.

> Τῶν ἐν Θερμοπύλαις θανόντων
> εὐκλεὴς μὲν ἁ τύχα,
> καλὸς δ' ὁ πότμος,
> βωμὸς δ' ὁ τάφος,
> πρὸ γόων δὲ μνᾶστις,
> ὁ δ' οἶτος ἔπαινος·
> ἐντάφιον δὲ τοιοῦτον
> οὔτ' εὐρὼς, οὔθ' ὁ πανδαμάτωρ
> ἀμαυρώσει χρόνος, ἀνδρῶν ἀγαθῶν.
>
> SIMONIDES.

Now the Athenians had sent messengers to consult the god at Delphi; and when they were come thither and had offered sacrifice, the priestess Aristonikê made answer to them, and said: [Herodotus VII. 140]

"O wretched people, why sit ye still? Leave your homes and the strongholds of your city, and flee away.

"For head and body, feet and hands, nothing is sound, but all is wretched.

VII.
"For fire and war, which are hastening hither in a Syrian chariot, will presently make it low.

"And other strong places also shall they destroy, and not yours only.

"And many temples of the undying gods shall they give to the flame.

"Down their walls the big drops are streaming, as they tremble for fear.

"And from their roofs the black blood is poured down, for the sorrow that is coming.

"But go ye from my holy place, and brace up your hearts for the evil."[1]

141. When the messengers heard these words, they were greatly afraid. But Timon, the son of Androbûlus, a great man among the Delphians, when he saw them thus utterly cast down, bade them take olive-branches and go again to the god. So they went, and said, "O king, look upon us who come now as suppliants, and tell us something better about our country, for, if not, we will stay here till we die."

Then the priestess spake and answered them: "Pallas cannot prevail with Zeus who dwells on Olympus, though she has besought him with many prayers.

---

[1] κακοῖς ἐπιδότατε θυμόν. The passage is ambiguous, and its meaning has been disputed. See Grote's History of Greece, vol. v. p. 82; Thirlwall's History of Greece, vol. ii. p. 294; and Rawlinson's Herodotus, vol. iv. p. 119.

"And his word, which I now tell you, is firmly fixed as a rock.

"For thus saith Zeus, that, when all else within the land of Kecrops is wasted, the wooden wall alone shall not be taken; and this shall help you and your children.

"But wait not until the horsemen come and the footmen. Turn your backs upon them now, and one day ye shall meet them.

"And thou, divine Salamis, shalt destroy those that are born of women, when the seed time comes or the harvest."

These words, as being more hopeful, the messengers wrote down, and went back to Athens and read them before the people. And the assembly was divided; for some of the old men thought that the god spake of the Acropolis, that it should not be taken, because long ago there had been a thorn hedge round it; while others said that he meant them to leave their city and betake themselves to the ships. But they who said this were troubled by the last words of the priestess, for all the soothsayers took them to mean that they should be beaten in a sea-fight at Salamis.

But among the Athenians there was a man named Themistocles, the son of Neocles, to whom the people gave, every day, more heed. This man came forward and said, "O Athenians, the soothsayers are wrong. If these words had been spoken

VII. of us, I am sure that the priestess would have said Salamis the *wretched*, and not Salamis the *divine*, if the people of the land were doomed to die there. The words are spoken not of us but of our enemies. Arm then for the fight at sea, for this is the wooden wall." And the Athenians believed Themistocles rather than the soothsayers, because they would not have them fight by sea or even lift a hand against the enemy, but besought them to flee away and dwell in some other land.

144 And at this time another judgment of Themistocles stood them in good stead; for many years before, when the treasury of the people was rich and they were going to share among the citizens the money from the silver-mine of Laureium, he prevailed with them not to give away the money, but to build ships with it for the war against Ægina. And so it was that this war saved Hellas, for it made the Athenians become seamen; and the ships then built were never used against the men of Ægina, but were now of benefit to all the Greeks. And now they resolved to build many more ships
145 to fight with the barbarians by sea. And with them all the Greeks who took the good side made a vow that they would put away all feuds one against the other and cease from war; for there had been several wars going on amongst them, but the greatest was that between the men of Athens and Ægina. They determined also to send

spies to Asia, to see how Xerxes fared, and to send
messengers to Argos and Sicily, to Kerkyra and
Crete, that all might come to the aid of their
kinsmen against the Persian.

So the spies went to Sardes; but they were 146
caught and were led away to be put to death.
When Xerxes heard it, he charged his spear-
bearers to bring them before him, if they were
yet alive; and when he saw them and knew the
reason of their coming, he ordered that they should
be led through his whole army, and sent away unhurt after they were tired with seeing everything.
And the king said that, if the spies had been killed, 147
the Greeks could not have heard beforehand of
all his great might, and yet they would do them
but little hurt by slaying three men; but now he
thought to have no trouble by marching against
them when the spies told them of his mighty army.
At another time, when he was at Abydos, he saw
ships with corn from Pontus sailing through the
Hellespont; and they who sat by were ready to
seize them, and waited only for the king's command. But Xerxes asked whither they were sailing, and they answered, "To thy enemies, O king,
laden with corn." Then he said, "Why, we are
going thither also. What harm do they do by
taking corn for me?"

After this, the messengers came to Argos, but 148
they spoke to the Argives in vain. Many tales

VII. were told about it, but their own story is this, that, when they first heard that the Persians were coming, they sent to Delphi to ask the god what it would be best for them to do, because they had lost many men in their war with the Lacedæmonians, and that the priestess said to them:

"O thou that art hated by thy neighbours, but dear to the undying gods,

"Keep thy spear beside thee, and sit still.

"Guard thy head, and the head shall save the body."

So, on the coming of the messengers, they said that, although the god forbade it, they would go out with the Spartans, if the Spartans would make peace with them for thirty years and give them 149 half the power. But the Spartans said that they had two kings, while the Argives had only one, and that they could not give him more than one vote out of three. Then the Argives were filled with anger, and bade the messengers leave Argos before the setting of the sun, if they would not be treated as enemies.

150 Such was their own tale; but another was told throughout Hellas, that Xerxes himself sent a herald to Argos who said, "O men of Argos, thus saith the king, We believe that Perses, from whom we are sprung, was the son of Perseus the son of Danaë, and of Andromeda the daughter of Kepheus. So then we are descended from you; and it is not

SYRACUSE.

right that we should go against those from whom
we spring, or that you should oppose us by aiding
others. Sit still then, and if things go as I
would have them, there are none whom I will
honour more than you." And so, when the messengers of the Greeks came, they asked the Spartans for an equal share of power, because they
knew that they would not give it. Now, whether
Xerxes really did so send a herald, I cannot say
with certainty; but this I know, that if all men
were to bring together their charges against others,
in order to make an exchange, they would gladly
go back each with his own burden, after stooping
to pick up that of his neighbour; and so it can
hardly be said that the Argives behaved worse
than all others. Still I can only say what has
been said by others; and the tale is also told that
the men of Argos in very truth called the Persians
against Hellas, because they were vexed at being
beaten in war by the Lacedæmonians.

Then also the messengers who had been sent to
Sicily came to Gelon the tyrant of Syracuse, and
said to him, "The Lacedæmonians and Athenians
have sent us to ask thy help against the barbarian;
for thou surely knowest that the Persian is bringing all the army of the East from Asia against
Hellas, pretending that he comes against Athens
only, but wishing really to make all the Greeks
his slaves. Thy power is great, and no little

VII. portion of Hellas is thine, because thou rulest
over Sicily. Help us then to deliver our country.
If we stand together, our arms are strong, and we
can match the enemy in battle. But if some
betray and others will not help us, then is it to be
feared that all Hellas must fall; for it is vain to
think that the Persian will not come against you,
if we are conquered. Take heed then in time.
By aiding us thou savest thyself; and a good
issue commonly follows wise counsel." But Gelon was angry, and answered vehemently, "What
grasping and selfish speech is this, O ye Greeks,
that ye ask my help against the barbarian?
When I sought your aid against the men of Car-
thage, and promised to open to you markets
from which you have reaped rich gains, ye would
not come; and, as far as lies with you, all this
country had been under the barbarians to this
day. But I have prospered; and now that war
threatens you, ye begin to remember Gelon. But
I will not deal with you as ye have dealt with
me. I will give you two hundred triremes and
twenty thousand hoplites, with horsemen and
archers, slingers and runners; and I will give
corn for all the army of the Greeks as long as
the war shall last. But I must be the chieftain
and leader of the Greeks against the barbarians.
Not otherwise will I go myself or suffer others
to go."

Then Syagrus the Spartan could not refrain VII. 159
himself, but said, "In very deed would Agamemnon the son of Pelops mourn, if he were to hear that the Spartans had been robbed of their honour by Gelon and the Syracusans. Dream not that we shall ever yield it to you. If thou choosest to aid Hellas, do so under the Lacedæmonians; and if thou wilt not have it so, then stay at home." Then said Gelon, "O Spartan friend, abuse commonly makes a man angry; but I will not pay thee back thy insults in kind. If ye cling to power, is it not likely that I should do so too, who lead many more ships and men than you have? But as ye are obstinate, I will thus far yield. If ye rule by sea, I will rule by land; if ye rule by land, then must I rule on the sea." But hereon 161 the messenger of the Athenians stood forth and said, "O king of the Syracusans, the Greeks have sent us not because they want a leader, but because they want an army. Now of an army thou sayest little, but much about the command: and when thou didst ask to lead us all, we left it to the Lacedæmonians to speak; but now that thou askest to rule by sea, then know that, not even if they should wish it, will we yield to thee in this. We grudge not to the Spartans their power by land, but we will give place to none on the sea. We have more seamen than all the Greeks; and we are of all Greeks the most

VII. ancient nation, and we alone have never changed our land; and in the war, of which Homer sings, our leader was the best who came to Ilium to set
162 an army in battle array." Then answered Gelon, "O Athenian, you seem likely to have many leaders, but few that may be led. But since ye will yield nothing and grasp everything, hasten home and tell the Greeks that the spring-time has been taken out of their year."

163 So the messengers sailed away; but the tale is also told that, as soon as Gelon heard that Xerxes had crossed the Hellespont, he sent Cadmus, a man of Cos, to Delphi, with much money and with friendly words, to watch and see how the war should go, and if Xerxes conquered, to give him earth and water, but if not, then to come
165 home again. But the men of Sicily say against all this, that Gelon would have helped the Greeks if he could, but that there came against Sicily at this time a great army under Hamilcar the son of Hanno, king of the Carthaginians; and that he therefore sent money for the Greeks to Delphi because he was not able to help them with men.

168 Now the messengers, who were coming from Gelon, came to Kerkŷra, and asked the people to aid them; and they answered them in fair words, but did nothing. For they manned sixty ships, and lay off the cape of Tænarus, waiting to see how the war would turn; so that, if the Persian

conquered, they might have favour with him for withholding so many ships from the battle; and if the Greeks gained the day, they might say that the Etesian winds hindered them from coming up in time.

But the men of Thessaly had taken the side of the Persians against their will; and when they heard that they were going to cross over into Europe, they sent messengers to the Isthmus, where many were gathered together from the cities who would not yield to the barbarian. And they came and said, "O ye Greeks, ye must guard the passes of Olympus, that so Thessaly and all Hellas may be safe from the enemy. We will do what we can; but you must also send an army to help us, and, if not, we must make our peace with the Persian. We, who lie in his path first, cannot all be sacrificed for those who will not aid us." Then they determined to send an army by sea, which sailed through the Euripus and then went by land from Alos to the vale of Tempe, which lies between Ossa and Olympus. There they pitched their camp and abode a few days, until a messenger came from Alexander the son of Amyntas, a Macedonian, to bid them depart lest they should be trampled down by the great host of the Persians. So they followed this counsel, chiefly because they learnt that there was another pass into Thessaly through the

country of the Perrhebians by the city of Gonnus;
and, marching down to the sea, they sailed back
to the Isthmus. And the men of Thessaly, when
they found themselves forsaken, went over altogether to the Persian, and were ever after most
useful to the king.

So the Greeks at the Isthmus took counsel
where they should fix the war; and the counsel
which prevailed was that they should guard the
pass in Thermopylæ, because it was a single pass
and narrower than the entrance into Thessaly or
the Peloponnesus. Nor did they know, until
they came to Thermopylæ and learnt it from the
men of Trachis, that there was yet another path,
by which those who kept the pass were at length
taken. And while the army went thither, the
ships were sent to Artemisium in the land of
Histiæa, because it was near at hand. For the
Thracian sea becomes narrow between the island
of Skiathos and the Magnesian land; and from
that point of Eubœa which is opposite to this
strait begins the Artemisian shore. Now the
pass through Trachis is about fifty feet wide,
where narrowest, but at Thermopylæ and Alpeni
there is room only for a single wheel-track; and
near Anthela it becomes again as narrow. Between these two spots there rises on the west a
rugged and steep mountain, and on the east is
marsh and sea. Here also are warm springs, and

an altar built to Heracles. There was also a wall VII.
to this pass, and gates, with which the Phokians
sought to shut out the Thessalians when they
came to dwell in the Æolian land. The greater
part of this wall had fallen by age, but many
thought that they should raise it again and meet
the Persian here, while they could get food from
the village of Alpeni.

Meanwhile the Delphians besought the god for 178
themselves and for their country, and the priestess
bade them pray to the winds, for these could
greatly befriend Hellas. With this answer they
cheered all who dreaded the coming of the Persian, and won for themselves undying gratitude.
And ten of the Persian ships found three ships of 179
the Greeks keeping watch at Skiathos, which fled
at sight of them. But the one which came from 180
Trœzen was taken; and the Persians led the
fairest man of the crew to the prow of the ship,
and there slew him for good omen, as being the
first and most beautiful of the Greeks whom they
had taken. Another which came from Ægina 181
gave them some trouble, for Pytheas, one of the
crew, fought fiercely until his whole body was cut
and wounded; and when he fell, the Persians
sought by every means to save him alive and to
heal his wounds with ointments and fine linen,
and showed him to all the army as one who had
done great deeds, and treated him kindly: but all

100   TALE OF THE GREAT PERSIAN WAR.

VII. 182 the rest they made slaves. The third ship, which
came from Athens, escaped to the mouth of the
Peneius, where it was taken by the Persians; but
the men had leaped on shore, and went by land
to Athens. All this the Greeks at Artemisium
learnt by fire-beacons from Skiathos, and they
fled in great fear to Chalkis to guard the Euripus,
and left watchmen on the high lands of Euboea.

184   Thus far the army of the barbarian had gone
without hurt; and its numbers, so far as I can
tell, were these. In the ships were fifty-one
myriads of men; and the Persian army, which
came by land, had more than one hundred and
eighty myriads of footmen and horsemen and of
185 Arabs who rode on camels. To these were added
all those whom the king had gathered in Europe;
and these could not be less than two-and-thirty
186 myriads. And the servants and traders, and all
others who followed the army, were more in
number perhaps than the fighting men; so that,
in all, Xerxes brought five hundred and twenty-
eight myriads of men as far as Thermopylae and
187 the shore of Sepias. But of the women, and of
all the beasts of burden, and of Indian dogs, it
would not be possible to count up the numbers:
so that to me the marvel is not so much that the
streams should fail, but that food could be found
for so great a multitude; for of corn alone eleven
myriads of pecks must have been consumed each

day, even if we count nothing for the women, the beasts of burden, and the dogs. And of all these myriads of men, none was more worthy than Xerxes himself, for beauty and for stature, to have so great power.

But when they came to the shore between Casthanæa and Sepias, in the Magnesian land, the ships that came first were moored upon the beach, while the rest lay beyond them at anchor and were ranged in rows eight deep facing the sea. So they lay all night; and at break of day the air was clear and the sea still, but soon a tempest rose with a strong east wind, which is called here the wind of the Hellespont. Then those who saw the storm increasing, and who could so take refuge, drew their ships up on the shore, and escaped; but all the ships which were out at sea were borne away and dashed upon the Ovens of Pelion, and all along the beach as far as Melibœa and Casthanæa. And the story is told, that at this time the Athenians prayed to Boreas, because an oracle bade them call on him who had married their kinswoman,—for Boreas had for his wife Oreithyia, the daughter of Erectheus; and so, when the storm rose, they offered sacrifice, and besought Boreas and Oreithyia to aid them, by destroying the ships of the barbarians as they had done before at Athos; and after this, they built a temple to Boreas on the banks of the river Ilissus. In this storm they who count the fewest say that there perished not less than four hundred ships, and men not to be told for number, and countless riches: so that this havoc was greatly a benefit to Ameinocles who had land in these parts, for from the shore he took up goblets of silver and of gold, and costly treasures of many kinds, until he became a very rich man. But of the corn ships and others that were destroyed, the number was never known; and the captains threw up a high fence with the wood of the wrecks, lest the Thessalians should fall on them in their evil plight, for the storm lasted for three days. At last the Magians offered sacrifice and appeased the wind, or else it went down of its own will. But the watchmen on the heights of Euboea ran down on the second day of the storm, and told to the Greeks all that had befallen the fleet of the Persians. And when they heard it, they poured out libations to Poseidon the Saviour, and hastened with all speed to Artemisium, thinking that very few only of the ships would come out to meet them. But when the wind ceased and the sea grew calm, the Persians dragged down their ships, and, sailing along the shore, doubled the cape of Sepias, and went into the gulf of Pagasæ. Of these ships, fifteen set out much later than the rest, and, chancing to see the ships of the Greeks at Artemisium, took them to be their own, and, sailing down, fell into the hands of their enemies; and all the men who were on board were bound with chains and sent as prisoners to the Corinthian Isthmus; but the rest of the Persian fleet reached Aphetæ in safety. And Xerxes went on through Thessaly and Achaia, and encamped in Trachis, in the Melian land; while the Greeks lay in the pass which is called Thermopylæ. Here there were gathered together three hundred hoplites of the Spartans, and one thousand of the men of Tegea and Mantineia; and others from the Arcadian Orchomenus, from Corinth and Mykenæ, and some also of the Thespians and the Thebans. Thither also had come many of the Locrians of Opûs, and of the Phokians, at the bidding of the Greeks, who told them that many more were coming up behind them, and that the men of Athens and Ægina were guarding the sea: so that they had no cause for fear, for it was no god who was invading Hellas but a mortal man, and no man lived who should never see evil, nay, that the greatest of men suffer the worst of evils; and so the Persian, as being mortal, should fall from his great glory. So they came to help the Greeks at Trachis; and the chief of all this army was Leonidas, the son of Anaxandridas, king of Sparta, with whom there came three hundred chosen men

VII. of Lacedæmon. And the Thebans he summoned to Pylæ, because it was noised abroad that they were greatly favouring the Persian, and he wished to know whether they would take his side openly or not. So they dealt craftily with Leonidas, and sent four hundred men.

These, then, were sent on first, while the rest remained behind, for the Carneian feast was at hand in Sparta, and the great games of Olympia fell also at this time. So they purposed to march when these should be ended, for they never thought that the strife in Thermopylæ would so soon be over. In the meanwhile, the Greeks took counsel with Leonidas, and some wished to fall back and guard the Isthmus; but the men of Phokis and the Locrians were urgent that they should stay, and send messengers for more help, because they were but a few men to fight with the great army of the Persians.

While they thus took counsel, Xerxes sent a horseman to learn their numbers and see what they were doing; and he came to their camp, but he could not see it all, for he was hindered by the wall which the Greeks had raised up again. But outside of it were the Lacedæmonians, and their arms were piled against the wall, while some of them were wrestling and others were combing their hair. And he marvelled at the sight, and having counted their numbers went back quietly (for none pursued him or took notice of him), and told Xerxes all that he had seen.

Now the king could not understand that they were making ready either to die or to slay their enemies, but thought that they were doing childish and silly things. So he sent for Demaratus and asked him what all this might mean; and he said, "When we first set out against Hellas, I told thee about these men, and thou didst mock my words when I said how these things would end. Yet it is most needful for me to speak the truth before thee; wherefore hearken now. These men are here to fight for the pass; and when they have to face a mortal danger, their custom is to comb and deck out their hair. Be sure then that if thou canst conquer these and the rest who remain behind in Sparta, there is no other nation which shall dare to raise a hand against thee, for now art thou face to face with the bravest men of all Hellas." But Xerxes believed him not, and asked how so few men could ever fight with his great army. And Demaratus said, "O king, deal with me as with a liar, if these things come not to pass as I say." But Xerxes would not believe him still, and four days he waited, thinking that they would assuredly run away; but when he found that they remained there in folly and lack of shame, he was angry and charged the Medians and Kissians to go and bring them all bound before

VII. him. So they hastened to take them, but many were slain; and although others came up, yet
211 could they not prevail. After these came chosen men of the Persians, who were called Immortals, with Hydarnes for their leader; and they thought to take them easily, but fared no better, for their spears were shorter than those of the Greeks, and their numbers were of no use in the narrow pass. And the Lacedæmonians fought bravely and wisely, and, pretending sometimes to fly, drew the barbarians into the pass, when they turned upon them suddenly and slew great multitudes, until
212 they all fled back to their camp. Thrice in this battle the king leaped from his throne in terror for his army; but on the next day he sent them forth again, thinking that the enemy would be too weary to fight. But they were all drawn out in battle array, save only the Phokians; and these were placed upon the hill to guard the pathway. So the Persians fared as they had done before, and then went back to their camp.
213 And the king was greatly troubled, until there came a Melian named Ephialtes, in hope of some great reward, and, telling him of the path which led over the hill to Thermopylæ, destroyed the Greeks who were guarding it. This man fled afterwards in terror to Thessaly, and the Pylagoræ put a price on his head, when the Amphictyons were gathered together at Pylæ; and at last he was

slain by a man of Trachis at Antikyra. There VII. 214
is indeed another story which says that two other
men showed Xerxes the path; but the Pylagoræ
put the price on the head of Ephialtes, and surely
they must have known best who betrayed the path
to the Persians.

Then Xerxes, in great joy, sent Hydarnes with 215
his men from the camp, as the daylight died
away. And all night long they followed the path 217
Anopœa, with the mountains of Æta on the right
and the hills of Trachis on the left. The day
was dawning when they reached the peak of the
mountain; and there the thousand hoplites of the
Phokians were keeping watch and guarding the
pathway, for they had charged themselves with
this task of their own free will. While the 218
Persians were climbing the hill, the Phokians
knew not of their coming, for the whole hill was
covered with oak trees; but they knew what had
happened when the Persians reached the summit.
Not a breath of wind was stirring, and they heard
the trampling of their feet as they trod on the
fallen oak leaves. At once they started up, and
before they had well put on their arms, the barbarians were upon them. But the Persians were
frightened as they saw men making ready to fight,
for Hydarnes had not thought to meet any; but
when he learnt from Ephialtes that these were
not the Lacedæmonians, he drew out his men for

battle. And the Phokians, covered with a shower of arrows, fell back to the highest ground, because they thought that the Persians were coming chiefly against them; and there they made ready to fight and die. But the Persians, taking no more heed of them, hastened with all speed down the hill.

210 In the pass itself, the soothsayer Megistias, as he looked upon the victims, first told them that on the next day they must die. There came deserters also, who said that the Persians were coming round; and as the day was dawning watchmen also ran to tell them the same thing. Then the Greeks took counsel, and some urged flight and went away each to his own city, while others remained 220 with Leonidas. But there is another story that he sent them away himself lest they should all be slain; and this tale I rather believe,—that he knew them to be faint-hearted, and so suffered them not to stay, but that it was not seemly for himself to fly. So he stayed where he was, and left behind him a great name, and the happiness of Sparta failed not. For the priestess of Delphi had told the Spartans when the war began, that either Lacedæmon must be wasted or their king must die. So Leonidas thought upon her words and sent them away, that so the Spartans might have 221 all the glory. And of this there is yet this further proof, that he sought to send away the soothsayer

Megistias because he was an Acarnanian, but Megistias would not go. Yet he sent home his only son who was with him in the army.

So all the rest departed, and the Thebans and Thespians alone remained. The men of Thebes Leonidas kept sorely against their will, as pledges for their people; but the Thespians would not save their own lives by forsaking Leonidas and his men; so they remained and died with them, and their leader was Demophilus, the son of Diadromes.

When the sun rose, Xerxes poured out wine to the god, and tarried until the time of the filling of the market, for such was the bidding of Ephialtes, because the path down the hill was much shorter than the way which led up it on the other side. Then the barbarians arose for the onset; and the men of Leonidas knew now that they must die, and on this day they came out into the wider part of the pass, for, before, they had fought in the narrowest place. As soon as the battle began, there fell very many of the barbarians, for the leaders of their companies drove every man on with scourges and blows. Many fell into the sea and were drowned; many more were trampled down alive by one another; and no thought was taken of those who fell. And the Spartans fought on with all their might, to slay as many of the barbarians as they could, before they should them-

VII. selves be slain by the men who were coming round the hill.

224 So they fought on till almost all their spears were broken and they slaughtered the Persians with their swords. At last Leonidas fell nobly, and other Spartans with him, whose names I learnt as of men whose memory ought not to be lost; and for this reason I learnt the names of all 225 the Three Hundred. Then over the body of Leonidas there was a hard fight in which fell many great men of the Persians, and among them two brothers of the king. But the Spartans gained back his body, and turned the enemy to flight four times, until the traitor Ephialtes came up with his men. Then the face of the battle was changed, for the Greeks went back into the narrow part within the wall, and there they sat down, all in one body except the Thebans, on the hillock where now the lion stands over the grave of Leonidas. In this spot, they who yet had them fought with daggers, and the rest as they could, while the barbarians overwhelmed them, some in front, some digging down the wall, others pressing round them on every side.

226 So fell the Thespians and the Spartans. Of the latter, the bravest man, it is said, was Diénekês, who, as the tale runs, heard from a man of Trachis, just before the battle, that whenever the Persians shot their arrows the sun was darkened by them,

and answered merrily, "Our friend from Trachis brings us good news. If their arrows hide the sun, we shall be able to fight in the shade."

They were all buried where they fell; and over those who died before Leonidas sent the allies away, were these words written:

> "Four thousand men of Peloponnesus
> Here fought with three hundred myriads."

But there was another writing over the Spartans by themselves, which said:

> "Tell the Spartans, at their bidding,
> Stranger, here in death we lie;"

and over the soothsayer were written these words:

> "This is the grave of the seer Megistias, whom the Medes slew
> When they had crossed the river Spercheius.
> Well he knew the fate that was coming,
> But he could not forsake the leaders of the Spartans."

Of these three hundred Spartans there is a story told, that two, Eurytus and Aristodemus, were lying sick in the village of Alpeni. These men would not make up their minds to do the same thing; but Eurytus called for his arms, and bade his guide to lead him (for his eyes were diseased) into the battle. So the guide led him and then ran away, while Eurytus plunged into the fight and was

VII. slain; and Aristodemus went back to Sparta alone.
230 Some say, however, that these two had been sent as messengers from the camp, and that the one loitered on his errand and was late for the fight, while the other hastened back and was killed. Now, if both had returned together to Sparta, I do not think that the Spartans would have been angry; but
231 coming alone, he was avoided by all. None would kindle a fire for him, none would speak to him, but every one called him Aristodemus the dastard. Yet this man made good his name, and fell nobly in the battle which was afterwards fought at Plataeae.
232 And yet one other of these three hundred was sent, they say, on an errand into Thessaly, and so was not in the fight. This man also the Spartans dishonoured, so that he slew himself in his misery.
233 Now the Thebans, as long as they were with the Spartans in the battle, were compelled to fight against the king. But when Leonidas with his men hastened to the hillock within the wall, they got away, and with hands stretched out went towards the barbarians with the truest of all tales, saying that they were on the king's side and were the first to give him earth and water, and that they were guiltless of the hurt which had been done to him, because they were in the battle sorely against their will. To these words the Thessalians also bare witness; so their lives were spared: but

some had the bad luck to be killed as they came
near to the Persians, and most of the others were
branded with the royal mark, beginning from their
chieftain Leontiadas.

After this Xerxes sent for Demaratus and said,
"Thou art a wise man, Demaratus, as I judge
from this, that all has turned out according to thy
words. Now tell me how many of the Lacedæmonians are left, and are they all warriors like
those who have been slain here?" Then he answered, "O king, the Lacedæmonians have many
men and many cities. One of them, which is
called Sparta, has about eight thousand men; and
these are all equal to the men who have fought
here. The others are not indeed so strong, but
yet they are brave men." Then Xerxes asked him,
"How shall we conquer these men with the least
trouble? Tell me, for thou knowest the secrets of
their counsels, because thou hast been their king."
And Demaratus said, "If thou really seekest my
judgment, O king, then I must give thee the best
counsel. Send three hundred ships to the Laconian coast. Over against it lies an island called
Kythêra, of which Chilôn, a very wise man, said
that it would be better for the Spartans if it were
sunk in the depths of the sea. He did not indeed
know of thy coming, but he feared lest any army
should seize it. Let thy ships then sweep their
coasts from this island and scare them, and so, with

VII. war at their very doors, there is no fear of their coming hitherwards to help the Greeks; and when the rest of Hellas is enslaved, then the Laconians will easily fall into thy hands. Otherwise this will be the issue. A narrow isthmus leads into the Peloponnesus, and there thou wilt have to fight greater battles than those which have been fought already."

236 But Achæmenes, the brother of Xerxes, who was admiral of the fleet, stood by, and, hearing this, feared that Demaratus would persuade him: so he said, "O king, thou art listening to a man who is jealous of thy good fortune, or perhaps a traitor. This is the way of the Greeks. They envy the prosperous, and hate every one who is better than themselves. Now, in our last mishap, four hundred ships have been broken; and if three hundred more are sent away, the enemy is at once a match for us. If all remain together, they cannot well be beaten; and the army on land and the ships at sea will greatly help one the other. Order thy own matters, and take no heed to the counsels of the enemy, their doings, or their numbers. They can take care of their own business, and we of ours. And if the Lacedæmonians do come out to fight, that is no 237 remedy for their present hurt." Then the king answered, "Thy words are good, Achæmenes, and I will do as thou wilt. Demaratus too has given

me his best counsel, but he is not so wise as thou art. For I never will believe that he is not my friend. His former words are my warrant, and so is this, that one citizen may envy another and will grudge him his counsel unless he be a very good man; and such men are rare: but it is different with a stranger to the man who is his friend. Let every one then take heed how he speaks evil of Demaratus, whom I have made my friend."

Then Xerxes went through the dead, and he ordered that the head of Leonidas should be cut off (when he learnt that he was their king and leader), and his body hung upon a cross. And this makes it clear, even if it had not been plain before, that Xerxes was wroth with Leonidas while he lived, more than with any other man; for the Persians always greatly honour those who have fought against them bravely.

Now it was from Demaratus himself that the Lacedæmonians first learnt that the king was coming; for when he was at Susa he heard that he was going against Hellas, and he longed to tell it to the Spartans, who had driven him away from being king. So we may shrewdly judge whether he told them in friendship or in mockery. Fearing then that he might be caught if he did it in any other way, he took a double writing-tablet, and, scraping off the wax, scratched upon the wood all that he wished to say, and then melted the wax again over the letters. So the guardians of the roads took no heed to an empty tablet; and when it reached Lacedæmon, they could make nothing of it, until Gorgo, the daughter of Cleomenes (who was now the wife of Leonidas), said that, if they scraped off the wax, they would find letters upon the wood. So they read the message of Demaratus, and then they sent to tell all the Greeks that the great king was coming.

CHAP. VI.

THE STRIFE OF SHIPS AND STORMS AT ARTEMISIUM.—THE
SIGHT-SEEING AT THERMOPYLÆ. — THE PERSIANS AT
DELPHI.

> Earth was quaking to her centre,
>   Heaven was all a sheet of flame,
> When the stroke of righteous judgment
>   On the haughty spoiler came.
> Then the peaks of high Parnassus,
>   Shivered in the tempest's blow,
> Showered a thousand craggy ruins
>   On the guilty ones below.
>
>   E. A. FREEMAN.

Now the ships of the Greeks were gathered together at Artemisium, two hundred and seventy-one in all. Of these the Athenians gave one hundred and twenty-seven, which the men of Plataeæ in their zeal helped them to man, for they themselves knew nothing of the sea. And the men of Corinth sent forty ships, and the men of Megara twenty. There were also ships from Ægina, Sikyon and Epidaurus, from Eretria and Trœzen. The Lacedæmonians also sent ten, while the men of Chalkis manned twenty ships which

VIII.   2 the Athenians gave to them. And the leader who had the chief power was Eurybiades the Spartan, for the Greeks said that they would obey none but the Spartans, and that they would immediately go away if the Athenians were to
3 rule. So the Athenians gave way nobly, for they sought before all things to save Hellas, and, knowing that it must fall if they strove among themselves for power, they resolved to bide their time; and this soon came, for, when they had driven back the Persians to Asia, the allies took away the chief power from the Lacedæmonians, because Pausanias, as they said, had grown wanton in his pride.

4 From Artemisium they saw the ships of the Persians at Aphetæ and the land full of men; and they determined to flee. In vain the Eubœans tried to persuade Eurybiades to stay until they could take their wives and children away. So they went to Themistocles, the general of the Athenians, and gave him thirty talents that he
5 might make the Greeks fight before Eubœa. Of these talents he gave five to Eurybiades, and so prevailed with him; but when Adeimantus the Corinthian stood out and refused to fight at Artemisium, Themistocles sent him a message, saying, "Thou shalt not leave us, for I will give thee more money than the king of the Medes would send thee for forsaking thy friends;" and

with this message he sent three talents of silver, and won over Adeimantus. So they stayed near Euboea and fought there.

And as the sun was now going down in the sky, the barbarians at Aphetæ saw that a few ships of the Greeks were lying in wait at Artemisium and were eager to take them; but they would not sail out against them, lest the Greeks should see them and flee away during the night, for their mind was not to let a man of them live. So they chose out two hundred ships and sent them round Skiathos, so that they might sail round Euboea and, coming to the Euripus without being seen, might attack the enemy in the rear, while they themselves should bear down on them in front so soon as they should see the signal which was to be set up. And after this they began to count the ships at Aphetæ.

Now in their army there was a great diver named Skyllias of Skionê, who in the storm at Pelion had saved many things for the Persians and taken a great many for himself, and who, wishing to go to the Greeks, had not been able to do so until now. But while they were counting the ships, he dived (as some say) into the sea at Aphetæ and came up at Artemisium, after swimming about eighty furlongs under the water. But of this man many other things are said which look much like lies, and I believe that he escaped

VIII. to Artemisium in a boat; and when he came, he told them of the great storm, and of the ships which were sailing round Eubœa.

9 Then the Greeks took counsel, and determined to wait where they were till midnight, and then to go and meet the ships which were coming round the island. And as no one came against them from Aphetæ, they sailed out themselves, when the day was now far spent, to make trial
10 of the enemy. When the Persians saw them coming, they thought them mad, and put out to sea, thinking easily to take them; and with their multitude of ships they surrounded the Greeks, so that the Ionians, who were with the king against their will, were grieved for the destruction which, as they thought, was now come upon their kinsmen; while the rest sought each to seize first an Athenian ship, and so to gain the prize from the king,—for the Athenians always counted most with the Persians.

11 So, when the signal was given for battle, the Greeks brought the sterns of their ships together, and then began the fight prow to prow, although they had but a little space. Then Lykomedes, an Athenian, took the first ship of the barbarians, after which nine-and-twenty more were taken; and the night came on, and the Persians fell back to Aphetæ, having fared not at all as they had
12 hoped. All night long there was heavy rain, for

it was midsummer, with much thunder from
Mount Pelion; and the dead, with pieces of the
wrecks, being carried towards Aphetæ, clogged
the prows of the ships and the oars. And the
men on the land were greatly afraid when they
heard this, and looked for death to all,—for
tempest and shipwreck had been followed by
battle, and after the battle again came storm and
thunder and torrents hurrying from the mountains to the sea; and a miserable night they
spent. But it was much more miserable for the
ships which were sailing round Eubœa, for on
these the storm fell more fiercely as they laboured
in the sea. Carried along by the gale, and not
knowing whither they were borne, they were
dashed against the rocks; and all this was done
by the god, that the Persian army might be
brought more nearly to the number of the Greeks.

Gladly the barbarians at Aphetæ saw the day
dawn; but, after so much buffeting, they were
well content to stay still. But to the aid of the
Greeks there came fifty-three Athenian ships;
and a message was brought that all the ships
sailing round Eubœa had been broken by the
storm. Falling in after this with some Cilician
ships, they destroyed them, and, when the night
came on, sailed back to Artemisium.

On the third day, the chiefs of the Persians,
vexed that so few ships should thus annoy them,

VIII. and dreading what the king might do to them, waited no longer for the enemy to begin the battle, but put out to sea about midday. And these things happened here at the same time that Leonidas and his men were fighting at Thermopylæ; and as they fought to keep the pass, so these fought to guard the Euripus, while the barbarians cheered each other on to destroy the
16 Greeks and force the passage. So they came on with their ships drawn up in a half-circle to surround the Greeks, who sailed straight to meet them. In this battle both fared much alike; for the ships of Xerxes were entangled by their own numbers, and dashed against each other; still they held out strongly, for they could not bear to be put to flight by so few. The Greeks also lost many ships and men, though their enemies
18 lost more. So both departed gladly to their place of anchoring; and the Greeks got back their dead and the broken ships, and began to think again of flight, for they had been roughly handled and half of the Athenian ships disabled.
19 Then Themistocles thought that, if he could draw away the Ionians and Carians, they would be a match for their enemies; and, gathering the generals together on the shore where the Eubœans were bringing down their cattle to the sea, he told them of his design, and bade all who wished to sacrifice to light a fire and offer some of the

Euboean cattle, since it was better that they
should have them than their enemies. Thus the
Euboeans lost their cattle, because they would
not give heed to the prophecy of Bakis which
said:

"When he that speaks in a barbarian tongue
shall cast a yoke into the sea,

"Take good heed to send away from Euboea the
bleating goats."

At this time came the scout from Trachis.
For two were placed, each with a boat ready,
the one at Artemisium to tell the men in Thermopylae if any evil befel the fleet, the other with
Leonidas to bring tidings to Artemisium if he
and his men fared ill. When they heard what
had happened, they tarried no longer, but set out,
the Corinthians first and the Athenians last. And
Themistocles, with some of the best sailing ships,
went to all places where they might get water;
and on the rocks he cut these words, which the
Ionians read when they came up the day after,
"Ye do wrong, O Ionians, by going against your
fathers and bringing Hellas into slavery. If ye
can, take our side. If ye cannot, then fight for
neither, and pray the Carians to do likewise. But
if this also be impossible, at least in the battle be
slack and lazy, remembering that ye are sprung
from us, and that we are fighting in a quarrel
which ye began." This Themistocles did, as it

VIII would seem, for two reasons: either he would win over the Ionians to their side, or he would make Xerxes suspect them and keep them back from any part in the battles which might be fought.

23 Soon after this there came a man of Histiæa to the Persians, and said that the Greeks had fled from Artemisium. And they guarded him with care (for they believed him not), and sent some swift ships to see. When these brought the same news, the whole fleet sailed to Artemisium, and thence to Histiæa, where they overran all the villages on the sea-shore.

24 Meanwhile Xerxes had been arranging a sight for the seamen. Twenty thousand of his men had been slain at Thermopylæ. Of these he left one thousand on the ground; the rest he buried in trenches under leaves and earth, so that they could not be seen. When all was ready, he sent a herald throughout his army, who said, "All who please may leave their posts and go to see how the king fights against those foolish men 25 who thought to withstand his power." On this, so many desired to go, that there was a lack of boats to carry them. And when they had crossed, they went over the battle-ground; and all knew the Lacedæmonians and Thespians, with the helots lying beside them: but not less did they see through the trick of Xerxes, for it was a thing to laugh at, when the thousand Persians lay by

themselves, and the four thousand Greeks were
gathered into a single heap. So all that day they
spent in seeing this sight, and on the day follow
ing went back to their ships, while the land army
went on its way.

At this time there came to the Persians some
men of Arcadia who wished to work for the king.
And when they were brought before him, they
were asked what the Greeks were doing. Then
they said that they were keeping the feast at
Olympia and beholding the contests of wrestlers
and horsemen. On hearing this, one of the Persians asked what the prize might be for which
they strove; and he was told that it was an olive-
wreath. Then Tritantæchmes, the son of Artabanus, could no longer keep silence, but said,
"Ah, Mardonius, what sort of men are these with
whom thou hast brought us here to fight, who
strive not for money but for glory!" And for this
saying the king held him to be a coward.

Meanwhile, after the death of Leonidas in
Thermopylæ, the Thessalians sent a herald to the
men of Phokis, whom they greatly hated because
the Phokians had done them much evil in war
in times past, and said to them, "Men of Phokis,
we are stronger than you. We were mightier
even before the Persian came; but now we are in
so great favour with the king that, if we please,
we can take your land away and make you all

VIII. slaves. Still, we bear you no malice. Give us
30 fifty talents, and no evil shall befall you." This
message they sent, because the Phokians were the
only people in those parts who did not take the
side of the Persians. And I believe that they
did not do so, merely because they so hated the
Thessalians; and that they would have joined the
king, if the Thessalians had not done so. As it
was, they made answer that they would give them
31 no money, nor be traitors to Hellas. Then the
Thessalians were very angry, and led the barbarians against them, through the country of the
Dorians which they did not hurt because they
32 were on the king's side. But when they came
into the Phokian land, they found that some of
the people had gone up to the tops of Mount Parnassus, and many more to the Ozolian Locrians,
to the city of Amphissa which lies above the Cris-
sæan plain. Then over the whole of Phokis the
storm of war burst, for the men of Thessaly led
the Persians everywhere, and burnt the cities and
33 the temples. Charadra and Tethrônium, Neon
and Hyampolis, Erôcus and Elateia, none were
spared, but all, with the rest, were burnt. At
Abæ also they set fire to the temple when they
had plundered its treasures, and slew some of the
Phokians whom they took as they drew near to
the mountains.
34 But when they reached Panopœ, the army

was divided, and the more part went on with Xerxes against Athens, and marched into Bœotia, of which all the people had given him earth and water. The others set off with their leaders to Delphi, to plunder the temple and bring all its wealth to the king, who knew the treasures which were there as well as he knew what he had left at home, for there was no lack of men to tell him. Onwards they marched, keeping Parnassus on the right, burning and slaying everywhere, so that the Delphians were dismayed, and asked the god whether they should bury his holy treasures or carry them away. And the god said, "Move them not: I am able to guard them." Then the Delphians took thought for themselves, and sent their women and children across into the land of the Achæans, while most of them climbed up to the peaks of Parnassus and to the cave of Corycus, and others fled to Amphissa. So there remained in Delphi only sixty men, and the prophet who was named Akêratus. As the barbarians drew nigh and were now in sight, the prophet saw lying in front of the temple the sacred arms which used to hang in the holy place, and which it was not lawful for man to touch; and he went to tell the Delphians of the marvel. But there were greater wonders still, as the barbarians came up in haste to the chapel of Athena which stands before the great temple, for the lightnings burst from

VIII. heaven, and two cliffs torn from the peaks of Parnassus dashed down with a thundering sound and crushed great multitudes, and fierce cries and shoutings were heard from the chapel of
38 Athena. Utterly dismayed and thrown together in the uproar, the barbarians turned to flee; and when the Delphians saw this, they came down from the mountain and slew many more, while the rest hurried with all speed to the Bœotian land, and said that two hoplites, higher in stature than mortal men, had followed behind, slaying and driving them from Delphi.

39 These, the Delphians say, were the two heroes of the land, Phylacus and Autonoüs, whose chapels stand near the great temple. And the rocks which fell from Parnassus lie in the sacred ground of Athena, into which they were hurled as they crushed the host of the barbarians.

CHAP. VII.

THE GREEKS AT SALAMIS. — THE FIGHT AND VICTORY. —
THE COUNSEL OF MARDONIUS.— THE FLIGHT TO SARDES.

> A king sate on the rocky brow
> Which looks o'er sea-born Salamis;
> And ships by thousands lay below,
> And men in nations; — all were his.
> He counted them at break of day —
> And when the sun set, where were they?
>   BYRON.

WHEN the ships of the Greeks sailed away from Artemisium, they anchored at Salamis, because the Athenians wished to take their wives and children away from Attica, and also to take counsel what they ought to do. They had looked to find all the Peloponnesians awaiting the enemy in Bœotia; but, instead of this, they learnt that they were strengthening the Isthmus, not caring for the rest of Hellas, if only the Peloponnesus could be saved. So the rest anchored at Salamis, while the Athenians went to their own country, and ordered all to take heed to their children and

Herodotus VIII. 40

41

VIII. households. These were mostly sent away to Trœzen, others to Ægina and Salamis. And this was done in haste, not merely because they sought to obey the words of Apollo, but because the priestess told them that the sacred serpent which guarded the Acropolis had refused to take the food which every month was placed before it. As this had never happened before, they were yet more eager to leave the city, which, as it seemed, the goddess had herself forsaken. When all had been removed, they sailed away to join the rest
42 at Salamis, whither also had come all the ships which had been commanded to meet at Trœzen. And many more ships were gathered here than had fought at Artemisium; and over all these was the same general, Eurybiades, who was a Spartan, albeit not of the royal race. The greatest number of ships, as well as those which sailed
44 best, were sent by the Athenians, who manned one hundred and eighty vessels by themselves, — for the Platæans did not help them at Salamis as they had done at Artemisium. These had been left in their own land, while they were trying to save their households before the coming of the enemy.

45 Of the rest, the Lacedæmonians sent sixteen ships; and the men of Corinth and Megara, of Chalkis and Eretria and Keos, furnished the same number as at Artemisium. There were also ships

from Sikyon and Epidaurus, Trœzen and Hermione, from Ambrakia and Leucas. And the men of Ægina sent thirty ships, while they kept the others to guard their own island. The Naxians sent four ships, which were made ready to help the Persians, but which they brought to Salamis at the bidding of Democritus. There were also a few ships from Styra and Kythnos, from Melos and Siphnos and Scriphos. All the other islanders had given earth and water to the king. And of all the Greeks who dwell beyond the Thesprotians and the river Acheron, the men of Kroton alone sent one ship to the aid of Hellas in this her time of danger. So all the ships together were three hundred and seventy-eight. And when all were gathered together at Salamis, the chieftains took counsel with Eurybiades where they ought to fight. Of Attica they took no thought, for the Athenians had already forsaken it; but, as they had done before, so now most wished to sail away to the Isthmus,—for they said that if they fought at Salamis and were beaten, they would be shut up and besieged in the island, where they could get no help; while from the Isthmus they could at the least flee into their own country. While they thus took counsel, there came an Athenian to tell them that the barbarian was already in Attica, and that everything in it was given to the flame; for the army of the Persians had now

30. gone through Bœotia, burning the cities of Thespiæ and Platææ, because these would not take the king's side, and had reached Athens, ravaging the whole land.

31. Three months had passed away since they had left the Hellespont; and they came to the city while Calliadas was archon, and found it empty, saving only the guardians of the temple and some poor men who had placed doors and planks of wood as a kind of hedge round the Acropolis, partly because they were not able to leave the city, but chiefly because they thought that this was the meaning of the priestess when she said
32. that the wooden wall should not be taken. So the Persians took their post on the hill of Ares which faces the Acropolis, and besieged it, shooting arrows rolled round with lighted tow against the palisade. Still the Athenians held out within it, although they were sorely pressed and saw that their wooden wall would not save them. Nay, they would not even hearken to the children of Peisistratus who besought them to yield, but rolled down huge stones on the barbarians if they dared to approach the gates, so that Xerxes for a
33. long time knew not what to do. But at last he found a way to enter in,—for the prophecy must be fulfilled that all the land of Attica should fall into the hands of the Persian. Near the chapel of Aglauros, the daughter of Kecrops, no watch

was kept, because the ground was there so steep
that they thought none could climb up it. Up
this way some of the Persians clambered; and
when the Athenians saw them, some threw themselves down the rock and perished, and others
fled into the temple, while the Persians hastened
to open the gates and slay the suppliants. After
this, they plundered the temple and burnt the
whole Acropolis.

Then, in the gladness of his heart, Xerxes sent
a messenger to Susa to say how he had taken
Athens, and to tell them of all his good fortune.
And, on the day after, he called the Athenians
who had followed him from their exile, and bade
them go up to the Acropolis and there sacrifice
after the manner of their country; whether it
was that he wished to obey some vision, or that
he was troubled at the thought that he had burnt
the temple. So they offered up the sacrifice;
and I tell these things for this reason. In the
chapel of Erectheus, the child of the earth, which
is built on this Acropolis, there is an olive-tree
and a well of salt water, which they say that
Poseidon and Athena left as tokens when they
strove together to see which of them should have
the land. This olive-tree was burnt along with
the chapel; but when the Athenians went up to
sacrifice at the bidding of the king, they saw a

VIII. shoot which had run up already from the stem to the height of a cubit.

56 When the Greeks at Salamis heard all these tidings, they were so frightened that some of the leaders would not stay for the ending of the council, but, hurrying to their ships, set sail and fled; while those who remained, decided that they must fight before the Isthmus. So the night came on, and all were scattered to their ships.
57 And when Themistocles reached his own vessel, Mnesiphilus, an Athenian, asked him what was the end of the council; and when he learnt that they were all to sail away and fight at the Isthmus, he said: "Well, if we leave Salamis, the men will go each to his own city, and Eurybiades will not be able to keep them, or any one else; and so the army will be scattered, and Hellas be ruined by our folly. If there is any way of doing it, try to upset their plans, and
58 persuade Eurybiades to stay here." These words pleased Themistocles; and, without waiting to answer them, he went straight to the ship of Eurybiades and asked to speak with him, and Eurybiades bade him come into the ship. Then Themistocles went up, and, sitting by his side, told him the words of Mnesiphilus as if they had been his own, adding many others, until Eurybiades agreed to call the chieftains to another
59 council on the shore. When they were met,

Themistocles rose, before Eurybiades could say why he had called them, and spoke urgently, until Adeimantus, the leader of the Corinthians, said, "O Themistocles, those who rise up in the games before their time are beaten;" and he answered gently, "Yes; but those who loiter are not crowned." Then, turning again to Eurybiades, he went on with his speech; but he did not say that the allies would run away if they went to the Isthmus, for he could not fitly accuse them when they were present; but he said, "It depends now upon thee to save Hellas, if thou wilt fight here, and not follow the advice of these men by taking the ships away to the Isthmus. Look at the matter on both sides. If we go to the Isthmus, we must fight on the open sea,— the worst thing for our ships, which are fewer in number and heavier; and even if we win the day, Salamis, Megara, and Ægina are lost. Nay, the land army of the Persians will go along with their fleet; and so, by bringing them to the Peloponnesus, thou wilt place all Hellas in jeopardy. But my counsel has this benefit, that, by fighting in a narrow space [1], we shall in all likelihood win the

[1] τὸ ἐν στεινῷ ναυμαχέειν πρὸς ἡμέων ἐστί. A complete revolution had been effected in Athenian naval tactics before the days of Phormion; and that which Themistocles desired for the Greek fleet at Salamis, brought both terror and destruction to the fleet of Nikias and Demosthenes at Syracuse. Mr. Grote has drawn out most forcibly and clearly the history and nature of the

battle; and by doing this, Salamis is saved, where we have placed our women and children. This is our concern, but it is your interest also; for we shall be defending your country just as well here as if we were fighting at the Isthmus, while the enemy will not be carried on to the Peloponnesus but (without going further than Attica) will make their escape as best they may, and Megara and Ægina will be saved, and also Salamis, in which, besides, an oracle tells us that we are to conquer our enemies. Reasonable counsels are followed generally by a good issue; without them, the gods will not fling good fortune in our faces." Then Adeimantus rose up in haste, bidding him be silent, because he had now no country, and charging Eurybiades not to listen to one who was only a wanderer; and these words he cast in his teeth because Athens was now in the power of the Persians. Then Themistocles was wroth, and spoke vehemently against him and the Corinthians, telling him that the Athenians had yet a nobler country and a greater city, as long as they had two hundred ships all well manned; but to Eurybiades he spake yet more earnestly: "By remaining here, thou wilt show thyself a brave man. By going away, thou wilt destroy all Hellas, for with the war on land the Athenians have nothing more to do; and if

changes in the naval tactics of Athens. History of Greece, voL iv. p. 409; vol. v. pp. 137, 181, 327, &c. &c.

thou wilt not stay, we will take up our people
from this island and sail to Siris in Italy, which
is ours from ancient times, and to which the
oracles have commanded us to send settlers. When
we are gone, ye will remember what I said."

Then Eurybiades agreed to stay and fight at Salamis, because he knew that they would be no match for the enemy if the Athenians went away; so they made ready for the battle. And the next day, as the sun rose, there was an earthquake both by land and sea; so they called on the children of Æacus to come and help them. Ajax and Telamon they brought from Salamis itself; but they sent a ship to Ægina for Æacus and the rest of his kinsfolk.[1]

Now Dikæus, an Athenian, who was with the Persians, being an exile, said that, while they were plundering Athens which had been forsaken by all its people, he chanced to be with Demaratus the Lacedæmonian in the Thriasian plain, and saw a cloud of dust coming from Eleusis, such as might be raised by myriads of men. While they gazed at this cloud, wondering what men they might be, they heard a voice which sounded like the cry of the mysteries; and Demaratus, who knew not the sacred rites of Eleusis, asked him what the voice said, and he answered, "O Demaratus, some great evil will

[1] See Livy, x. 47, xxix. 10, 11.

befall the army of the king, for, as all the men of Attica have left their country, it must be the voice of a god who is going from Eleusis to aid the Athenians and their allies. If the cloud goes towards Peloponnesus, the king himself and his land army are in jeopardy; if it turns towards the ships in Salamis, it is his fleet which will suffer. Every year the Athenians keep the feast here to the Great Mother and her Child, and any of the Greeks who will, may be taught these mysteries; and the voice which thou hearest is the cry which they use in this feast." Then Demaratus answered, "Say not a word of this to any one. If the king hears it thou wilt lose thy head, nor will any one be able to deliver thee. Keep thy counsel, and let the gods take care of his army." After this voice the dust-storm rose into a cloud and was borne on high in the direction of Salamis towards the ships of the Greeks; and so they knew that the fleet of Xerxes must be destroyed. Such was the tale of Dikæus, to which Demaratus and others bear witness.

66. In the meanwhile the Persians, who, after seeing the dead in Thermopylæ, had tarried for three days in Histiæa, sailed through the Euripus and in three days more reached the haven of Phalêrum; and the number of those who came to Athens by land and sea was not much less than the number of those who reached Sepias and Thermopylæ.

ELBURS.

For over against those who perished by the storms VIII.
and those who died in Thermopylæ, we must set
those who had not yet followed the king, the Melians and Dorians and Locrians, together with
all the Bœotians (except the men of Thespiæ and
Platææ), and the people of Carystos, Andros, and
Tenos, and of all the other islands, except the five
cities which have been already named.[1] For the
further that the Persian went, the more people
went with him.

When the ships had reached Phalerum, Xerxes 67
himself went down to the fleet, because he wished
to see it and to hear the judgment of those who
sailed in it. So the leaders and chieftains of the
nations were gathered before him, and they sat
down each as the king gave them honour, the
king of Sidon first, and next to him the king of
Tyre, and so with the rest. After which Xerxes
sent Mardonius to each of them to ask whether
they should fight by sea. So Mardonius went 68
to all, and all gave counsel to fight, except Artemisia, who said, "Tell the king, I pray you,
Mardonius, that this is the judgment of a woman
who has not shown herself a coward in the battles
off Eubœa, and who is bound to give him her
best counsel; and say to him, Spare thy ships,
for by sea their men are as much better than thine
as men are stronger than women. And what need

[1] See page 131. Herodotus viii. 46.

VIII. is there to fight by sea? Hast thou not Athens, for which thou camest hither, with the rest of Hellas? None stands in thy way; they who did so are gone, as it was but right that they should go. If then thou wilt keep thy ships by the land, or even if thou goest on to the Peloponnesus, all things will be according to thy mind, for the enemy cannot hold out long and will soon be scattered among their cities. They have but little corn, as I hear, in this island, nor is it likely, if thy army is sent to the Peloponnesus, that they who belong to it will care to stay and fight for the Athenians at Salamis. But if thou wilt fight, I fear that thy fleet may suffer and cause hurt to thy men on land; and ponder yet this one thing, O king! Good men have commonly bad servants, and evil men have good ones. And thou, who art the best of men, hast evil servants who call themselves thy friends, men of Egypt and Cyprus, of Pamphylia and Cilicia, who are of no use at 69 all." As she thus spake to Mardonius, they who were well-minded to her were grieved, because they thought that the king would punish her; and they who hated and envied her because she was held in great honour by the king, rejoiced that she would now perish. But when Xerxes heard it, he was greatly pleased with her judgment, and honoured her yet more. Still he followed the counsel of the rest, thinking that his men had

been cowards at Eubœa because he had not been
present, but now they knew that he would look
upon them while they fought.

When the order was given for battle, they put
out to sea over against Salamis; but there was no
time to fight that day, for the night came on before they had well arranged themselves. But they
made ready for the next day, while the Greeks
were in fear and trembling (and chiefly the men
of Peloponnesus, because they thought that, if
they should be beaten, they would be shut up in
the island and leave their own land unguarded).
That same night the land army of the Persians
moved on towards the Peloponnesus, where all
things had been done to prevent their coming in.
For when they heard of the death of Leonidas,
they hastened to the Isthmus with Cleombrotus,
the brother of Leonidas, for their leader, and,
blocking up the Skironid road, built a wall across
the Isthmus. This work was soon finished, as
the people were many myriads, and every one
worked with all their strength by day and by
night, carrying stones and brick, logs of wood,
and bags full of sand. Here were gathered the
Lacedæmonians and Arcadians, the men of Elis
and Corinth, Sikyon and Epidaurus, Phliûs, Trœzen, and Hermionê. The other Peloponnesians
cared nothing for the danger of Hellas, or, if we
may speak the truth, really took the king's side

VIII. 74 while they professed to take neither. Thus hard did they work at the Isthmus, as struggling for their last chance, and because they thought that they would win no great glory with their ships. In like manner the men in Salamis were afraid, not so much for themselves as for the Peloponnesus. For a time they spoke quietly in knots of men, marvelling at the folly of Eurybiades, but at last they burst out into loud voices; and an assembly was gathered, and there was much talk about the same things, the one side saying that they would not stay to fight for a land which had been already taken, while the Athenians and the men of Ægina and Megara besought them to remain.

75 When Themistocles saw that he could not prevail, he went secretly out of the council and sent to the Persian fleet a man named Sikinnus, who was his servant and the teacher of his children, and whom he afterwards enriched and made a citizen of Thespiæ. This man came with his message to the leaders of the Persians and said, "Themistocles, the general of the Athenians, has sent me, without the knowledge of the other Greeks (for he is well-minded to the king and would rather that ye conquered than the Greeks), to tell you that they are going to run away from dread of you. And now may ye win great glory by hindering them from escaping, for they do not agree among themselves, neither will they with-

stand you; and you will see those who take your side fighting against those who do not." Having thus spoken, Sikinnus departed; and the Persians, believing his tale, landed many men on the small island of Psyttaleia which lies between Salamis and the mainland; and at midnight they sailed with the western wing of their fleet inclining in towards Salamis, while they who were placed at Keos and Kynosûra also put to sea and filled the whole gulf as far as Munychia with their ships, that so it might not be possible for the Greeks to fly, and that, being caught in Salamis, they might pay the penalty for all the mischief done at Artemisium. And the men were placed in Psyttaleia because it lay straight in the way of the battle, and the men and ships would be carried thither by the stream; and so they would be able to take the ships and to slay the men. That night they never slept, but made ready for the fight in silence, that the enemy might not hear them.

Now I venture not to say that oracles are untrue, nor, after looking at such matters, do I wish to upset them when they speak plainly as Bakis speaks in this one:

"When men shall span with ships the sacred shore of Artemis who wears the golden sword, and Kynosûra on the sea,

"After they have sacked beautiful Athens in foolish daring,

VIII. "Then Divine Justice shall destroy strong Pride, the son of Wantonness,

"As he rages in his fury, thinking to bend all things to his will.

"For brass shall clash with brass, and Ares shall tinge the sea with blood,—

"Then the son of Cronos of the broad brow, and mighty Niké, shall bring to Hellas the day of her freedom."

Against such plain words I dare not speak myself, nor can I listen to those who do.

78. All this time there was a fierce strife of words among the generals in Salamis, for they knew not that the barbarians were encircling them with their ships, but fancied that they were still arranged as they had seen them in the evening.

79. And while they were still talking, there crossed over from Ægina Aristeides the son of Lysimachus, an Athenian who had been banished by the people, and whom I believe to have been one of the best and most upright men in Athens, having had good knowledge of his life. This man came to the council and called out Themistocles, who was no friend to him but altogether his enemy. But, in the greatness of the present sorrow, he put all those things out of mind, because he wished to speak with him and because he had heard that the Peloponnesians wished to take the ships away to the Isthmus. And when

he saw him, he said, "We may fight out our
quarrel hereafter: let us strive now who can do
most good to his country. It matters not now
whether much be said or little about the sailing
away from Salamis to the Isthmus. I have seen
with my own eyes and know that even if the
Corinthians and Eurybiades himself should wish
to flee, they cannot do so now, for the enemy are
round us in a circle. Go in and tell them so."
And Themistocles said, "Thy words and thy
tidings are both good, for thou sayest that thou
hast seen that which I most wished should happen. What the Medes have done, they have done
through me, for it was but right, when the Greeks
would not fight willingly, that they should be
made to do so against their will. But as thou
hast brought this good news, bear them in thyself; for if I say this, they will think my words
false and will not believe that the barbarians
are so doing. Tell them then thyself how it is.
If they believe, it is well; if not, it will make
no difference to us, for they cannot escape if, as
thou sayest, we are surrounded." So Aristeides
went in and told them, adding that he had
scarcely been able himself to escape the ships
which were surrounding the island. But again
there was yet more strife, for the more part of
the leaders would not believe his tidings, until
there came a Tenian trireme which had deserted

VIII. the fleet of Xerxes, and brought them the whole truth. In return for this, the Tenians had their name engraven on the tripod at Delphi among those who helped to destroy the barbarian. This ship, with the Lemnian vessel which had forsaken the Persians at Artemisium, made up the fleet of the Greeks to two hundred and eighty ships.

83 Then at last the Greeks believed and made ready for battle. And as the day was dawning, Themistocles cheered them on for the fight, putting everything in the fairest light to stir up men who were downhearted; and, bidding them be strong and of good courage, he told them to go on board their ships. And as they were embarking, the trireme came from Ægina which had been sent to fetch the children of Æacus. Then the Greeks put out to sea with all their ships, and

84 immediately the barbarians came forward to meet them. But while the other Greeks for some time backed water and even touched ground, an Athenian named Ameinias ran his ship into the enemy, and as it was thus entangled and could not get free, the rest came up to help him, and so began the battle. The Æginetans say, however, that the battle was commenced by the trireme which went to bring the children of Æacus; and the tale is also told that a form as of a woman was seen, which cried out in a voice

heard by all the army of the Greeks, "Good men, VIII. how long will ye back water?"

Fronting the Athenians were placed the Phœ- 85 nicians, who had the wing towards Eleusis and the west; and the Ionians, towards the east and the Peiræeus, faced the Lacedæmonians. Few of them, however, hung back in the battle, as Themistocles had sought to make them. Many of them, indeed, took some ships of the Greeks; but I will give the names of two Samians, Theomestor and Phylacus, of whom the former was made tyrant of Samos by the Persians, and the other received much land and was written down among the benefactors of the king.

Most of the Persian ships were lost in Salamis, 86 some being destroyed by the Athenians, others by the Æginetans. It could hardly have happened otherwise, since the Greeks fought in good order, while their enemies fell out of their ranks and did nothing wisely. Yet they were altogether braver here than they were in Eubœa, through fear and dread of Xerxes, for each man thought that the eye of the king was resting upon him. But how each fought on either side, we 87 know nothing as certain, except in the case of Artemisia, whose ship was chased by an Athenian vessel. Before her were only ships of her own side; and as the enemy was close upon her, she ran into a Calyndian ship in which was their

VIII. king Damasithymus. Whether she did so purposely because there had been any quarrel between them, or whether the Calyndians fell foul of her by chance, it is hard to say; but by this deed she profited in two ways. The trierarch of the Athenian ship, on seeing her run into one of the enemy's vessels, thought that her ship was a Greek one or else was deserting from the Persians, and so turned away to chase others. And, besides this, she won yet greater praise and glory from Xerxes who saw the deed with his own eyes, for some one said to him, "Dost thou see, O king, how bravely Artemisia fights, and that she has sunk a ship of the enemy?" But he doubted whether it really was Artemisia who had done this; and when they said that they knew her ship from the sign which it carried, Xerxes answered, "My men are women and the women men."

89. In this struggle Ariabignes the brother of Xerxes fell, and many great men of the Persians and the Medes; and some also of the Greeks were slain, but not many,—for these, not being crushed together in the fight, and knowing how to swim, escaped to Salamis. But the barbarians could not swim; and when the first ships turned to flee, then there followed a terrible destruction, for those which were drawn up behind pressed forward to reach the front and do something for the king, and so got entangled with the vessels which were

hurrying away. In this uproar some Phœnicians who had lost their ships came to the king and charged the Ionians with having destroyed their ships and betrayed them. But while they were thus speaking, a Samothracian vessel ran into a ship from Athens and sank it, while one from Ægina ran into the Samothracian ship. Then these Samothracians with the javelins drove the men of the conquering ship from the deck into the sea, and took their vessel; and this deed saved the Ionians. For Xerxes, on seeing it, turned to the Phœnicians in a rage, and commanded their heads to be struck off, that they might not lay their own cowardice to the charge of braver men.

So the barbarians fled; and as they sailed towards Phalêrum, the Æginetans met them boldly in the strait and destroyed those ships which made their escape from the Athenians in the battle. But all who could, hastened to Phalerum and joined the land army. In this fight the Æginetans and Athenians won the greatest glory, and among the men who were most honoured was Polycritus of Ægina, and the Athenian Ameinias who chased Artemisia. Had this man known whom he was pursuing, he would never have stopped until he had taken her or been taken himself; for there was a prize of ten thousand drachmas to the man who should take her alive, and all the Athenians were zealous against her, being vexed that a

VIII. 94 woman should come against Athens. But Adeimantus the Corinthian, as the Athenians say, fled at the beginning of the fight in great terror; and the rest of the Corinthians, seeing their leader hurrying away, made haste to follow him. But while they were opposite to the temple of Athena Skiras, a boat which no one was known to have sent[1] met them, and the men in it cried out, "So, Adeimantus, thou hast basely forsaken the Greeks, who are now conquering their enemies as much as they had ever hoped to do." But Adeimantus believed them not, until they said that they would go back with him and consent to die if their words were not true. Then they turned their ships about and joined the Athenians when the battle was ended. This is the Athenian tale; but the Corinthians maintain that they were amongst the foremost in the battle; and the rest of the Greeks confirm their words.

95 In the uproar of the fight, when the Persians began to fly, Aristeides the Athenian, who has been already named, landed a large number of hoplites

---

[1] τὸν οὔτε πέμψαντα φανῆναι οὐδένα. Mr. Rawlinson asserts that this was a "phantom ship:" Mr. Grote's words (History of Greece, vol. v. p. 197) do not imply a similar belief. Mr. Rawlinson's adopted translation appears drawn up to suit his supposition; for the words, "a very strange apparition," can hardly be taken to translate θείῃ πομπῇ; nor would the expression θεῖον εἶναι τὸ πρῆγμα necessarily mean "that there was something beyond nature in the matter." Herodotus, vol. iv. p. 339.

ESKIMO

on the island of Psyttaleia, and slew every one of the Persians who were upon it. So the battle was ended, and the Greeks drew up all the disabled ships which were there, on the shore of Salamis, and made ready for another fight, thinking that the king would bring up against them the ships that still remained to him. But the south-west wind carried many of the wrecks towards the shore of Attica which is called Colias, and so fulfilled the oracle of Bakis and Musæus and also the saying of an Athenian soothsayer many years before, that the women of Colias should bake their bread with oars. This saying no one had understood, but it came to pass now on the flight of the king.

When Xerxes knew all that had happened, he dreaded lest the Ionians should put it into the minds of the Greeks to go and loose the bridges at the Hellespont, or should sail away and do it themselves, leaving him to perish with all his army in Europe. But while he designed to fly, he wished to keep it secret from his own people as well as from the enemy, and sought to carry a mole from the mainland to Salamis, and tied Phœnician merchant-ships together to serve instead of a bridge and wall. All who saw him thus making ready for another fight, thought that he was altogether bent on remaining to carry on the war. But Mardonius saw clearly what he

VIII. was minded to do, for he knew the king's thoughts well. And while he was thus doing, he sent a messenger home to tell the Persians of all his misery.

98 These messengers go quicker than any other mortals. At the end of each day's journey stands a man and a horse ready to carry on the message; and neither snow nor rain, heat nor darkness, hinders them from doing their task as swiftly as possible. Thus the first man gives the message to the second, and the second to the third, until they reach the end, just as in the Feast of Torches which the Greeks keep in honour of Hephæstus.

99 Now the first message which reached Susa, to say that Xerxes had taken Athens, so delighted the Persians that they covered the roads with myrtle-branches and burnt incense and made merry with burnt offerings and feasting; but the second message so dismayed them that all rent their clothes and filled the air with their cries as they laid the blame upon Mardonius, not so much because they were grieved for the loss of the ships as because they feared for the life of the king.

100 And so the Persians went on mourning until Xerxes himself came home. But Mardonius, when he saw that Xerxes was greatly cast down by the issue of the fight and that he purposed to fly from Athens, knew that he would himself suffer for having persuaded the king to go against the Greeks. So he thought it better to run the risk

and enslave Hellas, or die nobly striving for a great end; and he went therefore to the king and said, "O king, be not grieved and cast down at what has happened; for that which matters most to us is a struggle not with wood but with men and horses. With these, not one of the men who think that they have utterly destroyed thy power by sea will dare to face thee; and they who have so dared, have paid the penalty. If, then, it seem good to thee, let us march straightway against the Peloponnesus. But if not, be of good cheer, for it is impossible for the Greeks to escape being made thy slaves and suffering for all the evil that they have done. This then is my counsel, if thy mind is fixed to go away thyself. Make us not, O king, a laughing-stock to the Greeks. Our power is not destroyed; we have nowhere shown ourselves cowards; and how are we, Persians, the worse, because Phœnicians and Egyptians, Cyprians and Cilicians have brought disgrace upon themselves? So, then, if thou must go, take with thee the greater part of the army; and I promise to make all the Greeks thy slaves, if thou wilt let me choose thirty myriads out of all thy host."

These words brought joy to Xerxes in his sorrow; and he said to Mardonius that he would give him his answer after taking counsel with others. So, together with the noblest of the

VIII. Persians, he sent also for Artemisia, because she alone before this seemed to know what ought to be done. When she came, he put all the others out, and then said to her, "Mardonius presses me to stay here and march against the Peloponnesus, telling me that the Persians and the land army are not in fault, and that with them we can win the victory. Or, if I go away, he undertakes to conquer all Hellas for me, if I leave him thirty myriads of men chosen out of my army. Now before the sea-fight thy counsel was good. Show me, then, in which way I can act

102 most wisely now." And she said, "O king, it is not easy to hit upon the best advice. Still, as things have gone, I think it best for thee to go away, and leave Mardonius with his thirty myriads to do as he has promised. If he shall accomplish all that he hopes and undertakes to do, it becomes thy doing, because thy slaves have done it. If things go against him, the harm is not great; for, while thou art safe and all thy house, the Greeks will have to do battle many times yet for their freedom; but if Mardonius falls, it matters not. The Greeks win no victory by destroying thy slave; and thou hast already done that for which thou camest, by burning the city of the Athenians."

103 With these words he was much pleased, for Artemisia happened to speak his own mind; and

if all, both men and women, had counselled him
to stay, I do not think that he would have done
it,—so terrible was his fear. Then he praised
her greatly and sent her with Hermotimus of
Pêdasa, to take his own children, who had followed him, back to Ephesus. After this he
called Mardonius, and told him to choose out
what men he pleased, and to do zealously as he
had promised. And when the night came, the
captains sailed away from Phalerum at the bidding of the king, and hastened with all the ships
as quickly as they could to the Hellespont, there
to guard the bridges till the king should come.
As they approached Cape Zôstêr, they took some
slender rocks, which here jut out into the sea, to
be ships, and they fled for a long way; but at
last they found out that they were not ships, but
rocks, and, coming into line again, sailed on in
good order.

When the day broke, the Greeks, seeing the
army where it was before, thought that the ships
also were at Phalerum, and made ready for battle.
But when they learnt that all were gone, they
hastened to go after them, but could not come
up with them, although they sailed as far as
Andros. There they took counsel; and Themistocles advised that they should immediately follow
the ships through the islands to the Hellespont,
and there destroy the bridges. But Eurybiades

VIII. held that this was the worst thing that they could do; for if the Persians should be so cut off and compelled to stay in Europe, they could never remain quiet, because, if they did, they could neither live there nor get back to their own land but all would die of hunger; and if Xerxes should act bravely, he might overrun the cities of Europe one by one, and eat up the corn of the Greeks, year by year, as it ripened. He thought, however, that Xerxes would not remain in Europe, now that he had been beaten in the sea-fight; and so it would be best to let him fly, and, after that, to carry the war into his own land. And with him agreed all the leaders of the Peloponnesians.

109 When, therefore, Themistocles saw that he could not hope to persuade the greater number, he turned to the Athenians, who were most angered at the flight of the Persians and wished to sail by themselves to the Hellespont even if no one else would go, and said to them: "I have often seen myself, and I hear that it generally happens, that men, who have been conquered, turn to bay when hardly pushed, and wipe out the old disgrace. Now our own safety, and that of Hellas, is a godsend to us, who have driven back so huge a swarm of men. Let us not chase them as they fly. For these things have been brought about not by us, but by the gods and

heroes, who were jealous that Europe and Asia should be ruled by one impious and unholy man, who, treating temples and houses in the same way, cast down and burnt the shrines of the gods, and, scourging the sea, threw fetters into it. Thus, then, have we prospered; and it is best for us to stay in Hellas and look to ourselves and our households. Let every one rebuild his house, and work hard to till and sow his ground, when we have clean driven the barbarian out; and when the spring comes, we can sail for the Hellespont and Ionia." This he said to leave himself a loophole with the Persians, if (as came about afterwards) he should suffer any wrong at the hands of the Athenians.

This judgment, then, they followed, for they believed him with all readiness, because to his old repute for wisdom he had added counsels which had all prospered. And as soon as they had agreed to do this, he sent in a boat some men, whom he could trust for keeping silence under any tortures, with a message to the king. Among these again was Sikinnus, the teacher of his children, who, on reaching Attica, went to Xerxes while the rest remained in the boat, and said: "Themistocles, the leader of the Athenians, and the best and wisest of all the Greeks, has sent me to say that, out of good-will to thee, he has held back the allies from chasing thy ships

VIII. and breaking up the bridges at the Hellespont: so go thy way in peace." After which, Sikinnus and his men sailed away again.

111 But the Greeks, having given up the thought of sailing to the Hellespont, remained at Andros and besieged it. For Themistocles had gone to the Andrians first of all the islanders and asked them for money, telling them that the Athenians were come with two gods named Persuasion and Need, and therefore they must give. But they answered that Athens was indeed a great city and had many excellent gods, but the Andrians were poor and weak, and that two worthless gods, named Poverty and Helplessness, would never leave their island, and so they could give nothing as long as these gods stuck close to them, since the power of the Athenians could not be greater than their own want of means. Hereupon the

112 Greeks besieged them, while Themistocles sent the same messengers to the other islands, with threatening words, telling them that, if they refused to give, he would bring the army of the Greeks upon them and destroy their cities. In this way he got much money from the men of Carystos and of Paros, who, hearing of the siege of Andros and that Themistocles had more weight than the other generals, gave through fear. Perhaps also some other islands gave, but it is not certain. Yet the Carystians were not better off

because they gave, although the Parians by their gift kept away the fleet of the Greeks; and Themistocles gained much money from the islanders without the knowledge of the other leaders.

After remaining a few days longer, Xerxes marched with all his army into Bœotia; for Mardonius wished to conduct the king on his journey, and it was now no fit time for fighting. So he thought to spend the winter in Thessaly, and, when the spring came, to go against the Peloponnesus. Then, in Thessaly, Mardonius chose out the men whom he wanted; and he took, first, the Persians who are called Immortals (except their leader Hydarnes, who would not leave the king), and after these the men who wore breastplates, with the thousand horsemen, then the Medes and Sakæ, Bactrians and Indians, both footmen and horsemen. Of these he took all, but from the other nations he picked out a few, either for stature or for their courage. But the Persians were the largest nation that he chose, men who wore chains and bracelets, and next to them the Medes, who were weaker than the Persians in strength only; and thus with the horsemen he made up his thirty myriads.

While Mardonius was thus choosing out his men and Xerxes lingered in Thessaly, there came an oracle from Delphi to the Lacedæmonians, bidding them demand recompense from Xerxes

VIII. for the slaughter of Leonidas, and take what he should give them. So they sent a herald forthwith, who hastened into Thessaly and coming to Xerxes said, "O king of the Medes, the Lacedæmonians with the children of Heracles who live at Sparta, demand recompense for murder, because thou hast slain their king while he was defending Hellas." Then the king laughed, and after some time pointed to Mardonius who chanced to be standing near, and said, "Well, then, my friend Mardonius shall give to you such recompense as may be fit." And with this promise the herald went away.

115 So Xerxes left Mardonius in Thessaly, and going on with all speed to the Hellespont reached the place of crossing in five-and-forty days, with little of his army left. All along their road they had seized and eaten the corn of the men through whose land they chanced to be passing; and if they found none they gathered grass to eat, and stripped off the leaves and bark of trees, and left nothing in their fierce hunger; and then came sickness and pestilence which wasted the army. Those who were sick Xerxes left behind, charging the men of each city to take care of them, and to feed them, in Thessaly, Pæonia, and Macedonia. Here also he had left the sacred chariot of Zeus as he went into Hellas, but on his return he could not get it again. The Pæonians had given it to

the Thracians, and when Xerxes asked for it, VIII told them that it had been stolen by the men who live by the fountains of the river Strymon. Here also there was a chieftain of the Bisaltæ in the land of Creston, who had refused to follow Xerxes and gone away to the mountain of Rhodopê, charging his sons not to march with him into Hellas. But they heeded not his words, or perhaps wished to see the fighting; and when all six returned home safe and sound, their father put out their eyes, and so they were rewarded.

When, from Thrace, the Persians reached the 117 place of passage, they were ferried as quickly as possible across the Hellespont in ships to Abydos, for they found the bridges unloosed by a storm. There they halted, and, finding more food than anywhere on their road, filled themselves as they could, and by reason of this and the change of water many of those who remained died. The rest reached Sardes with the king.

There is, however, another tale told, that in his 118 flight from Athens Xerxes went no further by land than to Eïon which is on the Strymon, and there left Hydarnes to guide the army to the Hellespont, while he himself went on board a Phœnician ship and sailed to Asia. On the way they were caught by the Strymonian wind, which raised a heavy sea and made the ship take in much water. Then, as the deck was crowded with Persians

M

VIII. who were with him, the king was greatly dismayed, and prayed the pilot to tell him if there was any hope of safety; and the pilot said, "There is none, unless we can ease the ship of the crowd within it." Then Xerxes, turning to the Persians, said, "Now, O Persians, show that ye care for the king, for my life depends on you;" and they, on hearing this, did obeisance and leaped into the sea, and the ship so lightened reached Asia in safety. As soon as they landed, Xerxes gave the pilot a golden crown for saving the life of the king, and then cut off his head for losing the lives of his men. This is the tale, but I do not believe it; for, even if the pilot had so spoken to Xerxes, not one in ten thousand will gainsay me, that the king would not have sent men who were Persians, and the noblest of the Persians, down from the deck into the body of the ship, and cast out into the sea a number of Phœnician sailors equal to that of the Persians. There is also yet this other proof that he went all the way by land, for when he reached Abdera he made a treaty of friendship with the people and gave them a golden dagger and turban; and, as the men of Abdera say, although I do not believe them, he there loosed his girdle for the first time since he left Athens, as thinking himself at last in safety.

CHAP. VIII.

THE GREATNESS OF THEMISTOCLES AND THE ATHENIANS.—
MARDONIUS AT ATHENS.—THE FEAST OF ATTAGINUS.

> Street and temple — scathed and shattered
>   All Athens's city lies;
> From its ruins, thick and choking
>   Clouds of smoke and ashes rise:
> None are there to mourn the ravage,
>   Gods and men have passed away:
> Through the shrines of blessed heroes,
>   Prowl at will the beasts of prey.

WHEN the Greeks found that they could not take Andros, they went to Carystos and having wasted the land returned to Salamis, and put aside the first-fruits for the gods, among which were three Phœnician triremes. Of these, one was dedicated at the Isthmus and remained to my time, the second at Sunium, the third to Ajax at Salamis itself. After this they shared the spoils and sent the first-fruits to Delphi. From these there was made the figure of a man (twelve cubits in height) holding in his hand the beak of a ship, which

VIII. stands close to the golden statue of Alexander
122 the Macedonian. When they sent these spoils to
Delphi, they asked the god in common if the first-
fruits given to him were enough; and the answer
was that he had enough from the other Greeks,
but that the Æginetans must pay that which was
due for the victory at Salamis. So they dedicated
golden stars which stand by the brazen loom near
the mixing-bowl of Crœsus.

123 After the sharing of the spoil, the Greeks sailed
to the Isthmus to give the prize for bravery to the
man who had done best in the war. So when the
generals placed on the altar of Poseidon the votes
by which they marked the first and the second
best men of all, it was found that each general
had given the first place to himself, but that
almost all had given the second to Themistocles,
who was thus shown to be by far the greatest.

124 This, however, the Greeks would not approve, and
sailed away each to his own land without giving
judgment; but none the less was the name of
Themistocles spread abroad through all Hellas for
his wisdom. And when, soon after this, he went
to Lacedæmon, the people received him gladly
and honoured him greatly, giving him a wreath
of olives for his wisdom and cleverness, and the
finest chariot in Sparta. And three hundred
chosen Spartans who were called the Horsemen
led him back as far as the land of Tegea; and he

is the first man whom the Spartans, as it would
seem, ever escorted on his road. But when he
reached Athens, Timodêmus of Aphidna, who was
his enemy, began to chide him vehemently, telling
him that the Lacedæmonians had honoured him
not for his own sake but because he was an Athenian. When Timodêmus had ended his words,
Themistocles said, "Well, if I had been a man of
Belbina I should not have been so honoured by
the Spartans; but neither wouldst thou have been
honoured even if thou hadst been an Athenian."

Now Artabazus, the son of Pharnakes, a man
of note among the Persians, had guided the king
as far as the Hellespont, with six myriads of the
men whom Mardonius chose out of the army.
And when he reached Pallênê on his way back
(as Mardonius was spending the winter in Thessaly and did not yet need him), Artabazus determined, now that he was near them, to attack the
men of Potidæa, who, after the flight of the king
and of his ships from Salamis, had openly revolted
against him, as also had all the others who dwelt
in Pallene. So he besieged Potidæa and also
Olynthus. This last place he took, and leading
all the men out to the lake slew them there, and
gave the city to Critobulus of Torone and the
Chalkidians. And, while he urged on the siege of
Potidæa, Timoxenus, the leader of the Skionæans,
agreed to betray the place to him; and whenever

VIII. he wished to write to Artabazus or Artabazus to him, they rolled the letter round an arrow and shot it into a certain place on which they had fixed. At last the trick was found out, for Artabazus, missing his mark one day, hit the shoulder of a Potidæan, round whom a crowd gathered, and finding a letter wrapped round the arrow, carried it to the generals. But they did not punish Timoxenus for his treachery, that the men of Skione might not be held traitors for all time to come.

129 When the siege had lasted three months, there was a great ebbing of the sea for a long time, and the barbarians, seeing that the water was quite shallow, crossed over to Pallene. But when nearly half of them had passed over, the sea flowed in again with a great wall of water, and those who could not swim were drowned, while they who could swim were slain by the Potidæans who came out in boats to kill them. This ebbing and return of the sea, the Potidæans rightly say, was caused by the Persians who were drowned, because they profaned the temple of Poseidon and the shrine which stands before the city. Those who escaped were led back by Artabazus into Thessaly.

130 But most of the ships which still remained to Xerxes, after they had ferried the king and his army across to Abydos, passed the winter at Kymê, and, when the spring came, sailed over to Samos, where some of them had wintered. But they

never ventured to go further westward, nor was
there anything to make them; but they remained
at Samos with three hundred ships, including
those of the Ionians, to prevent the Ionians from
revolting. The Greeks, they thought, would be
content to guard their own land, because they had
not chased them after the fight at Salamis. On
the sea, then, they were much cast down; but on
land they thought that Mardonius was sure to win
the battle. So, while they remained in Samos,
they tried to see if they could in any way harm
the enemy, and at the same time sought eagerly
to learn how things might go with Mardonius.

In the spring, the ships of the Greeks met
at Ægina, under the admiral Leotychides, of the
house of Procles, the child of Heracles; and the
leader of the Athenians was Xanthippus, the son
of Ariphron. Soon there came messengers from
Ionia, who had been to Sparta to ask them to deliver the Ionians from slavery, and now came with
the same prayer to Ægina. With much difficulty
they prevailed with them to go as far as Delos.
Beyond this the Greeks knew nothing of the land,
and fancied that every place was full of their
enemies, so that to sail on to Samos seemed to
them as great a thing as to sail to the Pillars of
Heracles. Thus the barbarians ventured not to
sail further west than Samos, and the Greeks
dreaded to sail further east than Delos; and that

VIII. which lay between was a land of terrors for both.

133 When Mardonius was setting out from Thessaly, he sent a man named Mûs to ask the will of all the gods whose oracles he might be able to visit. Why he did this is not clear, but in all likelihood it was only to learn what he ought to do in his own
134 matters. So Mûs went to Lebadeia to consult Trophonius, to Abæ of the Phokians, and to the
135 Ismenian Apollo at Thebes. After this he went to the Ptoan temple near Acræphia on the banks of the lake Copais. Into this temple three citizens followed him to write down the answer, whatever it might be. But the seer spoke in a barbarous tongue, and the Thebans marvelled to hear such sounds instead of their own language, while Mûs wrote down the words, telling them that the prophet was using the speech of the Carians,
136 and so went away to Thessaly. On reading the answers Mardonius sent to Athens as a herald Alexander, the son of Amyntas the Macedonian, not only because there was a bond between him and the Persians (for his sister was married to a Persian named Bubares), but because he had been a friend and benefactor to the Athenians; for so he thought that he would best gain over that great and strong people, who, as he supposed, had chiefly brought about all the evils which the king had suffered by sea. With these on his side he thought

truly that he would be master of the sea, and
on land he fancied that he was much stronger
already; and in all likelihood also the oracles
may have bidden him to gain over the Athenians
to be his friends.

So Alexander came to Athens and said, "Men
of Athens, thus saith Mardonius, There has come
to me a message from the king, saying, 'I forgive
to the Athenians all the trespasses that they have
committed against me; give them back therefore
their own land, and let them further take any
other land which they may choose, and let them
be free; and, if they agree to these words, build
up for them all the temples that I have burnt.'
Now therefore I must do with all my might as
the king commands, unless ye hinder me yourselves. And to you I say, why do ye thus madly
make war against the king? Ye cannot win the
victory, neither can ye hold out for ever. Ye
saw the great host of Xerxes and their brave
deeds; ye know the might which I have here now,
and even if ye be stronger and can conquer me
(which, if ye are wise, ye cannot think to do),
there will come soon another host far greater than
mine. Set not up yourselves then as equal to
the king, and so lose your land and imperil your
own lives; but make peace, for now can ye best
do so. Be free, making a covenant with us without craft or treachery. This, men of Athens, is

VIII. the message which I have brought from Mardonius. Of my own good-will to you I say nothing: ye knew it well long ago. But I pray you to yield to Mardonius, for I see that ye cannot make war against the king for ever. If I had not seen this, I would never have brought such a message to you. The power of the king is beyond that of mortal men, and his hand reaches far. Unless then ye agree now, while they hold out to you great and good things, I am full of fear for you, because ye lie in the very path of the war, and with your country as a battle-ground for both sides, ye must all perish. Yield, then, for the king does you a great honour by saying that to you alone of all the Greeks will he forgive their trespasses."

141 But the Lacedæmonians had heard that Alexander had come to make the Athenians yield to the barbarian, and were greatly afraid when they called to mind the oracles which said that they and all the Dorians should be driven out of the Peloponnesus by the Athenians and the Medes. So they too sent messengers who were heard at the same time with Alexander, for the Athenians had long put off to hear him, feeling sure that the Lacedæmonians would send a messenger as soon 142 as they heard of the coming of Alexander. So, when the Macedonian had finished speaking, the messengers from Sparta rose and said, "The

Lacedæmonians have sent us to pray you not to
listen to the barbarian or do otherwise than as ye
have done. For this would not be just or seemly
in any of the Greeks, least of all in you; and for
these reasons. Ye brought this war upon us at
no wish of ours; and this struggle which now
threatens to spread over all Hellas began from
your land. Yet more; it is not to be borne that
Athenians should help to enslave the Greeks,
when ye have always and everywhere striven to
make men free. But in your sufferings we suffer
also, because ye have now lost two harvests and
have for a long time had no homes. And therefore the Lacedæmonians and their allies promise
to feed your women and your households as long
as the war shall last. Let not Alexander then
prevail with you, by smoothing the words of Mardonius. A tyrant himself, he is likely to work
with other tyrants; and ye know that in barbarians there is neither faith nor trust."

Then the Athenians made answer to Alexander
and said, "We know that the power of the Medes
is much larger than ours, and there is no need
to cast this in our teeth. But in the struggle
for freedom we will beat them off with all our
might. It is useless even for thee to try and
make us agree with the barbarian, for we will
never do so. And now tell Mardonius what we
say, 'As long as the sun shall keep the same path

VIII. in the heaven, we will never make peace with Xerxes; but we will face him, trusting in the help of gods and heroes, whom he has insulted by burning their homes and shrines.' And never come again with such messages for Athenians, nor, under cloak of good advice, press them on to do abominable things, for we seek not that thou shouldest suffer any harm at our hands, when
144 thou art our guest and friend." Then turning to the Spartans, they said, "It was but doing like men that you should dread our making peace with the barbarian. But poorly indeed do ye seem to know the mind of the Athenians, for not all the gold throughout the world, not the richest and most beautiful land, could tempt us to take the part of the Medes and help to enslave Hellas. And even if we were willing so to do, there are many things to hinder us, and first and chiefly the shrines and dwellings of the gods which have been burnt and thrown down. And to take vengeance for this we must fight to the last rather than make peace with the man who has done such deeds. Yet more, the whole Hellenic race is of the same blood and speech with us; we share in common the temples of our gods; we have the same sacrifices and the same ways of life; and these the Athenians can never betray. Learn then now, if ye did not know it before, that, so long as but one Athenian shall remain, we will

never make any covenant with Xerxes. For your VIII
good will to us we thank you, and that ye so care
for our troubles as to wish to feed and support our
households. We are grateful for this, but we will
struggle on as well as we can, without giving you
trouble. Hasten then to send out your army with
all speed, for assuredly the barbarian will soon be
in our land, when he learns that we will not do
as he would have us; and we should hasten to
meet him in Bœotia before he can advance as far
as Attica."

On the return of Alexander, Mardonius set out IX. 1
with all speed against Athens, taking with him
all who lay in his road. And the Thessalians
repented in nowise of all that they had done
before. Thorax of Larissa guided Xerxes in his
flight, and now he openly suffered Mardonius to
pass into Hellas. And on reaching the Bœotian 2
land, the Thebans pressed him to stay there, telling him that there was no better place to encamp
in, and that if he remained there he could conquer all Hellas without a battle; for by mere
strength the Greeks could never win the day,
even if they should be of the same mind as they
had been before. "Send money, then," they said,
"to all the chiefs, and so break up their councils;
and after that thou wilt easily subdue all who do
not take thy side." But Mardonius would in no 3
way listen to them, for he had a strange longing

to take Athens, partly because the gods had blinded his eyes, and partly because he wished to send the news by fire-signals to the king at Sardes. So he came into Attica; but again the Athenians were gone, and he heard that most of them were in their ships at Salamis. Ten months had passed away from the time when Xerxes took Athens to the day when Mardonius came and found the city empty.

4 From Athens Mardonius sent a man of the Hellespont named Murychides with the same message as that which he had given to Alexander, because, although he knew that the Athenians had no good-will towards him, he yet thought that they would lay aside their madness now that he again 5 had their country and city in his power. When the message was brought to their council, one man alone, named Lykidas, said that the words of Mardonius should be set before the people. On hearing this they were enraged, and so were those who were not of the council; and, gathering round him, they stoned him to death, while they sent Murychides away unhurt. And when the Athenian women had heard of the tumult which had happened, they urged on one another, and, hastening of their own accord to the dwelling of Lykidas, stoned his wife and children.

6 Now the Athenians had remained in Attica as long as they thought that an army of the Pelo-

ponnesians would soon come to aid them; but
when they put off coming and the enemy was
said to be in Bœotia, they carried everything
away, and, crossing over to Salamis, sent messengers to rebuke the Lacedæmonians for suffering
the barbarian to enter Attica without a battle,
and to remind them how much the Persian had
offered to them on behalf of the king, and that,
if they did not at once send aid, the Athenians
must find out some way of escape for themselves.
But the Lacedæmonians were keeping a feast in 7
honour of the youth Hyakinthus whom Phœbus Apollo loved and slew, and before all things
they must needs attend to this. Their wall
at the Isthmus also was now rising high. So
the messengers of the Athenians, bringing also
others from the men of Megara and Plataea, came
to the ephors and said, "We have been sent to
tell you that the king of the Medes offers to give
us back our country and seeks to have us for his
friends in peace and war without craft or falsehood, and he is ready to give us moreover any
other land which we ourselves may choose. But
we feared the Hellenian Zeus, and it seemed to
us a terrible thing to betray Hellas, and so we
rejected his words, although the Greeks have
been unjust and traitors to us, and although we
knew very well that it was much more to our gain
to make peace with the Persian than war. Yet

IX. of our own free will we will never yield, and so have
we shown all honesty in our dealings. But you,
who then so greatly dreaded lest we should make
a covenant with the barbarian, when ye learnt
that our mind was firmly set not to betray you,
and now that your wall across the Isthmus is
nearly finished, care nothing for the Athenians.
You swore to march with us to meet the Persian
in Bœotia; you have broken your word and suffered him to enter Attica. The Athenians are
angry with you, for your deeds have been unseemly; and they charge you to send back an army
with us in all haste to receive the barbarian in
Attica, where the Thriasian plain is the fittest spot
to fight in, now that we have failed to meet him
in Bœotia."

8 To these words the ephors delayed to answer
from day to day, until ten days had passed.
Meanwhile all the Peloponnesians had been working zealously on the Isthmian wall; nor can I
say why on the coming of Alexander they were so
eager that the Athenians should not join the Medes
but now cared nothing for it, except that they
had now built their wall and fancied that they
9 needed them no more. At last they gave their
answer, and set out on this wise. On the day
before the last hearing, Chileüs of Tegea, a man
of great weight in Lacedæmon, heard from the
ephors what the Athenians had said to them, and

SPARTA

he answered, "Well, ye ephors, it is just thus. IX.
If the Athenians leave us and fight with the barbarian, the Persians have many ways of getting into the Peloponnesus in spite of your strong Isthmian wall. Listen to them, then, before they resolve on doing what may bring mischief to all Hellas."

This counsel they immediately weighed well, 10 and, without saying anything to the messengers, sent out five thousand Spartans while it was yet night, with seven helots to each man, under Pausanias, whose father Cleombrotus had died soon after he led away from the Isthmus the army which had been building the wall. So Pausanias was sent in the place of his cousin Pleistarchus, the son of Leonidas, who was yet a child.

In the morning the messengers went to the 11 ephors, intending to depart instantly each to his own people, and said to them, "Stay on, Lacedæmonians, keep feast and sport, after betraying your friends. The Athenians, whom ye have injured, will make their peace with the Persian as best they can; and when they have done so, they must march wherever the barbarian may lead them. And then ye will see what the issue must be to you." Then the ephors answered and sware to them that the army was already gone, and must, as they believed, be now in the sacred ground of Orestes, on their way to meet the

N

IX. strangers. And the Athenians asked them what they meant, for they did not know that they spoke of the Persians under this name; and, marvelling greatly when they learnt the truth, set out as quickly as they could, with five thousand chosen men of the Lacedæmonian Periœki.

12. When the Argives learnt that Pausanias with his men had left Sparta, they sent the best runner whom they could find to Attica, because they had promised Mardonius to hinder the Spartans from going out at all. And the runner came to Mardonius and said, "The Argives have sent me to tell thee that all the young men have set out from Lacedæmon, and that the Argives were not able to stop them; wherefore be wise in thy counsels." And so having spoken, he went home 13. again; but Mardonius, on hearing this, was in no way eager to remain in Attica. Up to this time he had waited to see what the Athenians would do, without hurting or wasting their land, in the hope that they would yield. But now he burnt Athens, and threw down and utterly destroyed every house and temple that had been left standing, and so departed from Attica before Pausanias and his men could reach the Isthmus. And he went away because Attica was not a good land for horsemen to fight in, and, if he should be beaten in the battle, he could only retreat through narrow passes which a few men might hold

against him. But while he was yet on the road to Thebes, there came to him another message that a vanguard of one thousand Lacedæmonians had reached Megara. Upon this he led his army to that city, in the hope of taking these before the rest came up; and his horsemen overran the Megarian land. This was the furthermost point of Europe which the host of the Persians reached; for, on learning by another message that the Greeks were gathered at the Isthmus, they went back through Dekeleia, guided by the men whom the chiefs of the Bœotians sent to lead him, by Sphendaleæ, Tanagra, and Scôlus, into the country of the Thebans. There, although they were on his side, he yet ravaged their lands, not at all because he hated them, but because he could not help it, since he must have some strong place for his army to fall back upon if the war should not go according to his hopes. And he stretched out his army from Erythræ to Hysiæ, and onwards to the Platæan land, by the banks of the river Asopus. However, he did not build the wall across all this space, but only for a distance of about ten furlongs on each front.

While the barbarians were labouring on this work, Attaginus, the son of Phrynôn, a Theban, called Mardonius, with fifty of the chief men among the Persians, to a great banquet which he

IX. 16 had made ready in Thebes. The rest of this tale I heard from Thersander, a great man among the Orchomenians, who told me that he had been invited to this feast with fifty men of the Thebans, and that they lay down to meat not separately, but one Persian and one Theban together on each couch. When the feast was ended, as they were drinking wine, the Persian who lay on the couch with him asked him in the Greek language who he was; and when he answered that he was a man of Orchomenus, the Persian said, "Thou hast sat at the same table and shared the same cup with me, and I wish to leave thee a memorial of my foresight, that thou mayest be able by wise counsel to provide also for thyself. Thou seest the Persians who are with us at this banquet, and the army which we left encamped on the river's bank. Yet a little while, and of all these but a very few shall remain alive." As the Persian said this, he wept bitterly; and Thersander marvelled at him and answered, "Is it not right that Mardonius should hear this, and the Persians who are of weight with him?" But the other replied, "O friend, that which Heaven is bringing to pass it is impossible for man to turn aside; for none will believe though one spake ever so truly. All this many of us Persians know well, but yet we follow, bound by a strong necessity; and of all the pains which men may suffer, the most hateful and wretched is this, to see the evils that are coming and yet be unable to overcome them." This story I heard from Thersander himself, who also added that he had told the tale to many others, before the battle was fought in Platææ.

CHAP. IX.

THE GATHERING AT PLATÆÆ.—MARDONIUS ATONES FOR THE DEATH OF LEONIDAS.—THE STORMING OF THE PERSIAN CAMP.—THE FLIGHT AND TRICK OF ARTABAZUS.

εἰς οἰωνὸς ἄριστος ἀμύνεσθαι περὶ πάτρης.

HOMER.

Herodotus IX. 17 WHILE Mardonius was encamped in Bœotia, all the Greeks who took the side of the Medes sent men to help him, and with him all marched against Athens except the Phokians. These took the king's side not of their free will but only of necessity, and a thousand of their hoplites joined Mardonius a few days after he reached Thebes, under Harmokydes, a man of great note among the citizens. As soon as they came, Mardonius placed them in the plain apart from all others; and immediately all the horsemen of the Persians rode up to them, and a rumour went through all the camp of the Greeks that the Phokians were to be shot down with arrows. The same rumour spread through the Phokians,

and Harmokydes, their leader, said, "It is clear, O
Phokians, that the enemy are about to slay us,
because, as I suppose, we have been slandered by
the Thessalians. Be strong, then, and of good
courage, every one of you, for better is it to die
fighting bravely for our lives than to be butchered
quietly like dogs; but let the barbarians at least
learn this, that they are attacking Greeks." So
when the horsemen had made a circle round them,
they rode up fiercely and stretched their bows as
if they were going to shoot, and one or two shot
their arrows. And the Phokians faced them,
being drawn up in one close mass, and the
horsemen wheeled round and drew off; nor is it
certain whether they went to slay the Phokians
at the request of the Thessalians, and then fell
back on seeing that they were ready to defend
themselves, or whether they did so merely to try
their courage. But as soon as the horsemen were
gone, Mardonius sent a herald to them, saying,
"Be of good cheer, men of Phokis; ye have shown
yourselves to be brave, and not such as I had been
told ye were. And now fight ye zealously for the
king, for, whatever benefits ye may do to us, ye
shall have yet more from him and from me."

In the meanwhile the Lacedæmonians reached
the Isthmus and encamped there; and when
the rest of the Peloponnesians who inclined
to the better side heard this, or saw that the

IX. Lacedæmonians had set out, they did not choose to be left behind: all therefore marched in one body from the Isthmus, when the sacrifices were said to be fair, and came to Eleusis, where they were joined by the Athenians who had crossed over from Salamis. Thence, when they had learnt again from the victims that the gods were kind, they went on to Erythræ in the Bœotian land; and, hearing that the barbarians were encamped on the banks of the Asopus, they drew themselves out in array on the slopes of Mount Kithæron.

20 And when they would not come down into the plain, Mardonius sent all his horsemen against them, under Masistius, a great man amongst the Persians, who rode upon a Nisæan horse with a golden bridle and brave trappings. So the horsemen rode up by their ranks to the Greeks, doing them much hurt by their arrows, and called them

21 women. It chanced that the Megarians were placed in that spot which was most open to attack, and where the horsemen could approach most easily. Thus they were hard pressed and sent a messenger to the generals of the Greeks, who came to them and said, "The men of Megara cannot by themselves receive the onset of the Persians and keep the ground where they were placed at the first; yet they hold out bravely and cheerfully, though they are sorely pressed: but if ye send not others to relieve us, we must leave

THE DEATH OF MASISTIUS.

our ranks." But when Pausanias asked who were willing of their own accord to go to this spot and take the place of the Megarians, none would go until the Athenians undertook to do so; and there went the three hundred chosen men, of whom Olympiodôrus, the son of Lampôn, was the captain. These, with the archers, placed themselves in front of the Greeks at Erythræ; and, at last, the horse of Masistius received an arrow in its side, and, rearing itself upright in its pain, shook Masistius from its back. Then the Athenians took his horse and killed Masistius as he strove to defend himself; but they did so with difficulty, for he wore a corslet of scale armour under a purple tunic. So they tried in vain to pierce the corslet, until at last some one, finding out the reason, wounded him in the eye; and so he died. All this was done without the knowledge of his horsemen, for they did not see him fall or learn what had happened while their retreat was going on; but on halting they found out their loss, and with a great cry turned back to recover his body. And the Athenians, seeing them coming up not by companies but in a single mass, called the rest of the army to help them; and while they were coming up, a sharp fight went on for the body of Masistius. As long as the three hundred stood alone, they were beaten and compelled to give up the body; but when the others came up, the

IX. Persians were again driven back, and, losing the body, had many more of their number slain. So they fell back about two furlongs, and taking counsel rode off to Mardonius because they had lost their leader. Then there was a great mourning throughout the army of the Persians, for all lamented for Masistius (and Mardonius mourned most of all), shaving themselves and their horses and their beasts of burden. And there was a great cry through all the host, and the sound of it went through all Bœotia, as for the death of one who, next to Mardonius, was of most note among the Persians and with the king.[1]

---

[1] Mr. Rawlinson rightly cites this passage among the instances of vivid pictorial description to be found throughout the pages of Herodotus: at the same time he remarks (Herodotus, vol. i. p. 145) that, "in common with the ancients generally, the historian for the most part neglects natural scenery." Volumes have been written in our own day on this supposed contrast between ancient and modern writers; and the greater merit of the latter in that art which has received the name of "word-painting" has been vehemently maintained by Mr. Ruskin, himself perhaps the most prominent of all painters in words. (Modern Painters, &c. &c.) Yet after all it may be fairly doubted whether this art will have any great permanence, and still more whether it has at all answered the purpose for which it was called into being. Its aim is to give to those who have not seen a natural landscape or a painted representation of it, a real idea of that scene or that picture. It is by some maintained already, and the opinion will rapidly gain ground, that the most elaborate descriptions give nothing more than general impressions. The most minute account of such pictures

But the Greeks, having withstood the onset of the horsemen and driven them off, became much more bold and cheerful, and putting the dead body on a car, they drew it along their ranks; and so wonderful was it for its stature and its beauty, that the men left their places and came forward to look upon Masistius. After this they determined to go down to Plataeae, which seemed to them a much better place to encamp in than Erythrae and to have more water. To this place, then, and to the fountain of Gargaphia, they resolved to go, and there place themselves in order. So they took up their arms and went along the lower slopes of Kithaeron to Hysiae in the Plataean land, and there drew themselves up by their nations near the fountain

---

as the "Old Temeraire," the "Slave Ship," the "Campagna of Rome," may lead us to create our own pictures to answer that description; but they will no more put us in the position of others who have seen those pictures, than the passing touches of the ancient poet will enable us altogether to realise the beauties of the ivy-covered Colonos. Yet probably the partial sketch of Sophocles will leave on the reader's mind an impression not less vivid than that which he may receive from any descriptions of the most elaborate word-painting. The enthusiasm with which Herodotus speaks of the beautiful climate of Ionia, and the description which he gives of the surprise of the Phokians at Thermopylae, show that he felt these outward beauties not less than Sophocles himself. In both the absence of more elaborate description may be caused as much by a consciousness of its uselessness, as by any want of the powers of appreciation.

IX. of Gargaphia and the sacred ground of the hero Androcrates, along some gently swelling mounds and level land.

26 In drawing up this order there arose a great strife of words between the men of Tegea and the Athenians, both claiming to have that wing of the army which the Lacedæmonians might not choose for themselves, and bringing up things done lately and long ago in support of their claim. And the men of Tegea said, "In every march of the Peloponnesians both in old time and in later days, the allies have ever given us this place, from the time that the children of Heracles sought, after the death of Eurystheus, to return into the Peloponnesus. Then, with the Achæans and the Ionians who were then in Peloponnesus, we went out to meet them; and the tale is that Hyllus would not suffer the armies to come together in battle, but asked for the bravest man among the Peloponnesians to come forth and fight with him in place of all. So they sware an oath that if Hyllus should conquer the champion of the Peloponnesians, the children of Heracles should return to their fathers' land, but if he should be beaten, then they should go away and not seek a return to the Peloponnesus for a hundred years. Then of his own will came forth Echemus, the son of Aëropus our leader and king, and fought with Hyllus and slew him. For this deed the Pelopon-

nesians gave us other great honours, which we
have still—and this also, that we should lead the
other wing whenever they went out to war. We
do not stand in your way, then, men of Lacedæmon; take whichever wing ye may prefer, but
the other we claim to lead as in the former days.
Nay, apart from this deed of Echemus, we deserve this post much more than the Athenians;
for many a sturdy struggle have we had with you,
O men of Lacedæmon, and many also with others;
but the Athenians have not deeds such as ours to
boast of, either in our own time or in the ages
that are past." To this the Athenians answered, 27
"We supposed that we were gathered here to
fight with the barbarian and not to quarrel between ourselves with words. But since the men
of Tegea think fit to balance their good deeds
in every generation against ours, we must also
show why, so long as we behave well, we deserve
to come before Arcadians. These children of Heracles, whose leader they say that they slew at
the Isthmus, we alone welcomed when they were
driven from one nation of the Greeks to another,
as they fled from the men of Mykênæ; and we
also put down the pride of Eurystheus, when with
them we beat in a battle the people who then had
the Peloponnesus. Yet again, when the men of
Argos went against Thebes with Polyneikes and
lay unburied on the ground, we marched against

the children of Cadmus, and recovering their bodies buried them in Eleusis of our own land. And we also did bravely against the daughters of the Amazons when long ago they came into Attica from the river Thermôdon; and in the labours at Troy we came behind none. But it is useless to go back to these things. They who behaved well then may be worthless now; they who were cowards long ago may now be brave. Enough then of the former days. For even if we had done no other good deed (and we have done many, perhaps beyond all the Greeks), yet, from what we did at Marathon, we deserve surely not this honour only, but others also, for daring to meet the Persians alone and conquering by one victory six-and-forty nations. But at such a time as this it is not seemly to be quarrelling for a place, and so we are ready, men of Lacedæmon, to stand where ye may think fit to place us; and wherever we are we shall strive to do our duty."

Then the Lacedæmonians cried out as one man that the Athenians deserved to lead the other wing more than any Arcadians; and so the men of Tegea were worsted in their claim.

After this they were drawn out for battle thus,— the new-comers along with those who had been there from the first. On the right wing were ten thousand Lacedæmonians; but five thousand of these were Spartans, who were guarded by five-and-thirty thousand helots, seven to each man. Next to themselves they placed the men of Tegea, fifteen hundred heavy-armed men, as a reward for their courage and greatness in times past. After these came fifteen hundred men of Corinth, close to whom stood the three hundred Potidæans who had come from Pallênê. Then came six hundred Arcadians of Orchomenus, and three thousand men of Sikyôn; then eight hundred Epidaurians, and one thousand men of Trœzen, next to whom were two hundred from Lepreum, with four hundred from Mykênæ and Tiryns, and one thousand men from Phliûs. Next to these stood three hundred from Hermione, then six hundred from Eretria and Styria, then four hundred Chalkidians and five hundred men of Ambrakia. Beyond these were placed eight hundred from Leucas and Anactorium, and then two hundred Palians from Kephallenia. Next to these were drawn out five hundred Æginetans, and then three thousand men of Megara, beyond whom were six hundred Platæans; and beyond all, and first on the left wing, stood the Athenians, eight thousand men, with Aristeides, the son of Lysimachus, for their leader.

All these, except the seven who served round every Spartan, were hoplites, and numbered in all thirty-eight thousand seven hundred men. And the light-armed were the five-and-thirty thousand helots belonging to the Spartans, and three for each of the other Lacedæmonians and Greeks, making together thirty-four thousand five hundred men; so that all the light-armed men in the army numbered seven myriads lacking five hundred.

30 And hoplites and light-armed together made up eleven myriads lacking eighteen hundred; but these were filled up by the Thespians, who remained after Thermopylæ, and who came without heavy arms. So all these were encamped on the banks of the river Asôpus.

31 When the barbarians with Mardonius had ended their mourning for Masistius, they also hastened to the Asôpus, on hearing that the Greeks were assembled in Platææ. There, facing the Lacedæmonians, Mardonius placed the Persians, who being many more in number fronted also the men of Tegea; but he picked out the strongest to stand opposite the Lacedæmonians, and the weakest he placed against the Tegeatans. This he did by the counsel and warning of the Thebans. Next to the Persians came the Medes, facing the Corinthians and Potidæans, with the men of Orchomenus and Sikyon; after these, the Bactrians in front of the Epidaurians, Trœzonians, and Lepreatans, and also of the men of Tiryns, Mykênæ, and Phliûs. Next to these stood the Indians, who faced the men of Hermionê and Eretria, the Styrians and Chalkidians. Beyond these came the Sakæ

in front of the Ambrakiots and Leucadians, the Paleans and Æginetans. And opposite to the Athenians, Platæans, and Megarians, he drew up the Bœotians and Locrians, Melians and Thessalians, with the thousand men of Phokis (for not all the Phokians had taken the king's side, but some who had fled to the heights of Parnassus aided the Greeks by coming down from the mountain and plundering the army of Mardonius and the Greeks who were with him). And facing the Athenians were also drawn up the men of Macedonia and the countries which lie near to Thessaly.

These were the greatest nations in the army of Mardonius, and had the highest name. But with these were mixed up men of other nations, Phrygians, Thracians, Mysians, Pæonians, and the rest; and of the Æthiopians and Egyptians were those who carry daggers and are called Hermotybians and Calasirians,—the only Egyptians who fight. These Mardonius took out of the ships while he was at Phalêrum, for they had not been reckoned amongst the footmen of Xerxes. So then the barbarians were, as has been said before, thirty myriads; but the number of the Greeks who were with them is not known, for they were never counted, but we may suppose that they made up five myriads more.

When all were drawn out by their nations and in their companies, then on the second day both

IX. armies offered sacrifice. The seer of the Greeks was Tisamenus, the son of Antiochus, whom, being an Eleian of the Iamid tribe, the Lacedæmonians had adopted into their own people. For when he had gone once on a time to Delphi, the priestess said that he should be five times conqueror in the greatest struggles; so he thought that she meant the great games, and, giving his mind to these, very nearly won the game of five contests against Hieronymus of Andros. And when the Lacedæmonians found from this that the priestess must have meant the strife not of games but of war, they sought with a great sum to obtain him for a leader in war together with their kings the children of Heracles. But he, seeing their eagerness, raised his price, and said that he would only lead them if they gave him all the rights of a citizen. But the Spartans would not hear of it, and at first cared nothing for the words of the priestess. But when the great peril of the Persian war hung over them, they agreed to do as he had asked. Then Tisamenus answered that he would not be content now, unless they gave to his brother Hêgias also all that he had demanded for himself. And they gave way to him in all, so grievously did they need him; and so Tisamenus became their soothsayer, and helped them to win five great battles, of which this one in Platææ was the first. And when he offered sacrifice, he told them that the signs were good if they stood in their own defence, but not if they crossed the river and began the battle.

Mardonius also was eager to begin the fight; but neither to him were the omens good if he advanced against the enemy. For he also had a Greek soothsayer, Hegesistratus, an Eleian of the tribe of the Telliadæ, whom the Spartans once bound and were going to slay, because they thought that he had done them great wrong. So he knew that he was in peril of his life, and resolved to do a daring and marvellous deed to escape not only death but horrible tortures before death. Somehow or other he got a steel knife and cut off the front part of his foot so as to let him draw the rest out from the stock to which it was fastened. So he fled from his dungeon by a hole which he had made in the wall, and, journeying by night and skulking in the woods by day, reached Tegea on the third night, although he had been sought by all the Lacedæmonians, who had marvelled to see the foot lying on the ground and the man himself gone. At this time the men of Tegea were not friendly to the Spartans; so when the wound was healed, Hegesistratus made himself a wooden foot, and showed himself openly as an enemy to the Lacedæmonians. However, he did not prosper in this enmity to the end; for they caught him at last as he was prophesying in

IX. 38 Zakynthus, and put him to death. But this was long after the fight at Plataea, where he offered sacrifice for Mardonius not only because he hated the Lacedæmonians, but because he had been hired at a great price. And when the signs would not allow him or the Greeks who were with him to fight, a Theban named Timagenidas counselled Mardonius to guard the passes of Mount Kithæron, telling him that more men were daily pouring in to help the Greeks, and that by so doing he
39 would catch many of them. Eight days had passed away since the armies began to face each other, when this counsel was given to Mardonius. And, as soon as it was night, Mardonius sent his horsemen into the passes of Kithæron which lead towards Plataea, and which the Bœotians call the Three Heads, but the Athenians name the Oak Heads. Nor did he send them in vain; for they caught five hundred beasts carrying corn from Peloponnesus for the army, together with the men who followed them. On these the Persians fell fiercely, and slew all, sparing neither man nor beast; and when they had taken their fill of slaughter, they drove away all that remained to Mardonius and his army.

40 After this, yet two days more passed, while neither side was willing to commence the battle. The barbarians came up indeed to the banks of the Asopus, but neither Greeks nor Persians at-

tempted to cross the river. Still the horsemen of Mardonius troubled the Greeks, for the Thebans, who were fierce on the king's side, urged them on vehemently. So for ten days nothing more happened; but on the eleventh Mardonius, vexed that the Greeks were daily growing stronger in number, took counsel with Artabazus, the son of Pharnakes, who thought that all the host ought at once to go to the wall of the Thebans, where much corn was stored up for the men, with food also for all the cattle, and there wait quietly. "We have much gold," he said, "both coined and uncoined, and also much silver both in money and in drinking vessels. Spare none of these, but send them about to the Greeks, and chiefly to those who are at the head in each city, and they will soon give up their freedom without facing the dangers of a battle." And so likewise thought the Thebans. But Mardonius was headstrong and would not listen, for he thought that his army was altogether stronger than the army of the Greeks. "Let us fight," he answered, "before our enemies grow more in number. As to the omens of Hegesistratus, let them alone, and seek not to force them; but let us go to meet the enemy as we should do in our own land."

None dared to speak against these words of Mardonius, for he it was and not Artabazus whom the king had left to be the general of his army.

IX. So he sent for the leaders of the companies and the captains of the Greeks who were with him, and asked them if they knew of any oracle which said that the Persians should be destroyed in Hellas. But all were silent, some because they knew no such oracle, others because they were afraid to speak. Then said Mardonius, "Since ye either know nothing or dare not tell out what ye know, I will tell you myself. There is an oracle which says that Persians, coming to Hellas, shall plunder the temple at Delphi, and then be utterly destroyed. But we are not going against this temple, nor shall we attempt to plunder it; and therefore we shall not for this cause be undone. Be glad, then, all ye who have good will towards the Persians, for we shall now conquer the Greeks." And so he bade them all make ready for the fight, for that he would begin the battle on the next morning as soon as the day should break. So the council was ended, and the night came on, and the guards stood at their posts. And when all was quiet through the camp and the men were in a deep sleep, then, in the late hours of the night, Alexander the son of Amyntas, the general and king of the Macedonians, rode up to the outposts of the Athenians and asked to speak with their leaders. So most of the watchmen waited there with him, while some went to say that there was a man come from

the army of the Medes who would tell them
nothing but sought to come to speech of the
generals, of whom he spoke by name. Then the
leaders followed the guards to the outposts;
and when they came near, Alexander said to
them, "Men of Athens, I charge you, tell not
these words of mine to any save Pausanias, lest
ye destroy me. I should never have spoken them
but because I greatly care for Hellas. I too am
a Greek by ancient descent, and I wish not to
see Hellas enslaved instead of free. Therefore do
I tell you that the omens are not fair to Mardonius and his army; otherwise he would have
fought with you long ago. Now, however, he is
resolved to take no further heed of omens and
victims, but to begin the battle as soon as the
day shall dawn, for, as I believe, he fears that
your numbers are daily becoming greater. Wherefore be ye ready, and even if Mardonius puts off
the battle, still tarry on, for he has but little corn
left. And if the war end as ye would have it,
then remember to deliver me also, for in my zeal
for the Greeks I have run this great venture, because I wished to show you the purpose of Mardonius, that so he might not take you unawares.
I am Alexander the Macedonian." So having
spoken, he rode back to the army and to his company; and the generals of the Athenians went to
the right wing and told Pausanias what they had

IX. heard from Alexander. Then Pausanias was afraid and said, "If we must fight as soon as the day dawns, then must ye Athenians face the Persians, while we stand in front of the Bœotians and other Greeks; and for this reason. Ye know the Medes and their way of fighting, for ye have done battle with them in Marathon. We have no knowledge of them, and are unskilled in their ways. But if the Spartans have never fought with the Medes, they have often fought with Bœotians and Thessalians. Take up your arms, then, and come to our wing, while we change to the left." Then the Athenians answered Pausanias and said, "Long ago, when we saw that you faced the Persians, it came into our minds to counsel you to do what ye now wish to do, but we were afraid that our words might not please you. But as ye have thought of these things yourselves, we gladly agree and are ready to do as ye would have 47 us." So both were pleased; and the day dawned as they were changing their ground. And the Bœotians, seeing what was going on, told it to Mardonius, who straightway made the Persians move to the other side so as again to face the Lacedæmonians. But when Pausanias saw by this that his purpose was found out, he led the Spartans back to the right wing, and Mardonius 48 placed the Persians again on his left. When all stood as they had been drawn up before, Mardonius sent a herald to the Spartans, who came to them and said, "O Lacedaemonians, the people of this land tell us that ye are the bravest of all men, and marvel that ye never fly from war or leave your ranks, but, holding your ground, either slay your enemies or are slain yourselves. All this, then, is a lie; for before the battle begins, we see you leaving your post and changing ground, wishing the Athenians to commence the fight, while ye place yourselves in front of our slaves. These are not the deeds of brave men. Nay, we have been sadly deceived in you. We thought that for your great name ye would send a herald saying that ye would fight with the Persians by yourselves; and not only do ye not say this, but yield ground before us. Well, we have begun this converse, not you; and so we will say yet more, what hinders us from fighting in equal numbers, you on behalf of the Greeks, because ye are held to be the bravest, and we Persians on behalf of the barbarians? If the others must fight, let them fight afterwards. But if there is no need of this, let us finish the strife; and whichever of the two shall conquer, let it be held that he conquers with his whole army."

So the herald waited for an answer; but none was given, and presently he rode away and told Mardonius how he had fared. And Mardonius was exceedingly glad, and ordered his horsemen

ix. to march against the Greeks; and they did much
hurt to their army by shooting their arrows and
lances against them, while the Greeks could not
reach them because they fought on horses. And
the Persians destroyed and filled up the fountain
of Gargaphia from which all the army of the
Greeks drew their water. Near this fountain only
the Lacedæmonians had been placed, while the rest
of the Greeks were near the river Asôpus; but
now that they were prevented by the horsemen and
archers from approaching the river, they were
50 compelled to resort to this fountain. Upon this
the leaders of the Greeks came to Pausanias on
the right wing, to take counsel on this matter and
on many others, for not only had they no water, but
there were other things more grievous still. Their
corn had almost failed them, and their servants,
whom they had sent to the Peloponnesus to bring
more, were caught by the horsemen of the Persians
51 and were unable to reach the camp. So the generals resolved that, if the Persians should again
put off the battle, they would retreat to an island
ten furlongs away from the fountain of Gargaphia,
in front of the city of Plateæ. Here the stream
which comes down in two courses from Kithæron
runs again into one, and so makes this island, which
is called Oëroê (as the people of the land say)
from a daughter of the river Asôpus. Thither they
purposed to go, that they might have plenty of

water and not be so vexed by the horsemen of the
enemy. So they made ready to depart as soon as
the second watch of the night should come, that
the Persians might not see them setting out and
send out horsemen to annoy them; and they purposed also, as soon as they had reached the island,
to send half the army to Kithæron to bring away
the servants, who had been sent to fetch food but
were shut up in the mountain.

All that day, then, they were grievously pressed
by the horsemen of the Persians; but as the day
ended, the enemy attacked them no more. And
when the hour of the night came which had been
agreed upon, and they set out on their march,
they forgot the place to which they had been
commanded to go, but, in their wish to escape from
the enemy, went straight to the city of Platææ,
and there gladly piled their arms before the temple of Hera. So when Pausanias saw them setting out from the camp, he supposed that they
were marching to the island of Oëroê, and gave
command to the Lacedæmonians to take up their
arms and follow those who were going before them.
This command all the captains were ready to obey,
except Amompharetus, the leader of the band of
Pitanê, who said that he would never fly from the
strangers and so bring shame upon Sparta. And
he marvelled at what was going on, because he
had not been present at the council. But Pau-

IX. sanias and Euryanax were greatly vexed that he
did not obey; and still more were they grieved at
the thought of leaving the band of Pitanê behind,
lest Amompharetus should be slain with all his
men. So they kept all their men still, and tried
to persuade him that he ought not so to do. While
they thus urged on Amompharetus, the Athenians
54 also remained quiet in their ranks, suspecting that
the Lacedæmonians had said one thing but meant
another. But when the army began to move, they
sent a horseman to see if the Spartans also were
preparing to set out, and, if not, to ask Pausanias
55 what ought to be done. In the meanwhile Pausanias and Euryanax failed to gain over Amompharetus, and they were in loud quarrel together
when the herald of the Athenians came. Presently
Amompharetus took up a piece of rock with both
his hands, and, placing it at the feet of Pausanias,
said, "Thus do I cast my vote against the counsel
of flying from the strangers." But Pausanias
called him a brainstruck madman, and, turning to
the herald who sought an answer to his message,
bade him tell the Athenians how matters stood
and ask them to take their stand near them.
56 So the herald departed, and the quarrel of the
Spartans was not yet ended when the day broke;
and then Pausanias, thinking (and, as the issue
showed, truly) that Amompharetus would never
remain if all the rest were fairly gone, made the

signal and led the others away through the hillocks, followed by the men of Tegea. But the Athenians went another way, for the Lacedæmonians, fearing the horsemen of the enemy, kept close to the slopes of Kithæron, while the Athenians turned lower down into the plain. At first Amompharetus, thinking that they would not dare to leave him, stuck to his old place; but as the men with Pausanias went further, and it seemed that they were really going away, he made his band take up their arms, and led them slowly to join the others who were waiting for him about ten furlongs away near the river Moloeis, where stands a temple of the Eleusinian Dêmêtêr. Here Pausanias had halted, that he might be able to go back and help Amompharetus if he should still refuse to move. But no sooner had he come up with his men than the barbarian horsemen again began to annoy them, for when they found the place empty where the Greeks had stood, they hastened on to overtake them.

When Mardonius heard that they were gone, he called Thorax of Larissa and his two brothers, and said to them, " Children of Aleuas, what say ye, now that ye see all this? You, who dwell near them, used to tell me that the Lacedæmonians never fled from battle, but were the bravest of men in war. Yet first you saw them trying to shift their place, and now, during the night that is past, we find that they have fairly fled. In very truth have they shown themselves to be worthless even among worthless Greeks, on the day in which they are doomed to do battle with those who in very deed are the bravest of mankind. You indeed, who know nothing of Persians, I can pardon for praising the Lacedæmonians, for whom ye have some fellow-feeling; but I am only the more astonished that Artabazus should have feared them, and given to me the cowardly counsel that we ought to march away and shut ourselves up in Thebes. Of a truth the king shall hear of all this from me; but there will be time enough to speak of this hereafter. Now we must hunt out these Greeks and punish them for all the evils that they have done to the Persians." So having spoken, he led his men across the Asopus, and then made them run in the track of the Greeks, who, as he thought, were flying. Thus he hastened to catch the Lacedæmonians and the men of Tegea, for he could not see the Athenians, who had gone down into the plain under the hillocks. And when the other barbarians saw that the Persians were gone in chase of the Greeks, they all arose, and, following as quickly as they could in no ranks or order, hurried with cries and screams as if they were going to tear the Greeks to pieces.

When the horsemen began to press him, Pausanias sent a messenger to the Athenians who said to them, "Men of Athens, we, the Lacedæmonians, have together with you been betrayed by our allies, who this night have fled just as the great struggle has come which is to decide whether Hellas shall be enslaved or free. We must help one another, then, as best we may. If the horsemen had come against you, then should we and the men of Tegea who have not betrayed their country have been bound to help you; but now they have come upon us, and it is fair only that ye should hasten to those who are in distress. But if ye cannot yourselves come to our aid, send some archers, and we will thank you for the help, as we believe that ye will grant us this kindness by reason of the zeal which ye have shown throughout the war." On learning this, the Athenians made all haste to go and help them to the best of their power; but as they were setting out, the Greeks who were on the king's side attacked them and hindered them from going. And so the Lacedæmonians, who were fifty thousand, and the men of Tegea (who were never separated from them), three thousand, being now left all alone, offered sacrifice, as being about to do battle with Mardonius and his army. But the signs were not good; and many of them were slain, and many more wounded. For the Persians placed their shields together and shot out their arrows

LX. without sparing them, so that the Spartans were greatly distressed; and Pausanias, looking away to the temple of Hera in Plataea, called upon the name of the goddess, and prayed her not to let them be disappointed of their hope.

62 While he yet prayed thus, the men of Tegea rose up first, and went against the barbarians; and immediately after the prayer of Pausanias there came good signs to the Lacedæmonians, who also rose up and hastened to meet the Persians, as they stood in front and shot at them with their bows. First, then, they fought against the fence of shields; and when this had fallen, there was a sharp fight for a long time, close to the temple of Dêmêtêr, until they pressed close and pushed one another, for the barbarians seized their spears and broke them off. In spirit, then, and strength of body the Persians were not weaker than their enemies, but they were without heavy arms, and had not the same skill and knowledge of war with the Greeks; and rushing forward singly or in small numbers, or mingled together in a wild strife, they fell into the hands 63 of the Spartans and were slain. But most of all they pressed the enemy where Mardonius himself fought on the back of a white horse with the thousand chosen Persians round him. And as long as Mardonius remained alive, they stood firm and slew many of the Lacedæmonians: but

presently Mardonius was slain and the chosen ix.
men that were with him fell, and then all the
others yielded and fled before the Lacedæmonians; for, having to fight with heavy-armed men,
they were most of all hurt by their dress, which
was not strong enough to defend their body.

Thus Mardonius paid the recompense for the 64
murder of Leonidas, as the priestess had spoken
to the Spartans; and so Pausanias the son of
Cleombrotus gained the most glorious of all victories. The man who slew Mardonius was called
Aeimnêstus, a man of great note in Sparta, who
afterwards, when there was a war with the Messe-
nians, was slain by them with his three hundred
chosen men in Stenyclarus.

When the Persians were turned to flight by the 65
Lacedæmonians, they fled in disorder to their own
camp and to the wooden fence which they had
made in the Theban ground. And a marvellous
thing it is that, although they fought by the grove
of Dêmêtêr, not one of the Persians entered her
sacred portion or died within it, but the most of
them fell in the common ground around the
temple; and I believe (if it be right to think at
all on matters such as this) that the goddess herself would not receive them because they had burnt
her temple at Eleusis.

Now Artabazus the son of Pharnakes had been 66
displeased at the first because the king left Mar-

P

LX. donius to rule the army, and before the battle he sought in vain to dissuade him from fighting. And so, being vexed at what Mardonius was doing, he took his men (and they were not less than four myriads) as soon as the fight began, charging them to follow him wherever he might lead them; and with this command he led them, as he said, to the battle. But as he went in front he saw that the Persians were already in flight, and so he wheeled his men round and fled, not to the wooden fence or into the walls of Thebes, but to the Phokian land, because he wished to reach the Hellespont as quickly as he could.

67 Of the Greeks who had taken the king's side, the Bœotians fought for a long time with the Athenians; and the Thebans did battle obstinately and fiercely, so that three hundred of their first and bravest men were there slain. But when they also were routed, they fled to Thebes, but not by the way that the Persians had taken. Of the other Greeks who were in the barbarian army not one 68 fought bravely, but all fled away together. And so it becomes clear that all the welfare of the barbarians depended upon the Persians, since even these ran away without fighting, because they saw Persians in flight. All fled, then, except the Bœotian and other horsemen, who kept close to their enemies and hindered them from falling on their friends; and the Greeks followed in their victory,

chasing and slaying the men of Xerxes. In the ix. 69
midst of this panic, a message was brought to the
other Greeks (who, being drawn up round the
temple of Hera, had taken no share in the fight),
that the battle was fought and the men of Pausanias were conquerors. On hearing this, without
falling into any order, the Corinthians hurried
by the hillocks and the lower mountain slopes on
the road which goes to the temple of Dêmêtêr,
while the men of Megara and Phliûs kept the
smoothest way through the plain. As these approached the enemy, the Theban horsemen saw
them coming up in disorder and, attacking them,
struck down six hundred, while they drove back
the rest and chased them to Kithæron. But the 70
Persians and the rest of their host who fled to
the wooden fence mounted the towers before the
Lacedæmonians could come up, and secured the
walls as well as they could, so that, when they
came, there was a fiercer fight against the wall,
which they were unable to take because they knew
nothing of this way of fighting. And even when
the Athenians came up, the fight was fierce and
long. At last, by their courage and their obstinacy, the Athenians clambered up and made
a breach through which the Greeks poured in.
First entered the men of Tegea, who tore down
the tent of Mardonius and plundered it, taking
among other things the manger of his horse,

IX. which was made of brass and very beautiful. This manger the men of Tegea dedicated at the temple of the Alean Athena; but whatever else they took they brought into a common store for the Greeks. But the barbarians no longer stood their ground in firm masses when the wall fell, and showed no more stoutness of heart, but ran about in frantic terror, being many myriads shut up in a scanty space. So the Greeks slew on, until of the thirty myriads (except the four which Artabazus had led away) not three thousand remained alive. In this battle there fell of the Spartans ninety-one men, of the Tegeatans sixteen, and of the Athenians fifty-two.

71   Among the barbarians, the bravest of the footmen were the Persians, and of the horsemen the Sakæ; and of all the men none, it is said, was so brave as Mardonius. Of the Greeks, the men of Tegea and Athens did well, but the Lacedæmonians did better; yet it is not easy to show how (for all conquered the men who were placed in front of them), except that they had to face the strongest of the enemy and conquered them. But by far the bravest among them was that Aristodemus who was disgraced for being the only one of the three hundred who returned home from Thermopylæ; and next to him came Poseidonius, and Philokyon, and Amompharetus. Yet, when they afterwards sought to fix who was

the best, the Spartans who were present judged IX.
that Aristodemus had shown his daring by leaving
his ranks and fighting with mad fury, because
he wished to fling away his life; but that Poseidonius did bravely although he did not wish to
die, and was thus far the better man. This,
however, was spoken from grudge and jealousy;
and so the others whom I have named were
honoured because they fell in this battle; but
Aristodemus lost his glory for seeking, as they
said, to die.

These were the men who won the greatest 72
name in Plataeæ; for Callicrates, the most beautiful not only of the Lacedæmonians but of all
the Greeks, died away from the battle. For, as
Pausanias was offering sacrifice, he was wounded
in the side by an arrow while he was sitting
down. So he was carried away, while the rest
fought; and, as the pains of death pressed him
hard, he said to Arimnestus of Plataeæ, that it
grieved him not to die for Hellas, but because he
had not been suffered to strike a blow in the
battle, and to do bravely for his country, as he
wished to do.

Among the Athenians, the man who won the 73
greatest name was Sophanes of Dekeleia, of 74
whom the tale is told that he carried an iron
anchor fastened to his breast-plate by a brazen

IX. chain, and with this, whenever he came near any of the enemy, he threw them out of their ranks, while he stood fast in his own; and when they fled, he took up his anchor and chased them. But another story is, that he bore the sign of an anchor on his shield which flashed everywhere and was never still, but not one made of steel hanging from his corslet.

76 And when the barbarians had been smitten by the Greeks in Plataeæ, there came a woman on a chariot with her handmaids, all arrayed in their fairest raiment; and, dismounting from it, she went towards the Lacedæmonians who were still slaying their enemies. When she saw that Pausanias was ordering everything, she drew near to him (for she knew his name before, and whence he came) and took him by the knees, saying, "O King of Sparta, save me, I beseech thee, from slavery. Thus far thou hast helped me, by slaying these barbarians, who had no care of gods or men. I am a woman of Côs and a daughter of Hegetoridas; and the Persians took me from my home by force." And Pausanias answered, "Be of good courage, not only because thou comest as a suppliant, but because (if thy tale be true) thou art the daughter of a man who more than all others is my friend among those who dwell in the parts of which thou hast spoken." Then he intrusted her to those of the ephors who

were present, and afterwards sent her to Ægina, whither she wished to go.

Immediately after this, the men of Mantineia came up, and were greatly grieved when they found that they were too late, and confessed that hey deserved to be punished. But, hearing that Artabazus with his men was flying to the Hellespont, they were setting out to chase them as far as Thessaly; but the Lacedæmonians would not suffer them so to do. So they went back to their own land, and then drove their leaders out of the country. And after them came the men of Elis, who also went home greatly grieved, and banished their leaders from the land.

While they were in the camp at Platææ, there went to Pausanias Lampôn, the son of Pytheas, a great man among the Æginetans, with a horrible prayer. Drawing near to him in haste, he said, "Son of Cleombrotus, thou hast this day done a work marvellous for its greatness and its glory, and Heaven hath permitted thee to deliver Hellas and to win a name beyond that of all the Greeks who are known to us. Finish then what yet remains for thee to do, that so thou mayest become yet more glorious and that the barbarians may dread to insult the Greeks hereafter. For when Leonidas died in Thermopylæ, Mardonius and Xerxes cut off his head and hung his body on a cross. Requite it therefore now to Mardonius, and thou shalt have praise not only from the Spartans but from all the Greeks." Then answered Pausanias and said, "O Æginetan friend, I thank thee for thy good will and forethought; yet thou hast missed the right judgment. For, having extolled my country and my deeds, thou hast brought them also to nothing by bidding me to insult a dead body and by saying that for such a deed I shall be the better spoken of. All this is fitter for barbarians than for Greeks, and we hate it even in them; and if such a thing be needed, then may I never please the men of Ægina, or any who may like such doings. It is enough for me to please the Spartans by right deeds and right words. Leonidas, whom thou urgest me to avenge, has, I tell thee, been mightily avenged already, and he, with all who fell in Thermopylæ, has been glorified in the countless numbers who have been slain here. Dare not then to approach me any more with such words as these or to give me the like counsel, and be grateful to me that thou goest away scatheless."

Then Pausanias commanded by a herald that none should touch the booty, but that the helots should gather everything into one common store. So they went through all the camp, and found tents adorned with gold and silver, and gilded couches, with drinking bowls and cups and goblets of solid gold; and on the waggons were sacks with gold and silver vessels. From the dead that lay on the ground they stripped off bracelets and chains and gilded daggers, for of embroidered garments no one took any heed. Of all this the helots stole much and sold much to the Æginetans, while they gave account of all that they could not hide; and hence began the great wealth of the men of Ægina, who bought gold from the helots, telling them that it was brass.

So when all had been gathered together, they set apart the portions for the gods. With that which was given to the god at Delphi they dedicated the golden tripod which stands on the three-headed brazen serpent close to the altar; and from the portion of the Olympian god they set up a brazen statue of Zeus ten cubits in height; and from that which was given to the Isthmian god was made a brazen figure of Poseidon seven cubits high. All the rest they divided, to each man his share according to his deserving,—the women, the gold and the silver, with all other things and the beasts. But it is not said what special gifts were set apart for those who had fought most bravely at Plataeæ; yet some, I suppose, were given. For Pausanias himself there was set apart a tenth of everything, women, horses, money, camels, and all other things in like manner. A tale is also told that Xerxes, when he fled from Hellas, left his furniture with Mardonius, and that Pausanias,

IX. when he saw it all blazing with gold and silver and embroidered hangings, commanded the cooks and bakers to make ready for him a banquet, as they had been wont to do for Mardonius. When all was ready he saw couches and tables of gold and silver all fairly spread and a banquet splendidly set forth; and then, marvelling at this magnificence and glory, he charged his own servants, by way of mockery, to prepare a Laconian feast. So the meal was made ready, but it looked not much like the other; and Pausanias laughed and, sending for the generals of the Greeks, pointed to the two banquets which were spread before them, saying, "O men of Hellas, I have brought you together that ye may see the madness of the Mede who faring thus sumptuously came to rob us of

83 our sorry food." Long after this many also of the Platæans used to find treasures of gold and silver and other things which had not been gathered by the helots.

84 The day after the battle the body of Mardonius disappeared; but none can tell for certain who took it. Many people of all sorts were said to have buried Mardonius, and I know that many received rich gifts from Artontes, the son of Mardonius, for the burial of his father; but the greater number seem to think that he was buried by a man of Ephesus.

85 After the sharing of the spoil, the Greeks buried

TOMB AT PLATÆÆ.

their dead according to their nations. The Lacedæmonians made three tombs, one for the chosen Spartans, amongst whom were Poseidonius and Amompharetus, Philokyon and Callicrates; another for the rest of the Spartans, and the third for the helots. In like manner the men of Tegea and Athens, Megara and Phliûs, buried their dead, each in a separate grave. Of all these the tombs were full: the rest, it is said, were empty; but those who were not present at the battle piled them up through shame, for the sake of the generations to come. Certainly there is among them a tomb which is called the sepulchre of the Æginetans, which, it is said, Cleadas, a Platæan, their friend, raised up at their desire ten years after the battle.

When they had ended the burial of the dead, they took counsel and determined at once to march against Thebes and demand the men who had taken the side of the Persians, and chiefly Timagenidas and Attaginus, who had been foremost in the matter; and if the Thebans should refuse to give them up, they resolved not to go away until they had pulled down their city. So on the eleventh day after the battle they went and laid siege to Thebes, charging them to bring out the men; and when they would not, they ravaged the land and made an onset against their wall. And so things went on till the twentieth day, when

IX. Timagenidas said to the Thebans, "Men of Thebes, since the Greeks seem resolved not to raise the siege until either they have destroyed the city or ye surrender us, let not the Bœotian land suffer more evil for our sakes. And if they ask for us only that they may get money, then let us give it to them out of the common treasury; for in common did we take the part of the king, and it was not done by us alone. But if they really wish to seize us, then are we ready to go and defend ourselves before them." On hearing this, the Thebans gladly and quickly sent a herald to Pausanias, saying that they would give up the

88 men; but when the covenant was made, Attaginus fled from the city, and Pausanias sent away his children unhurt when they were brought to him instead of their father, saying that the children could not be partakers of their father's sin. But the other men whom the Thebans gave up thought that they would be suffered to defend themselves and to win their freedom by money; and Pausanias, suspecting this, sent away all his allies as soon as he received them, and taking them to Corinth slew them there.

89 Meanwhile Artabazus was far away on his road from Platææ; and when he reached Thessaly, the men of that country called him to a banquet and asked him of the welfare of the army, having heard nothing of what had happened at Platææ.

But Artabazus, knowing that, if he were to tell them the truth, he should run a risk of destroying himself and all his army, made no answer to the Phokians, while to the Thessalians he said, "I am hastening, men of Thessaly, as ye see, with all speed into Thrace, being sent on weighty business from the army with the men who are with me. But Mardonius is close at hand and all his army with him: receive him as your guest and treat him kindly, and ye shall never have cause to repent it." And so having spoken, he led his army with all speed through Thessaly and Macedonia to the Thracian land, keeping the roads which were far away from the sea until he reached Byzantium, having left behind him many of his army who were cut to pieces by the Thracians on the march, or who died from hunger or worn out by toil. From Byzantium he crossed over in boats, and so got back into Asia.

CHAP. X.

THE FIGHT AT MYCALE. — THE MARVEL OF THE HERALD'S STAFF. — THE LOVES OF KING XERXES AT SARDES AND AT SUSA. — THE VENGEANCE OF PROTESILAÜS.

> τοιαῦθ' ὁρῶντες τῶνδε τἀπιτίμια
> μέμνησθ' Ἀθηνῶν Ἑλλάδος τε.
>
> ÆSCHYLUS.

Herodotus IX. 90. ON the same day on which the battle was fought in Plataea, the Persians were beaten also at Mycale in the land of Ionia. For while the Greeks who came by sea with Leotychides the Lacedæmonian were in Delos, there came from Samos heralds who had been sent by the Samians without the knowledge of the Persians and of Theomestor whom the Persians had set up to be their tyrant. And when they were brought before the generals, one of them spake and said, "O ye Greeks, we pray you, come and help us; for if the Ionians only see you, they will shake off the yoke of the Persians, and the barbarians will never withstand you. But even if they should do so, ye will never find such another prey again. Think of the

gods whom we worship in common, and deliver
from slavery men who are Greeks as ye are, and
chase away the barbarian. It is no hard task to
which we call you: their ships sail wretchedly and
are not fit to do battle with yours. And if ye think
that we are dealing craftily, we are ready to go
back with you in your ships and be pledges to you
for the truth of our words."

So the Samian continued to beseech him vehemently, until Leotychides, either wishing to know
by what name to call him, or by the ordering of
some god, asked the Samian what might be his
name, and he said Hegesistratus, "the man who
leads an army." Then breaking in upon the
speech of the herald, Leotychides spake in haste,
"O Samian friend, I take up the omen of thy
name; and thou canst return home when thou
hast given us surety that the Samians will in very
truth be faithful to us in war."

Then the Samians gave the pledge and sware
the oath, after which they all sailed away except
Hegesistratus, whom Leotychides kept because of
the omen of his name. And the Greeks tarried that
day where they were. But on the following day,
when Dêiphonus the soothsayer had told them
that the victims gave good signs, they set out from
Delos to sail to Samos; and when they drew near
to Calami, which is in Samos, they moored their
ships in front of the temple of Hera. But the

IX. Persians, when they learnt that the Greeks were coming, set out to sail to the mainland with all their ships except those of the Phœnicians, which they sent away altogether. This they did in their wish to avoid a fight by sea, in which they did not think themselves a match for their enemies; and so they sailed away, that they might be under the wing of the land army in Mycale, which Xerxes had left to guard Ionia. And this host numbered six myriads of men, of whom Tigranes, a man beyond all the Persians for stature and beauty, was the general. Here the captains of the ships purposed to draw up their vessels and throw a hedge round them, as a safe place to which they might

97 fly for refuge. So when they came near the temple of the Potniæ in Mycale, and to Gauson and Scolopoeis, where there is a temple of the Eleusinian Dêmêtêr, they drew their ships upon the land, and cast round them a rampart of stones and logs of wood, cutting down the fruit-trees, and then drove in stakes all round the rampart. Thus they made ready, counting all chances, whether they should win the day or be shut up within their rampart.

98 When the Greeks found that the barbarians were gone away to the mainland, they were vexed that they had thus escaped, and knew not whether they ought to return home or sail towards the Hellespont. At last they resolved to do neither of

these things, but to sail to the mainland, with ladders and whatever else might be needed for a sea-fight. And when they came near Mycale and saw no one sailing out against them, but the ships drawn up within the wall, while the army of the Persians stood in battle array along the beach, Leotychides approached the shore in his ship and called out to the Ionians, saying, "O Ionians, listen to my words, as many of you as can hear me, for the Persians cannot understand what I say to you. When the battle begins, first remember your freedom, and next to this the watchword 'Hêbê!' and give this password to all who may not hear it." These words followed the device of Themistocles at Artemisium, for either they might win over the Ionians without the knowledge of the Persians, or, if these understood them, would make them jealous of the Ionians.

After this, the Greeks went out from their ships and drew themselves up in battle array upon the land. Then the Persians, seeing them preparing for the fight and knowing that they had spoken to the Ionians, took away the arms of the Samians, whose faith they doubted because they had ransomed the Athenian captives who had been brought in the Persian ships and sent them back to Athens, having given them food for their journey. And the passes which lead to the heights of Mycalê they intrusted to the men of Miletus, because, as they said, they knew the country well, but really because they wished to get them away from the camp. While they dealt thus with those of the Ionians who, as they thought, would betray them if they had the power, they put their shields together as a defence against their enemies.

100 So the Greeks made ready and then went forth to meet the barbarians. And as they marched, a rumour went throughout the whole army, and a herald's staff was seen lying upon the sea-shore: and the rumour was that even at that hour a battle was being fought in the Bœotian land and that the Greeks were conquerors in it. And sure indeed are the tokens of those things which are ordered by the gods, since, on the very day in which Mardonius fell with his army in Platææ, there came a rumour to the Greeks in Mycalê which cheered their hearts and sent them forth more eagerly to the battle.

101 It so chanced also that at Mycalê as at Platææ there was a temple of the Eleusinian Dêmêter near the battle-ground. And the rumour was true that the Greeks with Pausanias had won the fight, for the battle at Platææ was fought early in the morning, and the fight took place at Mycalê when the sun was going down in the sky; and they assured themselves afterwards that both happened on the same day of the same month. Before this rumour came, they were afraid not so much

for themselves as for the Greeks in Bœotia lest
they should be beaten by Mardonius, for then
all Hellas would be in his power. But when
the rumour came, they hastened with the greater
speed to the conflict, and the barbarians also
hurried to the fight, for the islands and the
Hellespont lay before them as the prizes for that
day's battle.

So they came on; and, for the Athenians and 102
those who were next to them, the road lay along
the shore and on level land; but for the other half
of the army with the Lacedæmonians, along the
bed of a torrent and over hilly ground. While
these were going round, the men on the other wing
had already begun the fight; and as long as their
fence of shields stood upright, the Persians had
none the worse of the battle: but the Athenians
with their neighbours desired greatly that the work
might be done by them and not by the Lacedæmonians, and, cheering each other on to fight more
vehemently, presently changed the face of the
battle. Soon they dashed down the rampart of
shields and burst in a mass upon the Persians,
who stood their ground bravely for a long time
but at last were driven back to the wall; and
the Athenians broke in with the men of Corinth,
of Trœzen, and of Sikyon. When the wall
was taken, the barbarians stood no longer on
their own defence, but all turned to fly except

the Persians, and these fought bravely in little knots against the Greeks as they streamed into the camp. Of the Persian leaders two escaped, and the other two, Tigranês, the general of the footmen, and Mardontes, were slain.

103 While the fight still went on, the Lacedæmonians came up with the rest and helped them to finish the battle. And many of the Greeks also fell, chiefly among the men of Sikyon, whose leader Perilaüs was killed; and when the Samians in the Median camp, whose arms the barbarian had taken away, saw that the battle was doubtful, they did all that they could to help the Greeks; so that the other Ionians, seeing this, turned openly against the barbarians and fell upon them.

104 But the Persians fared worse at the hands of the Milesians. These they had sent to guard the passes, not only that they might not be able to do mischief in the camp, but that, if the battle went against them, they might have safe guides to lead them to the heights of Mycalê. Instead of this, they guided the Persians by roads which led them down to the enemy, until at last they turned round and slew them more fiercely than the other Greeks had done. And thus Ionia again shook off the yoke of the barbarian.

105 In this battle the Athenians won most glory; and among them the most honoured was Hermolycus, who fell afterwards in a war with the men

THE DEFENCE OF IONIA.

of Carystos. And when the Greeks had slain most of the Persians, whether in the battle or as they fled, they brought out the booty to the seashore; and then, having burnt the ships and the wall, sailed away to Samos. There they took counsel for the safety of Ionia, and how they might place the Ionians in some part of Hellas which they could defend, while they left Ionia to the barbarians. For it seemed impossible that they could stay to guard Ionia for ever; and if they did not do so, they had no hope that the Ionians would escape unhurt by the Persians. The Peloponnesians therefore thought that they ought to give to the Ionians the lands of those Greeks who had taken the side of the king. But the Athenians would not suffer Ionia to be given up to their enemies, or that the men of the Peloponnesus should take thought for places to which the Athenians had sent their people; and as they stood out obstinately, the Peloponnesians yielded. So they joined to themselves by a covenant the men of Samos, Chios, and Lesbos, and all the other islanders who were with them, and caused them to give pledges and to swear by an oath that they would abide by what they had promised and never break away from it. And then they sailed away for the Hellespont, to destroy the bridges which they thought to find still fastened.

107 Those of the barbarians (and they were but few in number) who had fled to the heights of Mycalê escaped afterwards to Sardes; and while they were on the road, Masistes, the son of Darius, who had seen the disaster of the army, reviled Artaÿntes, the general, with bitter words, telling him that he was worse than a woman and that he deserved every torment for having brought this hurt on the house of the king. Now there is no reproach among the Persians more vile than to be called "worse than a woman;" and Artaÿntes, after listening for a long time, at last drew his dagger to kill Masistes. But Xeinagoras, a man of Halicarnassus, who stood behind Artaÿntes, seized him round the body, when he saw this, and dashed him upon the ground; and in the meanwhile the spearbearers gathered round Masistes. Thus did Xeinagoras in order to win favour with the king for saving the life of his brother; and Xerxes afterwards gave him all Cilicia for a reward. Nothing further happened on the march, and in Sardes they found the king, who was tarrying there after his flight from Athens.

108 While he yet sojourned in Sardes, Xerxes sought in vain to win the love of the wife of his brother Masistes; and when he failed in this, he betrothed the daughter of Masistes to his own son Darius, and then departed to Susa, where he brought his son's wife into the palace. Then Xerxes began

to love her instead of her mother; and in no
long time Amêstris, the wife of Xerxes, saw the
daughter of Masistes wearing a robe which she
had made herself and given to the king; but
instead of being wroth with her, she determined to
destroy her mother. So she waited patiently till
the king's birthday came; and at the feast she
went up to Xerxes and asked him to give her
the wife of Masistes. Then Xerxes strove long
against Amestris; but on that day the custom of
the Persians is that the king should not say nay
to the prayer of those who come before him.
So he gave her, and sending for Masistes, he said,
"Thou art the son of Darius, and my brother; and
thou art moreover a brave man. Give up then the
wife whom thou hast now, for I like it not that
thou shouldest have her, and I will give thee my
daughter in her stead." And Masistes marvelled
and said, "O king, my wife is the mother of my
sons and of my daughters, one of whom thou
hast given in marriage to thine own son. Why,
then, dost thou wish me to marry thy daughter
and to give up my wife whom I greatly love? I
thank thee, O king, because thou hast thought me
worthy to marry thy daughter; but I can do none
of these things. Force it not on, then; there are
other men who deserve thy daughter better; leave
me to dwell with my wife in peace." Then was
Xerxes wroth and said, "Well, Masistes, thou

shalt not marry my daughter or keep thy wife, that thou mayest know how to receive my gifts." But Masistes answered only, "O king, thou hast not yet ruined me." But, even while they were talking, Amestris had sent spearbearers to fetch the wife of Masistes; and Amestris mangled her shamefully on her face and on her body and then sent her home. Then Masistes, knowing nothing of this, yet foreboding some evil, ran to his house, and seeing his wife thus torn and mangled took counsel with his sons and set out to go to Bactra with his army, that thence he might make war upon the king; and Xerxes, hearing that he was gone, sent after him and slew his brother with his children and all his army. Thus fared it with the loves of King Xerxes.

At Lectum, the Greeks, who had set out from Mycalê, were hindered for a while by winds from sailing further; but afterwards they reached Abydos, and found the bridges, for which they had chiefly gone thither, unloosed and broken. And upon this the Peloponnesians with Leotychides resolved to sail away to Hellas; but the Athenians under Xanthippus crossed over to the Chersonesus and laid siege to Sestos, into which, as being the strongest place in that land, Œobazus, a Persian, had brought the cables by which the bridges had been fastened; and with him were many other men besides the Æolians, whose city was.

THE CRAFT OF ARTAŸCTES.

And the ruler of this country was Artaÿctes, a Persian, a daring and impious man, who cheated the king as he was going to Athens, and stole the treasures of Protesilaüs the son of Iphiclus: for at Elæûs in the Chersonesus is his tomb with its plot of holy ground, where were goblets of gold and silver and much brass, with garments and other offerings. So Artaÿctes came to the king and said, "O king, there is here the house of a Greek who came against thy land and was slain, as he deserved. Give me this man's house, that others may learn hereafter not to come against thee." Then Xerxes easily suffered him to take it, not knowing at all the meaning of his words, and that Protesilaüs had come long ago into Asia to make war against the men of Troy; for Artaÿctes made Xerxes think that he had come against the Persians, because they hold that all Asia belongs only to the king. So he took the offerings and carried them away to Sestos, and ploughed up the sacred ground and profaned the holy place. And now the Athenians shut him up in Sestos unawares when he was not ready to endure a siege and thought not that the Greeks were coming. But the siege lasted long, and the autumn came; and the Athenians were vexed because they were kept away so long from home and could not take the wall. So they besought their leaders to take them home; but they answered that they would not go

IX. until either they had destroyed Sestos or the
Athenians should send for them.

118 But the men in the city were now so hard
pressed by hunger and famine, that they boiled
the ropes of their beds and ate them. And when
they had no more left even of these, the Persians,
with Artaÿctes and Œobazus, fled by night, letting themselves down from the wall where it was
least watched by the enemy. So when it was day,
the men of the city told the Athenians by signs
what had happened and opened their gates; and
some of them held the city while the rest followed after the Persians.

119 Now Œobazus had fled to Thrace; and there
he was taken by the men of Apsinthus, who sacrificed him, after their manner, to Pleistôrus, the
god of that land; and the rest who were with him
they slew in some other way. But Artaÿctes and
his men set out later, and were caught a little way
beyond Ægospotami. There they fought bravely
for some time, and some were killed, while the rest,
amongst whom were Artaÿctes and his son, were
120 taken alive and carried in chains to Sestos. And
the men of the Chersonesus say that a strange thing
happened to one of the men who guarded Artaÿctes,
as he was roasting dried fish. These, as they lay
on the fire, leaped and gasped like fishes newly
caught. But, while all who stood round marvelled, Artaÿctes called to the man and said to

him, "Fear not for this strange sight. It has not been sent for thee; but Protesilaüs who dwells in Elæûs gives me by this a sign that, though he is dead and his body wasted, he has power to punish the man that wrongs him. Now, therefore, I wish to make an atonement, and, in place of the offerings which I have taken from his temple, I will give a hundred talents to the god; and, as a ransom for myself and my son, I will pay to the Athenians two hundred talents when they have set me free." But for all his promises he could not prevail with their leader Xanthippus; for the men of Elæûs, in order to avenge Protesilaüs, demanded that he should be put to death, and this also Xanthippus was minded to do. So they brought him down to the sea-shore where Xerxes had fastened his bridge, or, as some say, to a hillock which is above the city of Madytos, and fastened him to some planks which they nailed together, after which they stoned his son to death before his eyes.

When this was done, they sailed away to Hellas, taking with them the booty together with the cables of the bridge, to be placed as offerings in the temples. And so the war ended for that year.

PART II.

ON THE
HISTORY OF THE PERSIAN WAR

Τὰ πολλὰ ἀπίστωι ἐπὶ τὸ μυθῶδες ἐκνενικηκότα

CHAPTER I.

ON THE HISTORICAL CONCEPTION AND METHOD OF HERODOTUS.

WHEN Herodotus undertook to tell the tale of the Persian war, he was in fact undertaking to write the history of the world. The recollections of his own childhood belonged to the later years of that great strife. The land of his birth had witnessed one of the noblest victories, and many of the worst disasters, which fell to the lot of the sons of Hellên. His own city had, as it was believed, sent forth the bravest woman and the wisest counsellor in the army of the great king; and the Persian satraps still gathered the tribute of the Asiatic Greeks in the days of his infancy.[1] His manhood was

The object and scope of his history.

---

[1] If we assume B.C. 484 as the most probable date for the birth of Herodotus, he was six years old at the time of the last event which he mentions in his history. See Sir G. C. Lewis's Credibility of Early Roman History, vol. ii. p. 501. Probably, therefore, his earliest recollections would belong to that year in which the battle of Mycalê practically decided the future relations of Greece and Persia. For, although twelve years passed away between this victory and the double defeat of the Persian fleet and army by Kimón on the banks of the Eurymedon, there can be no doubt that after the battle of Mycalê Persian ships were no longer permitted to enter the waters of the Ægæan Sea.

passed in that happier time during which no Persian ship of war was ever seen in the waters of the Ægæan,

From that time the claim of the Persian king to the whole Asiatic continent (Herodotus, i. 4) was practically set at nought. The tribute of the Asiatic Greeks was assessed as before; but there is no probability that it was levied after this date, while it is certain that it was not raised after the full establishment of the Athenian confederacy. Thucyd. viii. 56; Grote, History of Greece, vol. v. p. 460. The convention, which has received the name of the peace of Callias, simply ratified, after the battles of Eurymedon, a condition of things which had now virtually existed for many years. By it the Persian king engaged to send no ships of war westward of Phaselis or the Chelidonean islands. But the victory of Kimon had only completed the work which had been wellnigh accomplished by the battles of Salamis, of Platæa and Mycalê; and probably the Persians ceased to collect the tribute of the Asiatic Greeks from the time that their fleet could no longer with safety enter the Greek waters. The victory of Themistocles or Eurybiades cannot be said to have ended the work of the confederate Greeks; in one sense it only began it: for any symptom of strong disunion would have been the signal for renewed Persian aggression. But the Hellenic confederacy steadily maintained its ground; and the arrogance of Pausanias soon caused the transfer of the supremacy from Sparta to Athens. This change undoubtedly precluded all chance of a permanent Panhellenic union, of which there had been thus far some reasonable hope; but it probably tended to place the temporary preponderance of Athenian over Persian power in a stronger light. It proved that the Hellenic world was now committed to a rivalry between Sparta and Athens; but it showed also that Athens stood in no need of Spartan aid, not merely to defend herself, but to shield her Asiatic colonists and allies from barbarian violence. In the interval which passed before the outbreak of the Peloponnesian war, the character of her empire may have been changed; but it is certain that no Persian collectors dared to enforce the tribute assessed on the Asiatic Greeks from the days and when the Greek inhabitants of the coast were freed from all dread of robbery and cruelty, through the wisdom and might of Athens. But this time of freedom, so fair in its promise, so disastrous in its early close, led him back to the earlier day when the Greeks of Asia had not yet fallen under the sway of the kings who ruled at Sardes. In the space of little more than half a century[1], these Greeks had passed with their conqueror into the power of that mightier despot who had united the Persians and the Medes under a single sceptre. They had rebelled against a harder yoke than the Lydian had imposed upon them. Their rebellion had brought down prompt and fearful punishment; and their slavery had at length been broken by a war whose character and issue were as marvellous as they were unforeseen.

In this glorious result was closed for a time the rivalry of the Eastern and the Western world; and the many *Mingling of divine and human causes and agency.*

of Darius until the great Athenian efforts before Syracuse had issued in total ruin. For a period not very far short of seventy years (B.C. 477—412) the name and power of Imperial Athens had secured safety of land and person to every member of her confederacy. Herodotus, therefore, during his whole life, had no experience of the injustice and misery which attend on the supremacy of foreign tyrants, and his conviction of the great blessings of freedom (v. 78) could have been formed only from historical testimony, and not from any remembrance of his own of the previous fortunes of his country.

[1] The year B.C. 546 has been assigned as the most probable date for the taking of Sardes; but the chronology of the reign of Crœsus betrays too much its artificial composition to be received without some reluctance. On this assumption the interval between the fall of Crœsus and the battle of Marathon was a period of not more than fifty-six years.

R

aspects of that long struggle were all noted by the historian. It was a strife between the Greek and the Persian,—between Europe and Asia,—between civilisation and barbarism. In it the force of a centralising despotism was balanced against the free obedience to law,—the love of things noble and beautiful against the dread of a personal tyrant. It was the triumph of a society which placed no checks on the free growth of human intellect and affection, over one which could issue in nothing but an utter monotony of degradation.[1] Yet again, in this strife, the working of human agency was not wanting. The expulsion of tyrants by an oppressed and indignant people, their intrigues in foreign courts and lands, the jealousies of citizens and the feuds of cities, the obstinacy and cowardice of the many, the keen-sighted wisdom and the energy of the few, are motives of which he never wholly loses sight throughout his narrative. But by the side of this merely human action, or rather blended inextricably with it, there runs another chain of cause and effect, which is wholly and entirely divine,—which shows the moral forces at work amongst mankind,—and which vindicates the supremacy of the gods over the wisest, the wealthiest, and the greatest of men. The links in this mysterious chain must everywhere be visible; the necessity of tracing them out is paramount. This task may lead him into the region of marvels and miracles, of motives and thoughts which none probably could discover except those who feel them[2]; it may

[1] Thucydides, ii. 37.
[2] It is very difficult to understand how the secret thoughts

bring before him gods and departed heroes working visibly or invisibly among men; it may lead him to see in signs and portents in heaven or on earth the shadows of coming evil. But between these two intermingling chains of causes, each producing their own proper result, he feels no contradiction or inconsistency. He can pass without any sense of incongruity from the one to the other. The merest political motives may be accompanied by operations altogether marvellous or divine. Between these two classes of events there is no separation; the one is as true and as historical as the other.

If, then, in the events which led to the great Persian war, the agency of man may be discerned, and if adequate political motives[1] are assigned for civil or military undertakings, the working of divine power must throughout be still more clearly present and more vividly seen. The complications of the great struggle must be traced back to the first links in this twisted chain; and the supernatural principle must be vindicated in the persons of all who are brought upon the scene. Nothing is too wide or remote, nothing too

Prominence given to the divine element.

and designs of such men as Demokedes, Histiæus, and Xerxes, could become generally known in any age. The full knowledge, which Herodotus professed to have obtained of them in an age of very slender historical information, indefinitely increases the perplexity.

[1] Among these may be mentioned the aggressive tendencies of Oriental kingdoms, clearly implied in Herodotus (i. 46, vii. 8), and the intrigues of the Peisistratidæ, as not merely inducing the Persian satrap to comply with the request of Aristagoras, but as leading to the great enterprise of Darius and Xerxes.

insignificant to be embraced in the order of the narrative. The mention of a city or an empire, of a general or a king, leads naturally to a careful examination of their history and their fortunes.[1] And the religious belief, which underlies and even forms his historical sense, prevents him from losing sight of the thread of his story, which the modern reader, living under a different condition of thought, finds it sometimes most difficult to discern.

This religious sentiment imparts an epical unity to his history.
This theological or religious treatment of events and their causes gives to the history an unity which may not improperly be called epical, if we are careful not to attach to the term the ideas of poetry or romance.[2]

[1] Thus the mention of Egyptians, or Scythians, Medians, Babylonians, or any others, involves a sketch of their history and political conditions, with descriptions of their social life, their art, science, and religion. In the present volume those digressions and incidental narratives have alone been taken into account, which are directly connected with the main subject of the history. Little, therefore, or nothing is said on the very important topic of Egyptian history.

[2] All that can with safety be attributed to Herodotus in the execution of his work is the keener power of appreciation and expression which may have distinguished him from those with whom he lived. But there seems to be too great a tendency to impute to him faults or merits which really belong to the writers of a later age, and which cannot be said to have existed in his, because the opposite qualities had not then begun to offer any contrast. We may condemn, if we think fit, the epical conception of history which he shared with his countrymen; but we can scarcely follow Mr. Rawlinson (Herodotus, vol. i. p. 103, &c.) or Colonel Mure (History of Greek Literature, vol. iv. p. 352) in charges of credulity or romantic exaggeration, or excessive love of personal anecdote. To fasten these faults upon

It was no fondness for fanciful resemblances, no desire to embellish or to point a tale, but a religious faith, which led the historian to link together the several events in the long series of his narratives. From the first to the last is seen at once the working of men and the hand of the gods, and the operation of the latter was not of a kind to which he would be drawn by any impulse of human feeling. The jealousy of the divine being at the simple sight of human wealth or happiness[1], the punishment of the innocent for the guilty[2], the prostration of the gods before an irresistible necessity[3], are facts or doctrines which no man perhaps will be found to embrace with any eager consent of his will. He may believe that the course of the world is guided by a deity who has no sympathy with man, or by an irreversible order to which even that deity is subject, but he will not wish to believe the facts which establish such a theology with that eager welcome which hails the downfal of successful wrong.

In the most fictitious details, then, there was probably little conscious invention, and certainly no idea of deception and fraud. With such an historical method an abundance of material, self-created as it might seem, will never be wanting. Details grow up round the fact which they are intended to illustrate, as naturally and luxuriantly as the leaves and flowers on a plant;

him individually, or to imply that it was possible for him to have avoided them, would appear to be a serious error, for it would represent the historian as possessing a conscious art in his composition, of which, to say the least, we have no evidence.

[1] Herodotus, i. 32.   [2] Ibid. i. 13.   [3] Ibid. i. 91.

and, as we might also expect, the result will exhibit that peculiar beauty which, in a certain sense, we may regard as poetical and romantic. But this distinction did not exist in the mind of the historian; he believed the dream and the portent as much as he believed in a political intrigue, a battle, or a siege. The measure in which a more exact historical sense was being formed, and the degree to which it led him almost unconsciously to put aside some supernatural details, is a distinct and curious question[1]; but in the general sequence of double cause and effect his faith remains substantially unshaken.

Connection of mythical and historical causes.

Nor can we fail to see this as we trace the course of his tale, from the adventures of the Argive, Colchian, and Phœnician maidens, onwards through the war of Troy, to the history of the Lydian and Persian dynasties. The long conflict of races, and of Asiatic despotism with

---

[1] If the critical spirit of Thucydides led him simply to strip mythical tales of their marvellous features, and then to take the *caput mortuum* so left as authentic history (Thucydides, i. 9, &c.), we cannot be surprised that the criticism of Herodotus should be altogether more capricious and less determined. All that we can say is, that the growing conviction of a natural order which made some things possible and others apparently impossible, led him to question some fables which did not affect his own personal belief or the main course of his history. This will account for his rejection of the Greek tale respecting the founding of the Dodonæan oracle (Herod. ii. 57), or of the wholesale slaughter committed by the yet mortal Heracles, on the ground of physical impossibility, while yet he receives with eagerness the story of Phylacus and Autonoüs at Delphi (viii. 39), or of the mysterious sign vouchsafed to the Athenian Dikæus and Demaratus (viii. 65) before the battle of Salamis.

Hellenic freedom, begins with the wrong done to Inachus at Argos; and the retaliation is worked out at Tyre. But the balance is again left unequal by the piracy at Colchis; and the woes of Helen and the downfal of Ilium are the penalty. For a moment the chain would seem to be broken. The Lydian kings have nothing to connect them with the robbery of Io, or Europa, or Medeia. But the spread of Persian dominion called into action a power which was only slumbering. The victories of Agamemnon and Achilles were won on soil which was the heritage of the great king; and the avenging of Priam and Hector becomes a part of his inalienable birthright. Lydia, Egypt, Babylon, are conquered by his armies; the history of their kings and the fortunes of their people complicate the chain of cause and effect. The stream widens as it hurries on; but whether with the tyrant of Samos or the hereditary despots of Persia and Egypt, the same force is at work. The same being looks down with a jealous eye on their wealth and their power; and the pride of good fortune is followed by inevitable chastisement or ruin. Crœsus falls from a height of happiness to which no mortal man had before attained, in atonement for the sin of Gyges. The storm comes, but not without its warning. The gods speak in words of significant ambiguity, and afford the wisest counsels. Human advisers also are not wanting, and the historian delights to bring before us kings and generals with their good or evil genius by their side. The Athenian Solon bids Crœsus remember that death alone can place the seal of happiness on human life; and, in his turn, Crœsus, taught by his own calamity, becomes the teacher of Cyrus and Cambyses. Poly-

crates vainly seeks by self-inflicted sorrow to satisfy the
forebodings of the Egyptian king; and Xerxes hurries
to defeat and shame in spite of the wisdom of Artabanus.
In these instances, as in others, the good genius never
prevails. Orœtes lures Polycrates into his snare; the
craft of Demokedes draws even the wise Darius into
schemes which are not much to his liking. The words
of Mardonius outweigh with Xerxes the forethought of
Artabanus, of Demaratus, and Artemisia. But if the
pride of Cyrus called for vengeance at the hands of a
barbarian queen, if the crimes and the madness of
Cambyses placed the Magians on the throne of Persia,
if Darius returned defeated from his Scythian journey,
the Fates were still preparing to bring on Hellas the
vengeance due for the iniquities of Menelaüs and
Odysseus. The men of Athens had dared, with their
Ionian colonists, to assault the citadel of Sardes; and
the overthrow of Datis and Artaphernes at Marathon
gave a new force to the words which charged Darius,
before every meal, to remember the wrongs of the
Athenians. At length the hour came. The life of
Darius had closed amid the din of preparation for his
great scheme of vengeance. In him there was the wise
mind and the sober forethought which saved him at
once from excessive pride and excessive shame; and
therefore he incurred this punishment only, that he
was not suffered himself to lead his hosts against the
land of Achilles and Agamemnon.[1] But the reign of
Xerxes, the spoilt child of insolence and power, ushers
in the execution of an enterprise which was avenged

[1] Herodotus, vii. 4.

two centuries later on the fields of Issus and Arbela.¹ The nobles of Persia are gathered in council; the visions of Mardonius are balanced by the sober judgment of Artabanus. All the solemnity of Homeric imagery, the very language of the old epic poetry, is called in to heighten the great crisis on which are to turn the fortunes of Hellas and of the world. The childish folly, which rejected the words of Artabanus with anger and insult, is sobered down into grave misgivings during the dark hours of night. But the will of Zeus, or of the Fates more powerful than Zeus, may not be turned aside; and the dream stands over the couch of Xerxes as it had stood of old over that of Agamemnon.² The

---

¹ In the time of Herodotus, as well as in the ages which had gone before, this connection of causes was held to be a real one. When Alexander proposed to carry his arms against the Persian king, the claim of vengeance for the invasion of Xerxes was, as Mr. Grote has shown, set up in part to flatter his vanity, and partly with the political purpose of keeping the Greeks quiet during his absence. (Grote's History of Greece, vol. xii. pp. 68, 69.) When Isocrates in his panegyric speeches urged the same motive on Athens and Sparta, he addressed himself to the common sentiment at least of his own city; it had come to be little more than oratorical affectation in the mouth of the same orator, when he put forward the Macedonian Philip as the champion of united Hellas against the barbarian. Mr. Grote dwells strongly on the miserable change which had come over Isocrates from the time of the former speech, in which he expressed his real opinion, as well as that of others, on the nature of that policy which had brought about the peace of Antalkidas.

² Mr. Grote has remarked (History of Greece, vol. v. p. 14) that Herodotus seems to use ὄνειρον in the neuter gender, not ὄνειρος in the masculine. But this change from the Homeric

spell is again thrown over the king, and Artabanus himself yields to its power. There is nothing more to hinder him. From Susa to the Phrygian Kelænæ, from Kelænæ to Abydos, the great king advances with uninterrupted good fortune. Each day swells the numbers of his host; and the sea, which dared to hurt his bridge, is scourged and branded for its presumption. His march is not checked by the rugged deserts or the wild mountaineers of Thrace. The Spartan Euænetus and the Athenian Themistocles fall back before him as he approaches the gates of Thessaly; and through the Vale of the Peneius he advances to the passes of Pylæ, while his fleet sails on in its fulness of strength and glory to the Eubœan shores. But here the tide turns. The

gender is not apparently the result of a growing scepticism; and Herodotus appears to believe, not less than Homer, in the personified vision or dream-god who is sent from heaven to visit the minds of men in sleep. His dream is something which can move and speak, and has a power of judgment and discrimination. The expressions of the historian are not indeed altogether consistent. It is true that in the account of the first visitation he says that Xerxes in a dream beheld standing over him a man of more than mortal stature; but Mr. Grote (vol. v. p. 11) goes beyond Herodotus in saying that "the same dream and the same figure" appeared to him on the second night. Herodotus (vii. 14) merely says that the dream itself came and spoke to him; and the subsequent speech of Artabanus draws no distinction between the dream and the figure, of which indeed he makes no mention, and which he is not said to have seen when he lay down on the king's couch. The man was probably to Herodotus the embodied dream of whose personal existence he seems to have no doubt, while the fact that he speaks of a dream as well as of the figure betrays in its first stage the influence of a later philosophy.

overwhelming might of his army and his ships must be so weakened and brought down as to make it possible for mortal enemies to contend against them.[1] The unseen hand of the gods, the invisible force of the winds, must begin the work of destruction which the wisdom and bravery of their worshippers may consummate. Obstinate men block up the defiles of Thermopylæ and waste the blood of his bravest warriors, while the mighty Boreas so shatters his fleet that the rumour of its utter ruin is carried to his trembling enemies. The horrors of the storm are in some measure compensated by the slaughter of Leonidas and his comrades; but his rising hope falls again before the renewed wrath of the winds.[2] A mightier arm is stretched out against the men who, at his bidding, dared to approach the sanctuary of Apollo. The lord of light himself wields the sacred arms in defence of his shrine. Rocks torn from the summits of Parnassus beat down the invaders of his holy precincts. The blasphemy of the barbarian had reached its climax; and the havoc at Delphi was the prelude to a mightier destruction in the waters of Salamis. His hosts advance unopposed into the Athenian land. For a time they are kept in check by the few old men who guard the rock of the Virgin Goddess; but their wooden wall is overthrown by fire, and soon the tidings are sent to Susa that Athens is in the hands of the great king. The divine oracles had foretold his triumph: signs beyond nature foreshadowed his destruction. On the plains of Eleusis the Spartan Demaratus sees a cloud of dust raised by some mighty host, and learns from his

[1] Herodotus, vii. 188. [2] Ibid. viii. 12.

friend that the Sacred Mother is herself making ready to destroy the fleet of Xerxes. Throughout the narrative, almost every incident is now ushered in with its own peculiar signs. The disaster at Salamis determines the king to return home; and the Spartan demand of recompense for the slaughter of Leonidas prepares us for the coming doom of Mardonius. In dread of the wild Thracians, amidst the horrors of plague and famine, Xerxes hurries to the Straits of Sestos, while his generals revel in the halls of Attaginus. The end comes; but the signs which go before it are hidden from their eyes, and the man who alone can read them would announce it to them in vain. On the plains of Plataeae the two hosts are withheld from the onset by the warnings of their prophets; but Mardonius despises at length their omens and their words, and threatens Artabazus with the vengeance of the king, while the shadow of death is stealing over himself. And when the slaughter of the Persians is ended, and the Greeks have laid hands on their tents and couches, on their golden vessels and embroidered hangings, the Spartan king foreshadows his own future ruin, while, pointing to the two banquets, he draws the contrast between Spartan and Persian fare. The gods have fought against the barbarian; and they have done battle against him not only in the ancient land. At one and the same moment they are aiding in the fight at Plataeae, and cheering on Spartans, Athenians, and Ionians to the fight at Mycalê. The herald's staff thrown up by the waves upon the sea-shore is the token and the evidence that their kinsmen are conquerors far away on the Boeotian plain. The vengeance is indeed full. Athena has requited the insults done to her sacred citadel. The slaughter of thousands has atoned for the dishonour of Leonidas. Protesilaus has exacted a fearful penalty from the man who stole his treasures and defiled his tomb.[1] It remains only to show what is the home of a Persian despot, to disclose the loathsome scenes to which that man returns who had waged war against the heavenly guardians of Hellenic freedom; and the palace doors of Susa are opened to reveal the lust, treachery, and bloodshed which find a fitting consummation in the murder of the great king.

The historian says nothing of the contrast; but the images come before us of Athens rising to her imperial glory, and of her enemy struck down by the assassin's dagger, and we cannot choose but feel that the recompense of each is as it should be. *Epical contrasts*

The picture is drawn out in more minute detail. If the Greeks collectively reap the reward of the struggle, each state amongst them which chose the right side fails not to win its own special honour. There is a stately and even march in the events of the narrative. Great deeds are done on the same day in distant places, and the good success of the one is sometimes conveyed by marvellous tokens to the others. The same deities watch in different lands over the defenders of their country. From the Heracleium at Marathon the Athenians hasten to another home of the same hero in Kynosarges.[2] By his help they had beaten off their enemies at Marathon, and by it also they drove them away in terror from Phalêrum. The same day witnessed *and coincidences.*

---

[1] Herodotus, ix. 116. [2] Ibid. vi. 116.

the victory of Gelon over Carthaginians and Persians in Sicily, and the destruction of the barbarian ships at Salamis.[1] At Platæa and at Mycalê but a few hours passed between the death of Mardonius and the victory of Eurybiades; and alike in both places Dêmêter nerved the hearts and strengthened the arms of her children.[2]

Equal distribution of merit. In these several victories the highest praise is distributed to each Hellenic nation in its turn. Once only in the war does each state win an exclusive fame, unless Marathon makes an exception for the Athenians. But if there the name of Miltiades sheds a higher lustre on the valour of his countrymen, we may be forgiven for thinking that a purer and a more sacred glory rests on the brave band who came from the little city of Platæa. Such a feeling seems to have moved the Athenians in after days, when, in memory of their brotherhood at Marathon, the herald at every sacrifice united the names of Athenians and Platæans.[3] At Thermopylæ the Thespians are admitted to share in the glory of Leonidas[4]; at Salamis the greatest fame belongs to the men of Athens and Ægina together. Before Platæa the Lacedæmonians retrieve the reputation which their sluggishness or their piety had endangered[5]; while at Mycalê the paramount greatness of Athens[6] vindicates her title to that supremacy which for nearly seventy years banished the Persians from the lands of the Asiatic Greeks and the waters of the Ægæan Sea.

---

[1] Herodotus, vii. 166. [2] Ibid. ix. 101. [3] Ibid. vi. 111.
[4] Ibid. vii. 222. [5] Ibid. ix. 71. [6] Ibid. ix. 106.

CHAP. II.

ON THE EPICAL UNITY IN THE HISTORY OF HERODOTUS.

IF the preceding sketch fairly represents the historical method of Herodotus, we have before us a chain of epical causes which place the real causes of the Persian war in great measure out of sight. But if we speak of those causes on which the historian dwells most fully as being distinct from the real or true motives, we acknowledge at once the existence of different historical standards, and are driven to ascertain the historical conception which guided the mind of Herodotus. <small>In the historical conception of Herodotus.</small>

It is impossible not to see the harmony of that scheme of causation which begins with the rape of Io and Europa, of Medeia and Helen, and ends with the vision of Xerxes and the evil counsels of Mardonius. It is true indeed that in this very scheme the growth of an historical sense and the critical spirit of a later age are plainly discernible. But if in the tale of Io or of Helen we have a treatment very different from that of Æschylus or of Homer, and even if we assume that the historian was conscious of this difference, it is not the less certain that he accounts for the war and its issue on other motives than those which he incidentally admits to have been at work. The crafty plans of Demokedes and Histiæus are more than co-ordinate causes with <small>The sequence of events is chiefly ethical or religious.</small>

the intrigues of Hippias and the failure of Aristagoras at Naxos. These are not indeed put wholly out of sight; but the events turn rather on the home-sickness of slaves or exiles than on the plots of banished despots or the impulse of political ambition. The sequence throughout is either ethical or religious. It illustrates either the course of human acts and passions, or the working of unseen and heavenly powers. In the former case it is an advance on the critical standard of earlier times; but the connection is direct and intimate. If a careful examination of physical laws or facts, so far as they came before him, seems to lead him into something like scepticism, he still retains the old faith by which beings unseen are believed to defend and comfort, to deceive or destroy the sons of men. If a tyrant is driven out by the citizens whose rights and freedom he has trampled down, it is because his wealth and riches had roused the jealousy of the gods. If a king or general invades an enemy's land, it is because some ancient oracle or prophecy must be fulfilled. A series of aggressive wars originates in the appeal which a woman's flattery makes to a sense of kingly duty. If a nation or a tribe claims a post of honour on the battle-field, the claim is founded on good deeds done in the days of the Amazons or of Heracles.[1] He has not lost the faith which believed that Thetis arose to comfort her child from the depths of the green sea; and his narrative agrees most closely with the mental state to which agencies beyond nature appear the ordinary causes influencing the life of man. If he questions the

---

[1] Herodotus, ix. 26.

possibility of a dove speaking with human voice[1], or of crowds smitten by a single arm[2], he is not the less ready to believe that the dream came by the will of Zeus to deceive Xerxes, or that the deified heroes of Delphi were seen to slay the enemies of the gods.

Such motives and agencies the earlier ages had received not only without reluctance but with eager belief. The working of unseen powers formed the daily food of their minds; and a narrative which put this working out of sight or failed to bring it into paramount importance, would have met with neither praise nor credit at their hands. This age differed from the age of Herodotus in little more than a failure to see anything incongruous or strange in tales which contradicted the daily experience of their senses; but the absence of supernatural signs and wonders would as much have left a feeling of want in the mind of Herodotus as in the earliest hearers of the Homeric rhapsodists. *Growth of an historical sense.*

It is not then his method of arrangement which distinguishes him most pointedly from Thucydides, to whom a real historical criticism owes at once its birth and its perfection. The history of the Peloponnesian war has its special climax not less than the history of Herodotus. If the sacrilegious pride of the barbarian reached its height in the assault on Delphi, the downfal of Athenian greatness is not less traced from the conference and the massacre at Melos.[3] We may *Contrast between Herodotus and Thucydides.*

---

[1] Herodotus, ii. 57.

[2] Ibid. ii. 45. See also Grote, History of Greece, vol. i. p. 533.

[3] Mr. Grote's examination of the account given by Thucydides of the conference and massacre of Melos is among the most

rearrange the narrative of Herodotus; but by no process of selection can we bring it into harmony with the valuable passages of his history (vol. vii. pp. 149—161). Other writers had perceived that the conversation which he introduces before the siege was one which could not have taken place. But Dr. Thirlwall, while he denies to it any greater degree of historical truth, yet believes that the dialogue is one which Thucydides conceived might have passed on this occasion (History of Greece, ch. xxiv.), and inclines to think that the doctrines of the sophists lie at the bottom of the whole argument. Mr. Grote has shown not merely that Thucydides could have obtained no such full report as that which his narrative implies, but that the sentiments are strictly his own, as distinguished from those which, as he supposed, might have been expressed, and that far less are they the sentiments of the much calumniated Athenian sophists. The glaring contradiction to Athenian character manifest in this debate led to the plausible opinion of Dionysius of Halicarnassus, that Thucydides misrepresented their real language in requital of his own banishment. If there is little to support this conjecture, it is not the less true that the Athenian speakers here utterly belie the merits or the foibles of the Athenian people. And the very fact that Thucydides has not represented them as speaking somewhat more in harmony with their own ordinary sentiments and those of the sophists, proves that in this instance he has reverted to the epical or dramatic conception of his day. In order to heighten the effect of a crime which by a few months preceded the decree for the expedition to Sicily, he substitutes a bold and hardy ferocity in place of their general tendency to equivocate and to speak of fraud or violence by any rather than their real names, and leaves out of sight even the poor justification which the Athenians may probably have urged for their conduct. He wished to show Athens in her moment of haughtiest defiance before the commencement of her miserable fall; and he has so dramatised the whole narrative, that of the real sentiments of the actors on both sides we cannot be said really spirit of Thucydides. We may, if we please, maintain that political causes for the course of events are not omitted; but we can scarcely say that in his history supernatural phenomena are "mere excrescences, the omission of which leaves the historic narrative intact," or that " they are in no way interwoven with the narrative so that it should stand or fall with them."[1] We cannot omit the swarming of the

---

to know anything. He has in this instance departed from his own critical standard as much as Herodotus realised his own historical conception in the tale of the assault on Delphi; and the degree to which the old epical sentiment still influences the thought of such a writer as Thucydides, and in such an age, is the more surprising. It may serve to illustrate the enormous force with which it must have directed the mind of former generations.

[1] Rawlinson's Herodotus, vol. i. p. 91. I cannot but think that Mr. Rawlinson has expended a very unneccessary amount of labour in examining Colonel Mure's lists of defects or faults in the historical manner of Herodotus. If we speak of any writer as credulous, or as influenced by an excessive love of effect in exaggerated contrasts or historical combinations, we are either comparing him with others of his own time who were free from these faults, or else we project him beyond the age in which he lived. It is not perhaps too much to say that Colonel Mure was incapable of realising in any fulness the mind and language of a mythical age. His criticisms of the Iliad and Odyssey, or the Homeric Hymns, or of the narrative of Herodotus, are criticisms which might with some fairness be applied to works of fiction or of history put forth in our own day. Throughout he appears to regard as peculiarities of the man the universal characteristics of his age. To speak of his historical combinations as expedients to heighten a contrast or give force to a story, is to make him the inventor of that ex-

snakes before the citadel of Sardes and the feast which they supplied to the horses, and then say that the capture of the city and the very circumstances of the capture "are untouched by the omission."[1] Such a method may be applied as easily to the tales of the Iliad or the Odyssey; and in the residue we should have a story as plausible as that which Thucydides has culled from the tale of Troy. If from the account of the fall of Sardes we omit the prodigy of the snakes, with the parallel of the reign of fourteen years and the siege of fourteen days[2]; if we put aside the tale that

---

pedient. To dwell on "his love of the marvellous, as observed or imagined by him in the ordinary phenomena of nature apart from divine or preternatural agency," is perhaps to charge him with a fault of which he was guiltless, while his readiness to discern supernatural agency in natural phenomena, and still more in the fortunes of mankind, was the necessary result of the universal belief of his age. It is not difficult to multiply instances which either wholly or in part contradict Colonel Mure's positions; but it might be of more use to show that by adhering to his method of judgment we preclude ourselves from entering into the mind of Herodotus, and from measuring either the nature or the force of the influences which moulded it. See Mure, Critical History of Greek Literature, vol. iv. p. 352, &c.

[1] Rawlinson's Herodotus, vol. i. p. 91.

[2] The detection of artificial chronology at once proves that the age to which it relates cannot be considered strictly historical. Narratives which exhibit such chronology may be the merest fictions, or they may challenge an amount of belief second only to that which we accord to contemporary history. The tendency to trace historical coincidences (as in the battles of Salamis and Himera, of Mycale and Plataea) is not, it would seem, connected with this disposition to frame artificial chronological

a breach could only be made in the wall where Meles

schemes which has characterised the earlier ages of most nations of the world. Like the Greek genealogies, these artificial computations may embrace in their later stages periods of undoubted history; but they are in themselves no evidence, and their reckoning cannot be assumed as true, until we come down to times of contemporary witnesses. In default of such testimony, any striking chronological coincidence becomes a subject of extreme suspicion. In the case of Crœsus it leads us to doubt the length of his reign; in that of the Roman kings it leads us to question the very fact of their personality. The lives of unquestionably historical kings were included in the Egyptian system of Sothiac periods; but the chronology itself cannot be trusted, unless apart from the collateral evidence of contemporary writers or of genuine historical monuments. Grote, History of Greece, vol. iii. p. 455. The chronological scheme of the Etruscans was far less elaborate; but it requires a large faith to admit with Niebuhr (History of Rome, vol. i.: The Etruscans) that their soothsayers were enabled by previous calculation to fix on the year of the conquest by Sylla as the close of the national secular day. It is still more strange that he should have continued to attribute so much of historical truth to the early ages of Rome, after he had laid bare the utterly arbitrary plan of its chronology. (History of Rome, vol. i.: Beginning and Nature of the Earliest History.) Perhaps few fictitious schemes were more skilfully put together than the Fabian computation of Roman history down to the burning of the city by the Gauls. The simple plan of dividing it into three equal periods and assigning two of them to the kings, is followed up by the more ingenious device of placing the middle of the fourth out of seven reigns at the end of the first of these periods. Not less ingenious was the plan of fixing the precise length of the several reigns of Romulus and Numa, as well as of the kings who followed Ancus Marcius. (Niebuhr, History of Rome, ibid.) The only period which cannot be explained by reference to astronomical

had forgotten to carry the woman-born lion [1], and that a paroxysm of fear loosed the tongue of the dumb child of Crœsus, the circumstances of the capture are gone. The legend is, indeed, connected immediately with the oracles and signs previously given, and with the exquisite tale which vindicates the piety of Crœsus and the righteousness of Apollo; and to apply to it such a method is scarcely less dangerous than to accept the fact of a plague in the host of Agamemnon and the lonely musings of Achilles, while we put aside the vision of Thetis and her prayer to the father of gods and men. The difference lies in this, that we have no means of proving any statements in the Homeric poems, while we are able to test perhaps the greater number of the facts which are found in the histories of Herodotus. In these, while still maintaining the historical basis of his narrative, we can prove our right to reject either

or other arbitrary schemes, is the time of twenty-five years assigned to the reign of the last king, which, therefore, he thinks may have been its historical duration. He had forgotten that the schemes which, as he believes, guided their determination with regard to other reigns, left them no option but to give to the last whatever might have been left from the close of the preceding reign to the end of the second period of 120 years. By the side of this elaborate fiction, the plan of Anglo-Saxon chronology appears childish in its simplicity. An eight times repeated cycle of eight years, with the number forty as employed to express completeness, forms the basis of the computation. Lappenberg, History of England under the Anglo-Saxon Kings, vol. i. pp. 77, 109.

[1] Herodotus, i. 84. The story is but another version of the dipping of Achilles in the waters of the Styx. He fell by a wound in the only part of his body which the water had not touched.

mythical details or entire mythical episodes. We cannot do so with the great epics of the heroic age.

But if a religious or supernatural causation of events was imposed on Herodotus by the necessity of his time, if at the utmost we can only say that human and political causes, while not wholly put aside, are yet subordinate to causes of another kind, then to bring against him charges of credulity or superstition, of an excessive love of anecdote, and of exaggerations for the sake of pictorial effect, is to make use of erroneous terms. These peculiarities are not in him to be regarded as defects because we find a very different historical method in Thucydides; while the latter scarcely deserves credit for his higher critical standard, if we blame his predecessor for a lower one. The vivid imagination of Herodotus may have embellished, but it did not create, the exquisite legends of Crœsus and Cyrus, of Amasis and Polycrates.[1] The mightier genius of Thucydides may have strengthened, but it did not originate, the intellectual condition of his age. It was not merely "a poetic or romantic turn of mind"[2] which compelled Herodotus to give us the tale of Atys and Adrastus; it was not altogether his own philosophical temperament which led Thucydides to analyse the effects of plague or sedition on the morality of a people. The few years which separated the youth of Herodotus from that of Thucydides had removed the latter further from the faith of the heroic ages than the four hundred years which Herodotus believed to have intervened between

Intellectual condition of the age of Herodotus contrasted with that of Thucydides.

---

[1] See also Grote, History of Greece, vol. v. pp. 15, 16.
[2] Rawlinson's Herodotus, vol. i. p. 104.

himself and Homer.[1] It is difficult to regard it as "a happy chance which has given us, in the persons of the two earliest and most eminent of Greek historians, the two opposite phases of the Greek mind, religiousness bordering upon superstition, and shrewd practical sense verging towards scepticism."[2] The latter phase, in the youth of Herodotus, can scarcely be said to have had any existence; the former cannot be very closely connected either with piety or superstition. It was rather a condition of mind which assumed the mingling of things earthly and divine less as a stimulus to devotion than as the ordinary state of human life. Had Thucydides written the history of the Persian war when Herodotus wrote his, we should have had indefinitely less of that keen philosophical analysis which marks his own "immortal possession;"[3] and Herodotus, in the days of Cleon and Brasidas, would have thought of other things than legends which illustrate the causeless jealousy of the gods. The mental and political state which produced Pericles and Phormiôn was at work in all the actors in the Peloponnesian war. If we compare these with the Greeks of Herodotus in the struggle with Persia, we see that their motives and plans, their forms of thought and expression, are wholly different. The jealousy of the Tegeatans and Athenians is displayed in appeals to mythical exploits in the days of the Amazons and the Heracleidæ.[4] Themistocles has to force the meaning of an oracle, or to turn the religious sentiment

[1] Herodotus, ii. 53.
[2] Rawlinson's Herodotus, vol. i. p. 95.
[3] Thucydides, i. 22.   [4] Herodotus, ix. 26.

of his countrymen, in order to carry out his own wise designs.[1] But in the days of Pericles no claim is urged but such as may rise from merely public or personal services; and the Athenians are swayed by well-balanced probabilities of political success or failure. If the massacre at Melos is related by Thucydides under something of the form of an epical climax, the conference which precedes it, whether historically truthful or not, is a logical discussion as grave and calm as a debate of philosophers in the groves of Academus.

But it is another question how far the epical method of Herodotus affects the credit of his narrative, or what amount of historical fact it leaves to us. If tested by the standard of Thucydides, it would be small indeed. If every motive given must be purely human or political, to the exclusion of supernatural agency, the causes which produced the Persian war would be greatly reduced in number. From such a point of view we could scarcely say that the ruin of the Lydian monarchy was caused by the ill-advised aggression of Crœsus[2], while the necessity of conquest imposed on all Eastern despotism remains unnoticed. If the same necessity would adequately account for the efforts of Darius and Xerxes, then the intrigues of the Peisistratidæ would furnish rather an opportunity of which the Persians availed themselves than a predisposing motive for the war. We shall fail to meet with any recognition of conflicting forces, of forms of civilisation whose contact renders aggression and warfare inevitable, of antagonistic political ideas founded on difference of race or pro-

Its influence on the credibility of his history.

---

[1] Herodotus, vii. 143, &c.   [2] Ibid. i. 46.

duced by total diversity of circumstance; and we may therefore be tempted to regard as a defect in Herodotus himself this partial discernment of historical causes, until we remember that he had scarcely emerged from an age to which religious influences, exhibited under epical forms, were not only acceptable but indispensable. The influence of that age was shaken only in the cities and amongst thoughtful men: in the more remote districts those portions of Herodotean history which exhibit some approach to the criticism of a later time, would still have been unwelcome or repulsive.[1] And in his own mind the two methods of interpreting events were not very carefully distinguished. If, with some tendency to substitute a human for a supernatural sequence of things, he more frequently accepts marvels and prodigies with unquestioning belief, he was probably swayed unconsciously by the religious standard of his time. To doubt the intervention of Phylacus and Autonoüs at Delphi, would have offended the religious instincts of others as well as his own. But no such feelings were attached to the names of Io, of Europa and Medeia; and hence their history is presented under a disguise which utterly hides the spirit of the old heroic fables.[2] Myths, utterly unconnected one with the other, are introduced as connected causes for the political events of his own day, while every single

His treatment of the old mythical tales.

---

[1] The readiness of the men of Lystra to worship St. Paul as Hermes and St. Barnabas as Zeus, will show what strength this sentiment possessed in remote places, when a belief in the old mythology had long since been shaken elsewhere.

[2] Herodotus, i. 1, &c.

feature of the ancient legend is either obliterated or modified. The daughter of Inachus, changed into a heifer and chased by the gad-fly of Hera over the mountains where Prometheus is paying the penalty for his love of man[1], becomes an Argive maiden choosing foreign wares on the deck of a ship, and, possibly of her own free will, stealing away with Phœnician sailors. The child of the Morning, whom Zeus as a white bull bears away to the land of night[2], comes before us as the daughter of a Tyrian king whom Argives steal in retaliation for the rape of Io. And, more strangely still, the uncontrollable love which led the wise Colchian maiden to the Thessalian shore,—the atmosphere of portentous miracle which enwraps her mythical history from its commencement to its close,—the marvellous power which tames the fire-breathing bulls,—the devouring robe,—the dragon-chariot, are lost in the single statement that, by the robbery of Medeia, the Greeks reopened the causes of offence between the East and the West. But to deal thus with the craft of Demokedes and Histiæus, with the visions of Xerxes and the miraculous repulse at Delphi, would upset the whole

[1] It requires some little effort at first to believe that Herodotus is speaking of the same mythical beings who come before us in the Prometheus of Æschylus and the Medeia of Euripides, &c. Cf. Grote, History of Greece, vol. i. pp. 119, 543.

[2] Europa, herself, probably, an embodiment of the dawn, is the child of the light-giving Telephassa. The white bull is in the Veda a frequent appellation of the sun. Like Heracles and Endymion, she is borne away to the west, the "gloaming of the evening." See Max Müller, Comparative Mythology, p. 61, in Oxford Essays for 1856.

historical method of Herodotus, and deprive his work at once of its value and its charm. And if a more sceptical tendency here and there betrays itself, it is generally confined to those subjects of time and space in which the idea of a physical order was breaking in upon his mind. He is able to recognise the agency of Poseidon under the form of periodical earthquakes[1]; he believes that the winds may have been lulled after the shipwrecks at Artemisium because the storm was spent.[2] He accepts gladly and without question the coincidence of the battles of Plataeae and Mycale[3]; he doubts not the heavenly Phêmê, the divine Rumour, which cheered the Greeks on the Asiatic coast with the tidings of victory then scarcely achieved in Boeotia.[4] He is sure that the herald's staff was thrown up on the sea-shore as the visible token of the destruction of Mardonius; but, to give time for the passage of the rumour and the staff, he is careful to state that the fight at Plataea happened early in the day, while that of Mycale was fought as the sun was going down in the sky.[5] The victory of Gelon had indeed been won in Sicily on the same day with the battle of Salamis[6]; but it called for no explanation, as neither side during the fight was made aware of the good success of the other.

It is easy to take event after event, and to show that the details given by the historian are conflicting or

---

[1] Herodotus, vii. 129. [2] Ibid. vii. 191.
[3] Ibid. ix. 90. [4] Ibid. ix. 100.
[5] Ibid. ix. 101. It is not easy on any other supposition to understand why he should be at the pains to state this incident, which, except by way of explaining the wonder, is wholly unnecessary. [6] Ibid. vii. 166.

impossible, that the alleged causes are fictitious or in- *modern critical tests to the history of Herodotus.*
adequate, and that the true cause is frequently kept
altogether out of sight. But whether, and to whatever
extent, we may reject his details, it must be remembered that they are inextricably blended with the narrative. If we scruple to receive the marvels which embellish the history of Crœsus, we cannot safely believe more than that after a conflict with the power of Persia the prosperous Lydian dynasty was overthrown. If we reject the tale of the recovered ring, we can say nothing more of the death of Polycrates than that he was in some way or other entrapped by a crafty satrap and killed, even if we may believe so much. If we cannot admit the fable of the childhood of Cyrus, we shall substitute national aversion or rebellion to account for the fall of Median supremacy. And if, after rejecting the many details and stories which yield to the test of criticism, we still retain something more than a dry catalogue of facts, it is because we believe the man, and because we feel ourselves justified in according to him a belief which we refuse to yield to the lays of the old heroic ages. But this faith cannot be extended to those portions of his history which are constructed wholly on an epical or religious basis. We may perhaps believe that Xerxes sent a detached force to Delphi; but we cannot be sure, from the tale of Herodotus, how that force fared or whether the temple was plundered. Of the councils of Xerxes we know nothing, and are left with a probability, which applies equally to all wars, that it was not undertaken without forethought. We may maintain the truth of the policy of Themistocles, while we reject the story of the oracle, because we have

abundant proof of that policy as a fact in subsequent history as well as in that of Herodotus; and we readily believe that the necessities of the war with Ægina served his purpose better than a forced interpretation of the warnings of Apollo. But, except where we have such additional testimony, there will be left, when the process of rejection is complete, only that bare and lifeless residue which remains of Trojan history when Hector and Achilles have been banished from the tale.[1] We can scarcely say that with Herodotus, as with Livy, the prodigies and miracles form no essential portion of the narrative, unless we exclude the chronicles of the Roman kings and the early times of the republic. The prodigies of later Roman history are mere excrescences, and read like the official reports of men specially appointed to attend to them. If a statue moves or a cow speaks, no effect is seen in the deliberations of the senate or the action of the people; while in the history of Crœsus or of Xerxes the moral and religious element is everything.

<small>Introduction of Greek forms of thought into the description of Oriental society.</small>

Greek thought and feeling tinges many of the tales which Herodotus has given us of other lands. The speeches of Artabanus are full of early Greek philosophy; the debates on the overthrow of the Magian usurpers exhibit arguments which are the growth only of the Hellenic mind. Of several of his tales other versions exist, which betray a different conception; but to the beauty of Greek thought we owe not a little of the charm of his Oriental narratives. It seems strange, however, that the Greek colonies of the West, whether in Sicily or Italy, fail to carry with them this religious

---

[1] See the preface of Thucydides, i. 9, &c.

or didactic vein which runs through the early annals of the parent land. The history of Syracuse and Agrigentum exhibits no luxuriant overgrowth of mythical or epic legend. It has little to rouse the fancy or to provoke doubt; and where it does provoke it, the doubt rarely extends beyond historical inconsistency. The narrative is more credible, and less attractive; but it is not without its value as showing over what condition of society and course of events the halo of Greek legend has been thrown.

CHAP. III.

ON THE SOURCES OF INFORMATION ACCESSIBLE TO HERODOTUS.

Distinction between history and fiction. IT is not merely from its internal contradictions or improbability that the tale of Troy falls to the ground. That it may be made, by a process of selection and free interpretation, to furnish an eminently plausible narrative, has been proved by the introductory chapters to the immortal work of Thucydides. Helen and Hector, Paris and Priam, are to us mere creatures of fiction, not simply because Zeus and Hera, Thetis and Aphrodité, mingle freely with other actors in the tale. In the legends of the Crusading ages, Charles the Great becomes as mythical as King Arthur and his peers[1]; yet with the historical Charles the Great we are as familiar as with Pericles or Cæsar. But Charles the Great has come down to us in the pages of Eginhard: we have for his deeds and his policy the testimony of his own time. This testimony is wholly wanting to the legends of Achilles and Agamemnon. In the belief of Herodotus himself, four centuries had passed away before his birth from the composition of the Homeric poems; and even

---

[1] Cf. Milman, History of Latin Christianity, vol. vi. p. 345 (Ed. 2).

if we assume that they were written in the times of which they speak, we are driven to ask what change and havoc would, during so many ages, befall oral traditions which it would be the interest of all to warp or to embellish.

But Herodotus deserves and receives from us a wider and more generous credit than that which is warranted by the power of verifying certain statements in his history. He has to speak of a race broken up into many kindred tribes, under strange conditions of feud or friendship; and of all he has spoken with a singular impartiality.[1] He has had to tell us of a war of races in which the East and West, despotism and freedom, were set against each other; and he is as ready to acknowledge the merits of the despotic Persian as to admit the vices of his free kinsman.[2] He has shown himself almost wholly free from personal bias; he has as large an admiration for Dorian as for Ionian virtue. We can convict him of no interested motives in the performance of his task.[3] We are justified, therefore, under certain restrictions presently to be named, in according to him a ready belief on all points of which he had personal knowledge or on which he could exercise his own judgment, as also of all others in which he could avail himself of the testimony of eye-witnesses or of otherwise credible informants.

The impartiality of Herodotus is a strong argument for his credibility.

[1] Herodotus, vii. 152, &c.
[2] Ibid. vii. 238, &c.
[3] Ibid. vii. 139. His expressions imply that his judgment on the paramount merit of the Athenians was extorted by his conviction of its truth against the sense of his own interest, and in spite of the knowledge that it would be fiercely disputed.

Causes which tend to modify oral tradition.

If, however, we may generally admit his authority for contemporary events or in the results of his own observations, the case is greatly altered at every step which leads us backward. It is not merely that personal feelings may influence the form of tradition, but we may define the length of time during which the memory of various classes of events may be faithfully preserved. The motives and the words of men, apart from their results, have the greatest influence over those who hear them, and are impressed most forcibly on their minds. It is precisely here that the memory of a later generation fails, while a fair recollection may be retained of the objects which they aimed at or attained. There is a constant tendency to modify the details and features, and then to lose them, until there remains a barren fact from which all that gave it life and interest has been torn away. It is needless to enlarge on the wide difference between an age which derives all its knowledge from oral tradition, and another which rests wholly upon written history. The comparison of their condition presents a curious contrast. Sir G. C. Lewis quotes a remark of Mallet's, "that among the common class of mankind a son remembers his father, knows something about his grandfather, but never bestows a thought on his more remote progenitors."[1] In an age of oral tradition his knowledge of public affairs would follow the same rule. The period immediately preceding his own would come before him in something like its real outlines; but in an age of written records the time which a little precedes our own birth is that

---

[1] Credibility of Early Roman History, vol. i. p. 98.

with which we are least familiar. Its records have not yet been thrown into permanent historical forms, while its chief actors are passing away from the scene. The concerns of that time are less the subject of conversation than those of a more distant age, while few have reached so late a mark in the course of their historical study. Such a condition has this obvious disadvantage, that it deprives a man of that vivid realisation which almost turns the past into the present, and which must have wellnigh brought before the eyes of Herodotus every scene of the Persian war in its most minute detail. It checks the disposition to personal inquiry, and tends to hinder the intercourse of the rising generation with that which is passing away. But if in a time of oral tradition men realise more vividly the lives and fortunes of their immediate predecessors, there is danger that the picture may be partial or unfaithful. Personal motives, whether of favour or dislike, of jealousy or admiration, may enter in; their sympathies may be powerfully attracted towards the winning or the losing side; the imagination may fasten on one event to the distortion or depreciation of another.

A further difference is caused by the form in which the tradition is cast. If the vehicle employed is mere ordinary conversation, such as that which imparted to Herodotus the tale of Thersander and Attaginus, the chances of deviation from truth or of positive contradictions are indefinitely increased. If it be transmitted in a rhythmical or metrical form, the danger of alteration is comparatively slight, whatever may be the credibility of the events so recorded. The variations of Greek legend

Advantages of the poetical form for the perpetuation of tradition.

are great; but the oldest or the most beautiful tales might have been completely overlaid by the altered religious feeling of subsequent ages, if they had been intrusted to nothing more permanent than the common talk of the people. The metrical form of the Homeric poems was not indeed a guarantee against slight corruptions of text or deviations of detail during the times in which they were preserved by the memory of the rhapsodists; but it insured their substantial integrity then, and aroused a jealous care for the purity and completeness of the text after they were reduced to writing. The sufferings of Helen at Troy might have been abandoned for the strange version of Stæsichorus[1], but for the existence of a critical standard furnished by the poets themselves. At the least there is only one supposition on which we can conceive of a vast mass of legend as being faithfully preserved in a form devoid of metre or rhythm; and this alternative is supplied by the history of Sanskrit literature. When we learn that the power to repeat the whole Iliad and Odyssey from memory was no rare accomplishment among Athenian citizens[2], we are disposed to marvel at a feat which is by no means superhuman. The absence of a written literature and of a complicated form of society so circumscribes the memory that its powers in one definite direction become almost

---

[1] Grote, History of Greece, vol. i. p. 416. To the strange tale of the Egyptian priests, that Helen, during the war of Troy, was detained in Egypt, Herodotus yields as willing an assent as to their version of the founding of the oracle at Dodona. Herodotus, ii. 120, &c..

[2] Xenophon, Sympos. iii. 6. Grote, History of Greece, vol. ii. p. 195.

unlimited. But perhaps in no other instance than the Sanskrit has the system of oral tradition, as applied to a whole literature, been obstinately maintained after the introduction of writing and the existence of manuscripts; in no other instance has the preservation of the text been owing far more to the former than to the latter. But in this case the aid to the memory is supplied by converting the task into a religious duty; and the slightest perversion in the text of liturgical, grammatical, and devotional works incurs the ban of a religious anathema.[1] To this must be added an almost life-long training to which probably not even a Homeric rhapsodist would have submitted. Eight-and-forty years were spent by the most devoted class of students in achieving the gigantic task in which they were to train up others. And even with these conditions the effort would scarcely have been successful, unless an inviolable sanctity had been attached to every word and every syllable. Not only must the Veda be learnt

[1] In the transmission of the Veda, "the only difference in modern times, after the invention of writing, is that a Brahmin is not only commanded to pass his apprenticeship at the house of his Guru, and to learn from his mouth all that a Brahmin is bound to know, but the fiercest imprecations are uttered against all who would presume to acquire their knowledge from written sources. In the Mahábhárata we read, 'Those who sell the Vedas, and even those who write them, those also who defile them, they shall go to hell!' Kumárila says, 'That knowledge of the truth is worthless which has been acquired from the Veda, if the Veda has not been rightly comprehended, if it has been learnt from writing, or been received from a Súdra.'" — *Max Müller, History of Ancient Sanskrit Literature*, p. 502, &c.

orally, but all benefit is lost, and never-ending torments are the penalty, if any attempt is made to learn it in any other way. The memory of the Greek rhapsodists is almost inconceivable under the conditions of our modern society; but when every allowance has been made for the quickening of the faculty in proportion to the limitation of its range, their greatest feats sink almost into nothing beside the determined oral system which has preserved unchanged a literature altogether more vast in bulk, for perhaps three thousand years.[1] It is an achievement which could only have been accomplished by the despotic power of a sacerdotal caste, acting upon minds to whom such control was entirely congenial, and with a form of religious belief to which all change and progress were alike alien and repulsive.

Comparison of Greek and Mahometan tradition

Such influences extend but in a slight degree even to the epical literature of the Greeks, and in no way affect that mass of floating legend which ushers in the dawn of authentic history. The same national sympathies and jealousies, which might serve to guard the purity and completeness of the Homeric text, would here mould or modify those tales which formed the early annals of their country; and in the absence of

[1] Professor Müller inclines to regard the date B.C. 1000—1200 as too narrow and too recent for the earliest or Chandas period of Sanskrit literature, and maintains that we can only assign this date "on the supposition that during the early periods of history the growth of the human mind was more luxuriant than in later times, and that the layers of thought were formed less slowly in the primary than in the tertiary ages of the world."—*History of Sanskrit Literature*, p. 572.

any authoritative documents we are reduced almost to the same rules of judgment which we apply to the legends of Troy or the old theogonies. A close parallel is furnished in the early Mahometan history. The Coran comes before us, on conclusive proof, as being substantially the work of a single man[1]; and the religious faction which split up the followers of the Prophet is the strongest guarantee for the preservation, in their integrity, of documents which were compiled into a single volume by his own immediate successors.[2] But the Mahometan traditions which were subjected to no such ordeal, and which grew up with every successive change of thought or feeling, exhibit a luxuriance of miracle, marvel, and prodigy, which may vie even with the legendary history of the Persian war.[3] Most of them, indeed, we are able at once to reject, from the

---

[1] The "Life of Mahomet and History of Islam to the Era of the Hegira, by William Muir," contains an admirable introduction on the nature and value of Mahometan tradition. After admitting that "the real drawback to the inestimable value of the Coran" is its "want of arrangement and connection," he adds that, "bating this serious defect, we may upon the strongest presumption affirm that every verse in the Coran is the genuine and unaltered composition of Mahomet himself, and conclude with at least a close approximation to the verdict of Von Hammer, *that we hold the Coran to be as surely the word of Mahomet, as the Mahometans hold it to be the word of God.*"—Vol. i. p. xxvii. See also National Review, July 1858, p. 153.

[2] Mr. Muir notes, as conclusive evidence of the authenticity of Othman's version of the Koran, the absence of all opposition on the part of the followers of Ali. Vol. i. p. xvi.; but see at length pp. xix.—xxvi.

[3] Muir, Life of Mahomet, vol. i. pp. lxiii.—lxvii.

plain contradictions afforded by the Coran; while the rest stand either as plausible fiction or as mere probabilities.

with the traditions of mediæval Christendom.

This parallel is indeed the more valuable as showing the rapidity with which such fictions may grow up. The marvels attributed to Mahomet may all be matched and even surpassed by the miracles which attested the zeal and holiness of Benedict or St. Bernard, of Augustine or Columban. But marvels and prodigies formed the poetry of the middle ages. The preaching of the Gospel was announced by the despairing cries of baffled spirits[1]; the holiness of its preachers was attested by the homage of beasts and demons.[2] But it can scarcely be thought that the religion of Islam was as congenial a soil for the growth of miracle as the temper and circumstances of mediæval Christendom. The Coran gave little countenance to such representations; and two generations at most had barely passed away from the Prophet's death before a series of contemporary historians began to furnish means for detecting and refuting them.[3] But, in spite of these obstacles, miraculous narratives soon shed their false light on the life of this great teacher,

---

[1] Milman, History of Latin Christianity, vol. ii. p. 52.

[2] Montalembert, Moines d'Occident, vol. ii. p. 359. "Ceux-ci (les moines) vivaient naturellement dans une sorte de familiarité avec la plupart des bêtes fauves qu'ils voyaient bondir autour d'eux." After this historical statement, M. de Montalembert seems almost to Euémerise these stories by speaking of them as "touchantes légendes qui consacraient, *sous une forme poétique et populaire*, la pensée que la demeure des saints est le refuge inviolable de la faiblesse contre la force."—*Ibid.* p. 360.

[3] Muir, Life of Mahomet, vol. i. p. xxxii.

and invested not only his early years but the history of
previous generations with the vivid colouring which
cannot fail to be imparted by a profusion of minute and
plausible details. The gorgeous absurdities of the night
journey to Jerusalem were evoked by the recital of an
ordinary dream[1]; while the tendency to localise the incidents of a memorable career was developed as strongly
and as early as among the early Christians of Palestine.

But if the historian of Mahometanism is justified in rejecting not merely these miraculous legends, but the detailed events of times anterior to the Prophet or even of his earlier years, in exact proportion to the fulness of their detail, we are wielding a weapon which will fall with greater force on almost every part of Herodotean history except its close. If we accept the year 484 B.C. as that of his birth, the historian was only six years of age when the last event recorded in his narrative took place.[2] That he was born much earlier is most unlikely, even if we put aside the statements of Dionysius and of Pamphila. If his silence on the fate of the Æginetans at Thyrea, and on the occupation of Kythêra by Nikias[3], furnishes conclusive proof, if not of his death, yet of the completion of his work before the eighth year of the Peloponnesian war, still his own statements show that his final corrections must have extended to some time within three or four years of that date; and the lot of Gorgias or Isocrates is not the portion of many.

[1] Muir, Mahomet, vol. i. p. lxvii.
[2] See Sir G. C. Lewis, On the Credibility of Early Roman History, vol. ii. p. 501.
[3] Herodotus, vi. 91, vii. 235. See also Grote, History of Greece, vol. iv. pp. 307-8.

Herodotus not a contemporary historian.

In strictness of speech, then, it is no tale of his own time which Herodotus gives to us. His own careful inquiries and conscientious judgment may warrant our unquestioning acceptance of all statements the truth of which it was in his power to verify; but the element of uncertainty comes in even with the latest events in a narrative which closes so soon after the time of his own birth. If we may not safely forget the propensity to invent or alter details which is common to every age, still less may we put out of sight the peculiar circumstances of a generation whose native atmosphere was that of mythology. No testimony of earlier writers can be adduced in proof of his assertions. It becomes a superfluous labour to give a list of such earlier or contemporary authors, with whom probably Herodotus was even less acquainted than we are.[1] Of the Lydian Xanthus, as of Charon of Lampsacus, he seems to have known nothing, or at least to have made no use of their works.[2] With Hecatæus, if not with Hellanicus, he was undoubtedly more familiar; but even the former can lay no claim to the title of an historian, while the latter is but one of that large company whose labours were mostly confined to collecting the several versions of the heroic fables. At the least it seems impossible to disprove the opinion of Niebuhr, that, before the work of Herodotus was written, there was no writing in Greece which could be properly called historical.[3] The dog of Orestheus illustrated Ætolian genealogy to Hecatæus

---

[1] Rawlinson's Herodotus, vol. i. p. 39, &c.
[2] Ibid. vol. i. p. 43.
[3] Niebuhr, Lectures on Ancient History, vol. i. p. 168.

not less than the relics of the sow at Lavinium attested the legend of Æneas to Cato.[1]

The limits assigned by Sir G. C. Lewis to the possible authenticity of oral tradition are fully as wide as the evidence would seem to warrant.[2] Special circumstances may occur in the history of any people which may impress a series of events or a single event more forcibly on their memory. The institution of festivals or of civil or military offices, changes in the form of government, great national successes or calamities, must undoubtedly affect the common talk of the people, and may quicken the fidelity of their recollections. But the inconsistencies in such traditions as those of Harmodius and Aristogeiton[3] will deter us from placing too great a reliance on those which relate even to the most important political events; and we shall remember that the caprice of popular imagination might tamper with the history of even such men as Miltiades and Themistocles.

Circumstances which favour the permanence of oral tradition.

But if the nearness of Herodotus to the times of which he speaks is no conclusive guarantee for the details of the fight of Marathon or the assault on Delphi, and if all testimony of earlier writers is wanting, we can fall back only on his personal credibility, while examining events in Greek history which belong to any earlier generations than the one immediately preceding his own. To refer to public documents, to state regis-

Limits to the credibility of Herodotus.

[1] Mure, History of Greek Literature, vol. iv. p. 161.
[2] Sir G. C. Lewis, Credibility of Early Roman History, vol. i. p. 98, &c.
[3] Thucydides, vi. 53. Sir G. C. Lewis, Credibility, &c. vol. ii. p. 510.

ters, or other inscriptions, is to adduce evidence which is rather specious than real; and Mr. Rawlinson would seem to state more than what even a lenient historical standard would justify, when he asserts that "from these and similar sources of information Herodotus would be able to check the accounts orally delivered to him, and in some cases to fill them up with accuracy."[1] Nor is it easy to follow him when he says that "the independence of Phrygia under a royal line, affecting the names of Midas and Gordius, the wealth and order of succession of the last or Mermnad dynasty of Lydian kings, the enormous riches of Crœsus, the friendly terms on which he stood with Sparta, and his great devotion to the Greek shrines; the escape of Arion from shipwreck, the filial devotion of Cleobis and Biton, and the repulse of the Spartans by the Tegeans on their first attempt to conquer Arcadia, are all supported by this kind of testimony within the space of seventy chapters after the history opens."[2]

Authority of public monuments.

That Herodotus rests his alleged facts on such testimony is indisputable; the question turns simply on the value of the testimony, and we are tempted to forget that public monuments and inscriptions must be judged by precisely the same tests as those which are applied to historical narratives. As evidence of facts long anterior to their own date, they can have no weight; as proofs even of contemporary events, they require to be examined and checked not less strictly than the statements of individual historians. Mr. Grote rightly insists on the necessity of ascertaining whether the inscriber had an adequate knowledge

[1] Herodotus, vol. i. p. 56.   [2] Ibid.

of the facts which he records, and whether or not there may be reason to suspect misrepresentation.[1] The existence of contemporary writers at once imparts a different value to the public monuments of their time; in their absence we have to invest such records with an intrinsic infallibility, such as we should be unwilling to allow to them in any age. In the early period of history they are peculiarly liable to suspicion. The tendency of the people to receive mythical and historical facts with the same degree of belief, the temptation to forge or tamper with such documents to gratify national or personal vanity or malice, the habit of accepting, as genuine, records which referred to a purely mythical time, may well justify us in testing their credit by the statements of historians, rather than in receiving the latter on any proof which these monuments may furnish. Instances are not wanting whether of false inscriptions or of forged memorials. A sprinkling vessel, which Herodotus believed to have been the gift of Crœsus, was made by the forgery of a Delphian to testify to the piety of the Lacedæmonians.[2] Empty sepulchres raised on the battle-field at Platææ soothed the vanity of those Greeks whose fathers were not present at the fight.[3] It would scarcely be more rash to admit a fact without hesitation on the evidence of such monuments or inscriptions, than to accept as proofs of the historical existence of Heracles or Endymion, of Æneas or Niobe, the tombs and relics which were exhibited before the eyes of later historians and geographers.

[1] History of Greece, vol. ii. p. 56.
[2] Herodotus, i. 51. [3] Ibid. ix. 85.

We are not able to test by any collateral evidence such monuments as these, any more than the proofs which Euemerus adduces for the human life and exploits of Zeus before his deification.[1]

Nature and value of Greek genealogies.

Genealogies and official lists before the time of contemporary history are if possible even less trustworthy. If we accept the later names contained in them as historical, we do so not because they occur in the list, but because the list is supported by the authority of contemporary writers. We do not believe that Leonidas really lived and died because his ancestry is carried back through Heracles to Zeus, any more than we accept the personality of the historian Hecataeus because his sixteenth ancestor was a god.[2] The value of a Greek genealogy rose in proportion to its brevity; their faith in the reality of the superhuman stock was altogether stronger than their assurance of the truth of events which passed before their eyes. For historical purposes these genealogies are practically useless. We cannot tell where that which is mythical ends and where that which is historical begins. The existence of Hecataeus is no guarantee for the existence of even the third or fourth name from himself in the list of his ancestors. If the table of Spartan kings becomes historical in its later entries, we cannot make use of them before the existence of collateral testimony with more safety than the line of Athenian kings which closes as it began with a mere name.[3] The lists of public

[1] Diodorus, v. 44—46. Grote, History of Greece, vol. i p. 552.   [2] Herodotus, ii. 143.

[3] For a complete examination of the subject, see Grote, History of Greece, Part I. ch. xix.

officers, whether civil or sacerdotal, must be subjected to the same tests. The names of the earlier Athenian archons we must, in Mr. Grote's words, "take as we find them, without being able either to warrant the whole or to separate the false from the true."[1] A register was kept of the priests and priestesses at Argos and elsewhere; but the personality of Chrysis[2], who lived in the time of Thucydides, is no evidence for the historical character of her predecessors in the days of Orpheus or Melampus. The early chronology of the Olympiads is shrouded in the same mystery. The era begins with the victory of Corœbus; but of the reality of Corœbus we have no further evidence than a monument which was alleged to mark his grave.[3] The life of Pheidon, the great Temenid king of Argos, is assigned to several dates far removed from one another.[4]

To assume the existence of authentic records, wholly lost to us but corroborating these public monuments or inscriptions, is the dangerous and even desperate hypothesis of Niebuhr.[5] It is a supposition which, as applied to Greek history, is even less plausible than when it is used to explain the contradictory traditions of Rome.

No written records existed contemporary with the earlier Greek monuments.

[1] Grote, History of Greece, vol. iii. p. 67.
[2] Thucydides, ii. 2.
[3] Pausanias, v. 8, 3; viii. 26, 3.
[4] Grote, History of Greece, vol. ii. p. 423. Sir G. C. Lewis, Credibility, &c. vol. ii. p. 546.
[5] Lectures on Ancient History, vol. i. p. 169. He supposes that authentic "annalistic tables" furnished to Thucydides the dates of certain facts mentioned in his Introduction, as the building of the first galley, &c.; and the authenticity of these tables he "cannot allow to be attacked."

The legends of the mythical ages in Greece had long since been embodied in a poetical form; at Rome, perhaps because they were preserved in the ordinary speech of the people, their astonishing variations and their fragmentary beauty may tempt us to look upon them as relics of great national poems which are lost to us for ever. There is little evidence among the Greeks of that family pride which showed itself at Rome in pompous funeral orations and in bombastic family annals which fed their hereditary vanity; nor does Thucydides refer to such sources of information any more than the later historians of Rome.

Evidence furnished by works of art.

The offerings at Delphi, the votive statues in Tœnarum and elsewhere, cannot be brought forward as evidence for facts, when they themselves stand in need of other testimony to prove their genuineness. That Herodotus saw at Athens or Corinth or Babylon that which he says that he saw, is not to be disputed; but he has himself told us that the original inscriptions were sometimes displaced by forged titles, and that monuments were erected to commemorate that which had never happened [1]; and the tales which gave the history of these monuments are in some instances hopelessly inconsistent. In gratitude for the friendliness of Crœsus, the Lacedæmonians sent him a costly mixing bowl. It came too late, according to one version, for Crœsus was a Persian captive before it reached Samos [2], while the same event is stated by another version to have happened in the days of his father Alyattes.[3] If then we have any reason for believing in the order of suc-

[1] See before, p. 285.   [2] Herodotus, i. 70.   [3] Ibid. iii. 48.

cession of the last Lydian dynasty, it can be only because the facts may be regarded as sufficiently recent to be faithfully handed down by oral tradition. If the visit of Solon to the court of Crœsus is a mere legend which grew out of the epical tendency of the age, the existence of some statues at Argos can furnish no evidence for the tale of Cleobis and Biton, which thus becomes a legend within a legend. If again there is no reason for questioning the personality of Periander or Arîôn, the votive figure on Tænarum tells nothing of his miraculous escape from shipwreck. The miracle is of the essence of the tale; and to substitute for his deliverer a ship with a dolphin's sign is mere arbitrary invention. The war between Tegea and Sparta may be historical, but it is no more proved to be so by the fetters seen by Herodotus in the temple of Athena[1] than the wanderings of Æneas are proved by the relics which were exhibited at Lavinium. Nor could the tripod, which the confederated Greeks dedicated after the victory at Platææ, have enabled Herodotus to authenticate his list of the combatants in that battle. Mr. Rawlinson admits that the pedestal of this tripod, which still exists at Constantinople, has inscribed on it "the names not only of the Greeks who fought in that battle (as Pausanias mistakenly observes of the statue, v. xxiii. § 1) but of all who lent any effective aid to the Greek side during the war."[2] This fact would seem to lend some countenance to the supposition that the list on the tripod, even more than the list of Hero-

[1] Herodotus, i. 66.
[2] Rawlinson's Herodotus, vol. iv. p. 328.

dotus, is an epical representation, made up to give to all the Greek cities their share in the final glories of that war through whose course they had exhibited so wretched a picture of meanness and disunion. A list, which included allies who could only have given aid at sea, could not have enabled the historian to draw up a correct list of those who were engaged in a land battle. And while we wonder at the principle of selection which excluded from the inscription the names of the Lemnians, Crotoniats, and Seriphians, as having each contributed only a single vessel[1], we cannot but look on a collective enumeration of all the actors throughout a war as of no use in determining the combatants in each successive battle. The same difficulty extends to the inscription on the base of the statue of Zeus which was erected at Olympia, if, as Mr. Rawlinson gathers from a comparison of Herodotus and Thucydides, the "having borne any part in defeating the barbarian gave a claim for inscription."[2] Still less can it be admitted that the paintings of Mandrocles or the pillar of Darius prove the details of the Scythian expedition, or that the pictures in the Athenian Acropolis could have furnished a basis for historical descriptions of events in the Persian war.[3]

Value of Egyptian or Assyrian monuments.

But, if there is a dearth of Hellenic monuments and inscriptions, or, at the least, if those of which we have any knowledge appear lacking in authority, a contrast so striking would appear to be presented by foreign inscriptions as to induce an inference that his history

---

[1] Rawlinson's Herodotus, vol. iv. p. 486.
[2] Ibid. vol. iv. p. 408. [3] Ibid. vol. i. p. 56.

of the Greek states is the least authentic portion of his narrative. The bricks of Nineveh and Babylon have been made to yield their unwilling testimony to his list of Oriental despots and his catalogue of their exploits and their conquests; the annals of Cyrus, of Cambyses and Darius, are established by the gravings of the iron pen on the rocks of Behistun. The palaces and sepulchres of Assyrian and Persian kings are held to teem with memorials still unread or even undiscovered, which are to establish every doubtful point in the Jewish chronicles yet more surely than they uphold the general credit of Herodotus.

Of no historical documents whatever can it be said with truth that they are devoid of interest and value. It would be both useless and absurd to depreciate the importance of the discoveries which have been already made in the mounds of Birs Nimroud and Khorsabad; and it would be presumptuous to define the limits of future researches. It may, however, be not unprofitable to ascertain, so far as we may be able, the degree of light which these discoveries throw on that portion of the Herodotean narrative which is of paramount interest and importance,—the history, namely, of the Hellenic world in Europe and in Asia. The infinite superiority of Greek thought as exhibited in their legends, their art, and their religion, is no reason for turning aside from careful examination of winged and human-headed bulls; the glories of the Parthenon need not interfere with the appreciation of the barbaric magnificence of old Assyrian palaces. But after all due weight is given to the verification of the lists of Eastern despots, and of the order and course of their expeditions, that which is
(marginal note: Extent of their authority and of the evidence furnished by them.)

of never-dying interest for ourselves, that which makes the age of Themistocles and Miltiades not less real to us than our own, must be the battle of Hellenic freedom against Oriental slavery, the history of that intellectual and moral growth which has left an impression, perhaps never to be effaced, on the civilisation of Christendom. And therefore we must believe that it is of more moment to us to learn the real mind and purposes of the great leaders of Athens or Sparta and the condition of Athenian or Platæan citizens, than to determine the nature of the Magian revolution or the name of the Assyrian king who fell before the hosts of Kyaxares and Nabopolassar.

Limited range of Assyrian and Persian inscriptions.

On these subjects of Hellenic and European interest the researches at Nineveh and Babylon throw no light whatever. The records, so discovered, have a narrower range; but within that range they establish results which must be welcomed by all who would not lightly cast aside the credit of the father of Hellenic history. There can be little reluctance to accept fresh proofs of the suspected falsehoods and forgeries of Ctesias, little inclination to resist the evidence which shows that the usurpation of the Magian Smerdis was founded on a rivalry of religion, not of race.[1] But the worn or mutilated inscriptions of Behistun, which indicate the antagonism between Persian dualism and the elemental or Fetiche worship of the Magians, impart no information on such subjects as the Scythian expe-

---

[1] The history and nature of this usurpation has been well brought out by Mr. Rawlinson, in his essay on the subject, vol. ii. p. 553, &c.

dition of Darius or the suppression of the Ionian revolt. They tell us nothing of the motives which led to the long struggle between Greece and Persia, of the intrigues of Atossa, of Demokedes, or of Histiæus. Still less do any of the inscriptions, brought to light in the great seats of Oriental power, supply a conclusive settlement of those points in Jewish history over which any special uncertainty may rest. To bring up Assyrian records in proof of the general fidelity of the historical books of the Old Testament, is almost a superfluous labour; and no information yet produced would serve to establish more. The identity of Kudurmapula with the Chedorlaomer of Genesis is confessedly conjectural.[1] There is no sufficient proof that the Astyages of Herodotus is the Median Darius of the book of Daniel.[2] The lists of the early Babylonish kings cannot be presented with any conviction of their entire authenticity or any certainty in the order of their succession.[3] Still more brief and obscure are the oldest records of the Assyrian kings; and it is admitted that the bricks of Khileh-Shirgat in no way compensate the loss of the Assyrian history of Herodotus.[4] If again the name of Sargon is proved to introduce a new dynasty after the death of Salmanassar, the annals of the reign of his son Sennacherib break off before the period of his expedition against Hezekiah at Jerusalem.[5] So also, while the inscriptions sufficiently attest the might of Nebucadnezzar and his subversion of the Jewish kingdom, it would seem that they are silent on

[1] Rawlinson's Herodotus, vol. i. pp. 436, 446. [2] Ibid. p. 418.
[3] Ibid. p. 440.   [4] Ibid. p. 452.   [5] Ibid. p. 478.

the subject of that retribution which sent him forth for years to dwell amongst the beasts of the field.[1] And when their full weight has been assigned to all these monumental records, when we admit that they establish the credit of Herodotus over Ctesias, and of the Jewish history over that of Herodotus, to what does the knowledge so gained amount? The driest and most meagre dynastic lists, the bald enumeration of conquests or defeats, are welcome and valuable; but they remain mere tables of kings and dry catalogues of conquest still. Do we learn as much of Sennacherib from the records of the palace of Kouyunjik as from the vivid picture of the Jewish historian? Lists of kings and generals present to us history in the dullest form which it can be made to assume; yet, if they can be authenticated, they furnish an invaluable test for judging the records of a prehistoric age.

[1] Rawlinson's Herodotus, vol. i. p. 516.

CHAP. IV.

ON THE SUPERNATURAL MACHINERY IN THE HISTORY OF HERODOTUS.

ONE other class of monuments yet remains, which, if not of much weight in determining the order of events, would yet, on the assumption of their genuineness, very clearly illustrate the condition of popular feeling and the line of policy adopted at the time of which they may speak. These monuments are the oracular responses, obtained either from the Delphic and other shrines, or hawked about by professed soothsayers. But the mention of them brings up subjects of controversy which it may not be easy to settle and into which it is unnecessary to enter at any length. Apart, however, from the moral or theological difficulties connected with them, there can be no question that, if the fact of their delivery could be established, they would go far to prove the reality of many events of which we cannot now speak with certainty. If Crœsus really obtained from Delphi such answers as those which are introduced into the story of his life, it would be difficult to resist the conclusion that he was the aggressor in the struggle which ended in his ruin. If the Spartans were really told that their success in the Persian war depended on the death of their king, it would serve in great measure

Difficulties connected with the oracular responses.

to explain the strange conduct of Leonidas in the passes of Thermopylæ.

Amount of evidence necessary to prove the fact that they were delivered in the form which has been handed down.

But it is obvious that evidence almost indisputable is required before such documents can be received as proving even the fact that such answers were delivered. Nor has this demand any necessary reference to the question of their inspiration whether by heavenly or diabolic influence. The admission must be made that they were not always inspired either in the one way or the other, if by inspiration be meant the faculty of discerning the real events of the coming time. And this admission renders it absolutely necessary to separate by the most stringent tests the false oracles from the true.[1] Whether such a process will leave any as belonging to the latter class, is a question the decision of which may well precede the assertion of any supernatural agency. It may therefore be the more regretted that any attempts should be made to put the matter to a wrong issue; nor is it easy to see what is gained if, with Mr. Rawlinson, we impute to the oracles an exclusively diabolical inspiration. In support of this conclusion he recurs to the instance of the maiden mentioned in the Acts of the Apostles, to the fact that oracles began to fail soon after the publication of Christianity, and to the general conviction among the early fathers that the oracles were so inspired.[2] But in what respect do such

---

[1] By true oracles as distinguished from false I mean those of whose *delivery* we have adequate proof. The character of their contents is another, and very frequently a less important question.

[2] Rawlinson's Herodotus, vol. i. p. 92. It may be noted that Mr. Rawlinson appears to confine the inspiration of the oracles

opinions differ from the belief of St. Clement in the existence of the Phœnix[1], or from the unbelief of Bede and Augustine in the reality of antipodes?[2] and how can the former be enforced without involving the assertion of other opinions which none would now care to defend? Still more unnecessary does it appear to connect the oracular inspiration with the tales of modern mesmerism.[3] In either case the question must turn on the truth of the facts; and mesmerism is likely to fare but ill, if it cannot undergo the test of criticism with better success than the ancient oracles. To allege the introduction of Christianity as the sole cause for the failure of the oracles, while another had at least a co-ordinate influence, is scarcely consistent with a sound criticism. If Plutarch mentions that in his time the oracles were consulted only on private questions and for the interests of individuals, he was not speaking of a state of things for which Christianity alone was responsible. The decay and the extinction of Hellenic freedom and nationality sealed the doom of the Hellenic oracles. Henceforth they were of necessity confined to the solution of private difficulties, because all public action and all national enterprise was annihilated. The

to that which may be supposed to proceed from evil spirits, and to take no account of that better aspect of right moral teaching by which alone they could in the long run have maintained their influence through many centuries of years. See Grote, History of Greece, vol. v. p. 16.

[1] Epistle to the Corinthians, chap. xxv.

[2] See Alban Butler's Lives of the Saints: St. Zacharias, March 15.

[3] Rawlinson's Herodotus, vol. i. p. 188.

result, which may have been forced on by the preaching of the Gospel, was insured by the political degradation of the preceding ages. And when we speak of Hellenic oracles, we do in fact speak of all. The Roman and the Italian sought for aid and counsel not from the human mouthpiece of an unseen god, but from visible signs whether in the heavens or on the earth. He was under the sway of a sacerdotal system which was worked for purely political ends.

Manifold character of the Greek oracles.

But even in the days of their highest glory the action of the oracles was confessedly very varied. If the responses appeared sometimes to justify an unquestioning faith, there were others which were mere utterances of earthly fraud. With this changing and uncertain character, common caution would require very clear and forcible evidence, not of the truth of their predictions but of the fact of their enunciation, or, in other words, that they should be subjected to a test which can be met only by the testimony of contemporary writers. With such a criterion, there is perhaps not one oracular response of which we can affirm with any certainty that it belongs to the time in which it is alleged to have been uttered. We know that at the commencement of the Peloponnesian war the soothsayers fed the hopes and fears of their countrymen by such predictions; but, with one exception, we do not know the nature or the form of those prophecies. From this one (in which, however, we learn that there was a doubt as to the authority of the version), we know as a fact that Thucydides was acquainted before the time with the announcement that a Dorian war should come with either a famine or a plague.¹ The ambiguity, which made it applicable to other wars besides the one then beginning, tells in this instance its own tale. We also know that before the influx of the country people into the Athenian walls there was a line which warned them not to meddle with the Pelasgic ground ² ; but the faith which the great historian displays in this almost solitary instance was grounded on an idea of political prescience in the seer which was altogether his own. Of the few remaining oracles which are mentioned in his history, some belong to a time for which he had no contemporary evidence ³ ; while the greater number appear to be dictated under that foreign influence, supported by strong party feeling at home, which is betrayed by the promise of the god to aid the Spartans to the utmost throughout the war.⁴ In the case of Pleistoanax his restoration to his country is enforced by the threat that otherwise the Spartans should turn the earth with a silver ploughshare.⁵ The expression is held to mean simply the

---

[1] Thucydides, ii. 54. [2] Ibid. ii. 17.

[3] Among these are to be reckoned the answers given to the Athenian Kylon (i. 126), to the poet Alcmæon (ii. 202), to Hesiod (iii. 96).

[4] Thucydides, i. 118, 123 ; ii. 54.

[5] Thucydides, v. 16. See Dr. Arnold's note on the passage. In the time of Pleistoanax, the expression may have been equivalent to the Latin phrase "aureo hamo piscari." Some generations earlier it might have received some such accomplishment as the older oracle to the Spartans,

δώσω τοι Τεγέην τοσσίκροτον ὀρχήσασθαι
καὶ καλὸν πεδίον σχοίνῳ διαμετρήσασθαι.

Herodotus, i. 66.

payment of a heavy penalty. Two generations earlier, some literal fulfilment would probably have been invented for it; but Thucydides knew that the answer was given simply in furtherance of personal designs and as the discharge of a previous debt.

<small>Classification of the oracular responses.</small>

The same character and influence is prominent in not a few of the oracular responses which occur in the pages of Herodotus. In these, however, there is this difference, that we cannot ascertain the fact of their having been given at the time to which they are referred, or, at the least, that they were given in the form in which they have come down to us. They may indeed be classified under several heads, and they carry with them very different degrees of credibility. Some are mere puzzles wrought out by the ingenuity of a mythical age; some are nothing more than the expression of a shrewd and politic ambiguity. Others again serve simply for the carrying out of state intrigues, while another, and this the largest class, seems to be the form under which the events of which they speak were represented after their occurrence. And in all these, as there is certainly no heavenly inspiration, so neither is there any need to suppose that other influences were at work than those which produce falsehood, craft, or treachery in the great mass of mankind.

<small>1. Enigmatical answers.</small>

The strange tale which relates the discovery of the bones of Orestes[1] serves well to explain the way in which these oracular details grew up around popular legends. It may be impossible to trace out the process, but the result may be strictly compared with the di-

---

[1] Herodotus, i. 67.

dactic narratives which were associated with the names of Solon and of Crœsus, of Demaratus or Polycrates. The tale belongs to a war which precedes all contemporary history, and for which, at the utmost, nothing more can be claimed than a high degree of probability, while the subject of it is a man whose name and adventures are scarcely less mythical than those of Prometheus and Deucalion. In itself it is a mere riddle, and its object is to account for a result which is capable of another and a very simple explanation. To the same class belong the elaborate answers which illustrate the story of the Corinthian Kypselus[1], and the defeat of the Spartans by the men of Tegea[2]; and we set them down at once as the mythical form under which alone the popular mind could receive and retain the traditional history. But no such antecedent objections apply to the larger class of responses, which express nothing more than a shrewd and prudent ambiguity; and the fact of their delivery will be received without any excessive scepticism. No great risk of detection was incurred by the soothsayer who told Peisistratus, as he drew near to Athens to recover his lost power, that the net was spread out to receive its booty.[3] It was no unsafe prediction which told Crœsus that the passage of the Halys would be followed by the ruin of a great power.[4] A guarded calculation of probabilities suggested perhaps the greatest number of the answers which the god returned to the kings and chieftains who came to ask his will or learn their destiny. The wisdom which inspired the

II. Ambiguous answers.

[1] Herodotus, v. 92.
[2] Ibid. i. 62.
[3] Ibid. i. 66.
[4] Ibid. i. 53.

priestess at Delphi had not deserted the guardians of the Sibylline books who told Maxentius that, when he came to fight with Constantine, the enemy of the Romans should perish.[1] A prohibition might be safely given which was grounded on a known or suspected impossibility; and the name of Zeus might without fear be used to deter the men of Cnidus from their wish to convert a peninsula into an island.[2] Pictures of wealthy plains and fruitful flocks might well be held up as temptations to the men who were bidden to colonise the distant shores of the Libyan Kyrênê.[3] And this commoner method of dealing with important public or national questions may serve to indicate the almost universal method by which the doubts and troubles of private men were answered or evaded. There is no more reason to doubt that Crœsus consulted the god of Delphi than that the meanest Bœotian sought to learn his fate at the cavern of Trophonius; but a very clear contemporary proof would alone justify the belief that the later answers to Crœsus were ever delivered at all. The tales themselves betray a curious amount of latent scepticism. Before committing his faith to any, Crœsus puts all the oracles to a test which nothing but supernatural aid could enable them to meet successfully, and, with but two exceptions, we are told that all the answers were untrue.[4] The faith of Herodotus himself is grounded not on the uprightness and honesty of the divine interpreters, but simply on the

---

[1] Gibbon, Roman Empire, ch. xiv. Milman, History of Christianity, vol. ii. p. 349.
[2] Herodotus, i. 174. [3] Ibid. iv. 154, 157. [4] Ibid. i. 49.

wonderful minuteness of predictions whose subsequent fabrication it was scarcely possible for him to detect. With the tales of Crœsus and Mardonius and the detected forgeries of Onomacritus before him, he could scarcely have done more than express his reluctance to reject or to admit any scepticism in others, for predictions so distinct and unequivocal as those of Bakis.[1]

Yet more must his faith have been unconsciously shaken as he recurred to the political or private intrigues which the Delphian priestess had furthered with no unwilling aid. Chiefly by her instrumentality, if we are to believe the tale, the Alcmæonidæ brought about the overthrow of the sons of Peisistratus[2]; through her corruption Demaratus was driven from the Spartan throne to take refuge in the courts of Susa.[3] Such instances of utter venality may well make it a matter of wonder that any faith could have survived, even in the age of Herodotus, in oracles which could speak so corruptly or so falsely. Yet that faith was retained to many a later generation; and, if we have no reason to question its sincerity, we must look elsewhere for its justification. To suppose that any one could really have trusted an oracle because it solved a riddle of a tortoise and a ram, is not less absurd than incredible. The fable indicates a genuine conviction, and when his glory had departed from him, Crœsus admitted his own folly and the wisdom and goodness of the god.[4] But if the whole action of the oracles had been such as was exhibited in their corrupt or ambiguous responses,

IV. Answers extorted by political and personal influence.

V. Answers which enforce a moral principle.

[1] Herodotus, viii. 77.
[2] Ibid. v. 63.
[3] Ibid. vi. 66.
[4] Ibid. i. 91.

such faith must have been almost an impossibility. If they possessed any real influence, that influence must have been moral. They must have served, however feebly or fitfully, to uphold a higher standard of practice, a clearer distinction between right and wrong, before those who shrank from the former and sought to confound the latter. The known instances of such interference may be few; but their occurrence warrants the belief that there must have been many of which we know nothing; and we can be at no loss to account for the hold which they possessed over the minds of men, when we read such a tale as that of Glaucus, the son of Epikydes[1], and still more the parable which saved the life of Pactyas.[2] It must have been no light blessing which taught men, feebly perhaps, but still really, to restore to the debtor his pledge and to let the oppressed go free. An influence so gained it would be monstrous to set down to diabolical agency. It was an influence lawfully and righteously acquired, although it may have been unrighteously and corruptly exercised. We may be sure also that the general action of the oracles was of this kind; and when their authority began to decay, we may well believe with Dr. Arnold that in the general immorality which increased as the faith in the old mythology grew weaker, the change was greatly for the worse, and that, whatever may be the falsehood of the oracular predictions, "there are yet specimens of their moral doctrine preserved, which exhibit a purity and wisdom scarcely to be surpassed."[3]

[1] Herodotus, vi. 86. [2] Ibid. i. 159.
[3] Arnold, Later Roman Commonwealth, vol. ii. p. 397.

But, if the tales of Pactyas and Glaucus illustrate the beneficent action of the Hellenic oracles (and we may note that in the Italian divination this action is wholly wanting), those answers which seem to be fabrications after the fact are eminently deceptive and misleading. They are so interwoven with the whole thread of the tale, and furnish so often the very turning point of the narrative, that it becomes almost impossible for the historian to exclude them altogether from his survey of the time; and if on these grounds he rejects some, there is yet the tendency to accept others which rest on no better evidence. If we put aside the oracular answers and the didactic legends which surround Crœsus in his glory and his humiliation, the history of his reign becomes brief indeed. We may speak of the Lydian king who subdued the Asiatic Greeks, but whose yoke lay so light upon them that his conquest is not reckoned as the first subjugation of Ionia.[1] We may say that his

VI. Predictions made up after the event.

---

[1] Herodotus speaks of the conquest by Crœsus as a subjugation to tribute (κατεστράφατο ἐς φόρου ἀπαγωγήν), and so explains the meaning of his words that up to this time the Ionians had been free. Their self-government seems not in other respects to have been interfered with. Herodotus, i. 26. Grote, History of Greece, vol. iii. p. 353. Herodotus speaks of three Ionic conquests, the first being that of Crœsus (i. 92), the second taking place on the suppression of the revolt of Pactyas (i. 169). Grote, History of Greece, vol. iv. p. 273. The third ensued on the failure of the great revolt under Aristagoras (Herodotus, vi. 32). Yet this mere transference from Lydian to Persian rule, although not brought about by any special resistance of the Ionians themselves, was more truly a conquest than the comparatively nominal dependence to which Crœsus had reduced them. Their immediate revolt under Pac-

wealth and his power rendered a conflict with the growing empire of Persia inevitable, and that, whether from his own aggression or from the ambition of the Persian king, he was involved in a struggle which ended in his ruin. We may perhaps say also that, after the custom of Oriental conquest, he lived to be the friend and the counsellor of his conqueror; but anything beyond this becomes mere conjecture or fiction, when we have further acknowledged that the missions which he sent to Delphi may perhaps be considered historical, " though the oracular responses recited by Herodotus bear, for the most part, indubitable marks of subsequent fabrication."[1]

The oracles of little use as historical documents.

With a people whose form of thought was so strangely influenced by the mythical speech of earlier ages, it becomes especially difficult to mark any particular time as the beginning of authentic history. It may be safer to leave the question in uncertainty until we arrive at a period for which we have strictly contemporary evidence. In fixing on the first recorded Olympiad (or B.C. 776) as such a date, Mr. Grote admits that he may "appear lax and credulous rather than exigent or

tyas proves that it was so felt by them; and the expression of Herodotus (i. 99) may be interpreted as well of the transfer from Crœsus to Cyrus as of the original Lydian conquest. In vi. 32, he confines the first conquest to Crœsus; but there were really four conquests, unless we refuse to take into account that which followed on the fall of the Lydian dynasty, and which the Ionians clearly felt to be a real slavery.

[1] Sir G. C. Lewis, Credibility of Early Roman History, vol. ii. p. 525.

sceptical;"[1] and, although his singular powers of discernment have led him, in innumerable instances, to detect legend where others had seen history, and to place beyond doubt many points which others had left uncertain, yet he appears to have felt the temptation to make use of these oracular answers in his historical narrative, and sometimes to have yielded to it. At the least it is difficult to avoid the impression that he relates as facts not merely the mission of the Lydians to Delphi (for of this there is perhaps little doubt), but the answers which Herodotus places in the mouth of the priestess. This mission is placed in historical contrast with the advice of more prudent counsellors who warned Crœsus "that he had little to gain and much to lose by war with a nation alike hardy and poor."[2] And while marking the scepticism implied in the strange test of Crœsus, he wonders that it should have escaped the notice of Herodotus, who relates the judgment on Glaucus for having tested the oracle.[3] It is true, as Mr. Grote urges, that this scepticism is put forward by Xenophon as constituting part of the guilt of Crœsus; but it seems not less certain that Xenophon had lost that higher moral instinct which Herodotus retained comparatively uncorrupted. Like the men of Kymê when they were ordered to surrender Pactyas[4], Glaucus consulted the god on a simple question of primary

[1] History of Greece, vol. i. p. xl.
[2] Grote, History of Greece, vol. iv. p. 254.　　[3] Ibid.
[4] Mr. Grote regards the conduct of Aristodicus to ascertain the real mind of the oracle as a piece of "ingenuity." It ought surely to be regarded rather as an instance of a very deep moral faith. History of Greece, vol. iv. p. 271.

morality. The Kymæans sought to betray a suppliant, while Glaucus wished to justify his own dishonesty. The reply in each case harmonises singularly with the answer which the Moabitish soothsayer made to Balak. "Give up the suppliant and abide the consequence, that ye may learn how to come again with such a question," is the reply of the oracle at Branchidæ, and it differs little indeed in spirit from the words of Balaam that on the subject of sacrifice God had shown every man that which was good.[1] "To tempt the god with evasion of a debt is a sin as great as perjury," was the answer of the Delphian priestess to Glaucus, and it agrees strangely with the words of Butler while speaking of Balaam, that second thoughts on a plain matter of duty are a mere effort to explain it away.[2]

Oracles relating to

But not only do the several responses from Delphi

---

[1] It is well known that Bishop Butler, in his Sermon on the Character of Balaam, lays great stress upon the passage of Micah (in ch. vi.) as showing the nature of Balaam's moral convictions. In Dr. Smith's Dictionary of the Bible (s. v. Balaam), Bishop Butler's application of the words is asserted to be groundless; while it is maintained that the question and answer following the fifth verse are propounded not by the Moabitish seer but by the prophet himself. Such a conclusion will not much affect Bishop Butler's estimate of Balaam's character; but it seems to make the exhortation to remember the consultation of Balak an introduction to nothing: and unless the question and answer are referred to the Moabitish soothsayer and king, it is difficult to understand why the prophet should in this context ask his countrymen to remember Balak and Balaam, rather than any other enemies of the nation who are mentioned in the Pentateuch.

[2] Butler, Sermons (VII.), vol. ii. p. 85.

appear, in Mr. Grote's narrative, as substantial portions *the last dynasty of Lydian kings.* of the history of Crœsus: they are the moving causes of his military preparations and his political alliances.¹ The capture of Sardes on the fourteenth day of the siege is mentioned without a notice of the artificial chronology which balances it by a reign of fourteen years²; while the release of Crœsus and the subsequent favour shown to him by Cyrus are removed from the region of probabilities into that of certainty.³ It is, therefore, the less easy to see why the statement, that no one noticed the prophecy of vengeance on the fifth descendant of Gyges until after its fulfilment, should be any reason for concluding " that the history of the first Mermnad king is made up after the catastrophe of the last."⁴

It may perhaps be doubted whether the evidence is *Oracles relating to the taking of Athens by Xerxes.* sensibly greater for the oracles which came from Delphi to the Athenians before the battle of Salamis. In this case, as in that of Crœsus, the fact of the consultation is doubtless historical; and in both, the first answers, though very different in length, are simply ambiguous utterances, fully justified by the circumstances of the time. The question is, whether the subsequent details are equally true? In the advice of Timôn to the Athenians, when awestruck on the receipt of the first answer, Mr. Grote traces the underhand working of the leading Delphians on the priestess⁵; but we must suppose a further influence from Themistocles himself,

---

¹ Grote, History of Greece, vol. iv. p. 255, &c.
² Ibid. p. 259.   ³ Ibid. p. 260.
⁴ Ibid. p. 263.   ⁵ Ibid. vol. v. p. 82.

before we can account, on purely human grounds, for the special suggestion contained in the second response.[1] Mr. Grote, however, sees "every reason to accept the statement of Herodotus as true, respecting these oracles as delivered to the Athenians, and the debated interpretation of them. They must have been discussed publicly in the Athenian assembly, and Herodotus may have conversed with persons who had heard the discussion."[2] But while thus accepting this supernatural warrant for the adoption of a course of action in which Themistocles had previously determined to persevere, he doubts whether the oracle, which intimated that either Sparta must be conquered or a king of Sparta perish, was in existence before the battle of Thermopylæ.[3] In this case it could not possibly have furnished any motive for the conduct of Leonidas in the pass. Yet this Delphian response is represented as having moved him to keep his post, not less forcibly than the laws of his country and the shame which attends a leader who has failed.[4]

These answers do not affect the conduct of Themistocles.

But if the uncertainty which must continue to rest on all incidents connected with these oracular answers excludes from the domain of history much with which we may not part willingly, yet the strictest sifting will fail to reduce the early history of Athens to a level with the misty traditions of the Lydian dynasties. Crœsus himself, though unquestionably historical, is in his own

---

[1] The use, namely, of the happy-omened θείη in place of some such epithet as σχετλίη. Herodotus, vii. 143.
[2] History of Greece, vol. v. p. 84.
[3] Ibid. pp. 84, 85.   [4] Ibid. p. 124.

person a mere name.[1] The exquisite legends which invest that name with an undying charm spring altogether, as Mr. Grote has remarked, from the disposition to surround persons really historical with fictitious and fanciful details. All that we know of him and of his kingdom may be summed up in a few sentences, which must fail to bring before us one single life-like image. But when every mythical detail has been swept away, when all the marvels which gather round the glories of Salamis and Plataea have been banished from the mind, a light altogether more full and clear breaks upon the pre-eminent greatness of Themistocles. The keen discernment of all political contingencies, the marvellous power of shaping means to ends, the prudence to plan, the determined will to execute, all become the more conspicuous when every prodigy and mysterious portent has been cast out of the tale. In that border land between the mythical and historical ages, where truth and fable are either mingled together or lie side by side, it is scarcely possible to separate accurately the overgrowth of fiction which clings round the living tree, scarcely possible to determine how far such a man as Themistocles was rather a parent of the coming age than a child of the time that was passing away. It is hard to decide what measure of influence oracles and portents and prodigies had upon that commanding mind which bent all wills to its own; and perhaps it may be wiser to leave the question unanswered. Thus much only, perhaps, we may affirm, that of such influence there is little sign or none; that his career, as related by Herodotus, mar-

---

[1] Grote, History of Greece, vol. iii. pp. 202—205.

vellously agrees with the sketch of Thucydides; and
that every feature in his character points to the mental
condition of a later age. From the beginning of his
course to its close he exhibits that knowledge of the
real strength and weakness of Athens which marked,
perhaps still more wonderfully, the life and policy of
Pericles. The Delphian responses serve, in his case,
only to illustrate the method by which he guided the
religious prejudices or convictions of his countrymen,
and to contrast his position with that of the man who,
after him, raised to its greatest height the fabric of
Athenian power. Themistocles appeals, indeed, to the
sense and the courage of his fellow-citizens; but he
appeals also to the force of an epithet in the mysterious
verses of a Delphian priestess.[1] He will not let them
swerve from the path in which alone he sees hope and
safety; but he is compelled to extort a sanction for his
own decision from the same ambiguous authority. That
to these grounds of encouragement he must have added
arguments still more akin to those of Pericles, that he
must have convinced his countrymen, as he had convinced himself, of the stubborn vitality of Athens so
long as she continued in her own proper path, is certain
from the results which he brought about. The mental
condition of his time has deprived them of their prominence; but we may be sure that he realised their
future victory over the Persians as clearly as Pericles
saw that Athens must come out triumphant from the
struggle with Sparta, if she remained true to his counsels.[2] Pericles died with his power and influence almost

---

[1] Herodotus, vii. 143.   [2] Thucydides, ii. 65. 7.

unimpaired; but his warnings were unheeded. Themistocles achieved his gigantic task, and died with a traitor's fame in the land of the barbarian.

He lived before the full light of contemporary history. Whether that light would have removed some part of the dark cloud which rests upon his memory, is a question of practical not less than of historical interest. The condition of Athens, during the generations immediately preceding the really historical age, may favour, however slightly, an attempt to answer it. Of the motives and actions even of the best among the barbarians we can speak only with doubt and much uncertainty, as long as we are confined to pictures drawn from barbarian sources. But in the Hellenic world, and still more in Athens, there was much in the words of poets and statesmen to raise the standard of historical truth; there was more, in the order and freedom of their political life, to insure something like consistency of character, and to preclude any incredible abandonment of feelings and convictions which have grown up with our youth and been strengthened with every year of our manhood. And in this Hellenic world we have to deal not with the secrets of Eastern palaces or the dark mazes of Persian iniquity, but with a people whose poets had shed some light even on times long since passed away; for whom Tyrtæus had invested the Messenian wars with something of reality; for whom Solon had urged on the struggle with Megara for that little island which was now to be immortalised by the victory of Themistocles and the tragedy of Æschylus.

Poetical literature of the Greeks before the historical age.

CHAP. V.

ON THE CAUSES AND INCIDENTS OF THE PERSIAN WAR.

Authority of Herodotus in Greek and barbarian history respectively.

If a few sentences may comprise all that we can be said to know of the history of Crœsus, the accounts given by Herodotus of times and countries still more distant can rest upon no surer foundation. Oral narratives, obtained from people of whose language he was ignorant, and which he could not compare with the statements of other historians, cannot be expected to furnish very safe grounds for historical conclusions. His own scrupulous fidelity was no safeguard against the misrepresentations or falsehoods of his informants; and on his authority alone but little faith could have been placed in the lists and exploits of Babylonian, Assyrian, Median, and Egyptian kings. A comparison of his narrative with the historical books of the Old Testament and with the statements of writers varying so greatly in degree of credibility as Ctesias, Manetho, and Berosus, may prove to us not only his unwearied diligence in amassing his materials, but the general correctness of the information so gained, as well as the perfect fidelity of all his descriptions. Still (after every acknowledgment has been made for the light thrown on these distant times by the recent discoveries of

Eastern excavators) the scantiness of our knowledge of the great Oriental dynasties becomes apparent on a perusal of the essays which Mr. Rawlinson has appended to his translation of the first book of Herodotus. The monuments of Borsippa and Khorsabad fail to carry us beyond bare probability or mere conjecture in many important parts of the history; and the testimony of Babylonish bricks has to be filled up by the statements of writers, of whom some at least cannot claim on these subjects any higher authority than Herodotus himself. It is not likely that future discoveries will present us with more detailed accounts than those of Sennacherib and Nebucadnezzar; and even of these we have but the driest of chronicles, which attest their greatness but fail to give us any living picture of the time. Probably even the shattered relics of their cities and palaces may enable us to realise their social life better than annals, however elaborate, which illustrate the monotony of Oriental despotism. That these discoveries have placed beyond question some points which the conflicting statements of historians had left uncertain,—that they have enabled us to fill up many important gaps,—that they have corroborated historical statements in the Old Testament, and established the authority of Herodotus, and still more of Berosus and Manetho, over the fictions and falsehoods of Ctesias, are benefits which cannot be undervalued; but the results so attained are meagre indeed when contrasted with a page of living history. Of their general poverty Mr. Rawlinson's Essays furnish abundant proof. Of the earlier kings little more than the names have been disinterred from the Babylonish monuments; and of these many are read but imper-

Historical value of recent Assyrian discoveries.

fectly, or are altogether illegible.[1] Of the long line of kings who followed Kudurmapula, we are told that "little is to be learnt from the inscriptions with regard either to their foreign or their domestic history,"[2] while "nothing certain has been ascertained" "on the subject of the Arabian dynasty which, according to Berosus, succeeded the Chaldæans on the Euphrates."[3] The same darkness still covers the origin of Assyrian independence; and a list of mere names is all that we can be said to possess until we reach the days of Tiglath-Pileser.[4] Passing over the scanty chronicles of his descendants, which have been obtained from bricks and vases, we derive from the same sources a knowledge somewhat more full, but still grievously scanty, of the new dynasty of Sargon.[5] The annals as yet discovered tell us only of the first eight out of the twenty-two years which made up the reign of his son Sennacherib[6]; nor do they give us any information different in kind to that which we possess of earlier periods. It is not far otherwise with the dynasties of Babylon. The era of Nabonassar, not being the expression of any great astronomical facts, must be taken to mark the commencement of its greatness; but we do not know whether he acquired regal power or left it to his children; and Mr. Rawlinson perceives no light in the history of his successors, until the Assyrian Esarhaddon took up his abode in Babylon, and so caused the Jewish king Manasseh to be brought before him there instead of at Nineveh.[7] The period of its highest grandeur is marked by the names

[1] Rawlinson's Herodotus, vol. i. pp. 440, 441. [2] Ibid. p. 447.
[3] Ibid. p. 449.   [4] Ibid. p. 467.   [5] Ibid. p. 473.
[6] Ibid. p. 476.   [7] Ibid. pp. 481, 482.

of Nabopolassar and his son Nebucadnezzar; but of the former we have but scanty historical notices, of the latter a well-detailed list of expeditions and conquests, without any of those personal characteristics which mark the narrative of the book of Daniel. Less clear are the notices, furnished by the inscriptions, of his feeble and degenerate successors[1], and the details of the fall of Babylon before the army of Cyrus have to be obtained by a comparison of less convincing and trustworthy authorities.

But the admission must be made that if walls, bricks, and vases have yielded at best a scanty harvest, they present to us an eminently plausible, if not a perfectly authentic history. A narrative more completely divested of all improbable matter could scarcely have proceeded from Thucydides himself. The ruins of Nineveh and Babylon have yielded up fragments of a history as destitute of marvellous and supernatural incidents as that which the great historian of Athens has extracted from the tale of Troy; and these fragments have over this plausible fabrication of Thucydides the immeasurable superiority that they are genuine expressions of the men who did the deeds of which they have preserved the memory.

Character of the historical information obtained from them.

And thus from the narrative of Herodotus must be rejected at once the abundant personal details, the rich luxuriance of fable which sheds on his Eastern stories their vivid and gorgeous colouring. It is but a poor exchange for these splendid fictions to speak of a Median dynasty which was displaced by a line of Persian

Its bearing upon the history of Herodotus.

---

[1] Rawlinson's Herodotus, vol. i. p. 517, &c.

kings, of expeditions against the monarchs of Lydia and Babylon from which the tales of the piety of Crœsus and the treachery of Zopyrus are rigidly excluded.[1] Yet this dry skeleton is all that remains after his records of the Median and Persian kingdoms have undergone the test of historical criticism. The legend of the birth of Cyrus and his early years then points only to that common yet mysterious source from which have sprung kindred tales in many lands which could not have borrowed from each other's wealth. It is an offshoot from that ancient tree which has produced the legends of Romulus and Chandragupta, of Bellerophon and Kunala, of Sinbad and Aristomenes.[2] The rise of

---

[1] Rawlinson's Herodotus, vol. i. p. 526.

[2] The points of resemblance between the tales of Cyrus and of Romulus have been traced out by Sir G. C. Lewis (Credibility of Early Roman History, vol. i. p. 408). It is also true that some other Roman stories are strikingly like tales which occur in Greek writers; among these specially may be compared the tale of Sextus Tarquinius at Gabii with the treachery of Zopyrus at Babylon, and the counsel given to Sextus by his father with that which Herodotus puts into the mouth of Thrasybulus (v. 92; Livy, i. 54). The tale of the Horatii and Curiatii has a suspicious likeness to that of Othryades (Livy, i. 24; Herodotus, i. 82). But, after all, it would seem that, except where the evidence of imitation is overwhelming, the idea of borrowing or stealing from the legendary wealth of other nations must be abandoned. Sir G. Lewis refers to a passage of Gibbon (Decline and Fall, ch. xlii.) in which the progenitor of the Turks is shown to have been exposed in infancy with the same good fortune as Cyrus or Romulus. The resemblances of national legends in the most distant times and countries furnished the groundwork of the science of comparative mythology; but it would be a miserable waste of ingenuity if we should seek

Deiokes and the Median power expresses only the common idea of the primary origin of all sovereignty in any age or country.[1] And these tales are constructed to fasten on one or the other version a charge of wilful copying. Such a charge becomes ludicrous when applied to such tales as those of Joseph, of Bellerophon, and of Kunala the son of Asoka, and is scarcely less absurd when brought against those of Samson, Heracles, and the Persian Rustam, of the Egyptian Rhampsinitus and the Arabian story of the Forty Thieves, and still more against another tale which closely agrees with another part of the legend of Romulus. The discovery of the royal birth of Cyrus and of the twin founders of Rome is found in the legend of Chandragupta, along with differences of detail which preclude all possibility of imitation. See Max Müller, History of Sanskrit Literature, p. 290. Such theories of theft or forgery hang, as Mr. Dasent has well remarked, "on what may be called a single thread." (Popular Tales from the Norse, p. xliii.) Tales which account for facts that might strike an ordinary observer in any country, are found in the most distant lands to turn on one and the same incident, where no communication subsequent to the dispersion of the original race can by any possibility be proved. The Norse story which explains how the bear lost his tail, is identical with the African story which recounts how the hyena fell into the same condition. The absence of a tail in both might well strike a race of hunters; but Mr. Dasent puts a puzzling question to those who uphold a theory of transference or imitation, when he asks how we are "to explain the fact that both Norseman and African account for it in the same way,—that both owe their loss to the superior cunning of another animal?" (Popular Tales from the Norse, p. li.) The remnants of a common store exist among Aryans and Turanians, among Greeks and Teutons, Hindus, Arabs, and African Bechuanas; and they seem to lead us, more rapidly almost than the fragments of primæval language, to the common stock of the widely severed races of Europe, Africa, and Asia.

[1] Grote, History of Greece, vol. iii. p. 310. Niebuhr Lectures

on the same system of artificial chronology on which have been framed the early annals of Etruria, of Egypt, of Britain, and of Rome.[1] They exhibit popular notions of national character; but these notions are not always consistent. To Cyrus the Persians owed that exemption from tribute which they dignified with the name of freedom; but although with him they emerged from a state of poverty and hardship, their old way of life, we are told in one legend, was not abandoned. Although the story of Astyages represents Cyrus as tempting the Persians by a day of feasting after one of toil, yet, when the Lydian Sandanis seeks to deter Crœsus from his desperate enterprise, he speaks of the Persians as of men inured to all severity, whose garments are made of leather, who eat whatever they can get, who drink no wine, and have no figs or anything else that is good.[2] But when the ravenous greed of Cyrus drives him against the land of the Massagetæ, the contrast is transferred to the wandering hordes of Queen Tomyris. It is the entreaty of Crœsus that he should seek to tempt their poverty by the sight of wine and dainties such as they had never seen[3]; and Queen Tomyris completes the contrast when in her bitter reproach she charges Cyrus with murdering her son by that juice of the grape with which Persians were wont to fill themselves till they were mad.[4]

Historical residuum

With Cyrus, then, not less than with Crœsus, the full

on Ancient History, vol. i. p. 35) thinks that the legend indicates the manner in which a Median (not a Greek) may have conceived the origin of regal power.

[1] See note 2, p. 260.
[2] Herodotus, i. 71.   [3] Ibid. i. 207.   [4] Ibid. i. 212.

stream of legend shrinks, as we seek for historical *In the legends of Cyrus.* truth, to a shallow and scanty rill. His whole personal history falls to the ground; there remains a bare recital of conquests over Median, Lydian, and Babylonish kings, as well as over nations so distant and so little known that it becomes rash to determine their extent or their results. There were tales which, in place of the draught of blood, made him die peacefully in his bed at Pasargada.[1]

The same luxuriance of legendary detail has overspread the strange history of the reign of Cambyses, of the murder of his brother Smerdis, of the usurpation of the Magi and their overthrow by the seven Persians. *The reign of Cambyses and the Magian usurpation.* Something of the history of this time we learn from the inscriptions at Behistun[2]; but are the words there carved on the rocks to measure the trust with which we may receive this narrative? If they teach us that this usurpation was a religious and not, as has been generally supposed, a national rebellion, they compel us not less to reject almost every portion of the story as given by Herodotus. Of the mutilation of the Magian by Cambyses, of his discovery through the agency of Phædymê (which Mr. Grote recounts as historical incidents[3]), of the conspiracy of the Seven (which Niebuhr interprets to mean a confederacy of the seven

[1] Xenophon, Cyropædeia, viii. 7. It might however be said that Xenophon invented the version which he has so well worked up at the close of his historical romance.

[2] See the inscription as given by Mr. Rawlinson, in his Herodotus, vol. ii. p. 590.

[3] History of Greece, vol. iv. p. 301.

Y

families which formed the original nobility of Persia[1]), the inscription at Behistun says absolutely nothing. To the version of Herodotus, who represents Darius as the last who joined the conspirators, it gives the most complete contradiction. Darius asserts unequivocally that no one dared to say anything concerning the Magian until he arrived.[2] To the seven he makes no reference, unless possibly in the words that "with his faithful men" he fell on the Magian and slew him; and the legend of his election by the trick of his groom is put aside by his assertion that the empire of which Gomates dispossessed Cambyses had from the olden time been in the family of Darius. The incidents so rejected are the chief and essential features in the narrative of Herodotus; and the rock inscription must, on the supposition of their truth, have made to them at least some passing allusion, if not some direct reference.

The conspiracy of the seven Persians.

The debates of the seven conspirators fall before another test. As speeches of Oriental chieftains, they are an impossibility. They have not even the merit of the legend of Deiokes, in so far as it exhibits the possible origin of despotism in Media or in any other country, while their expression of Hellenic thought[3]

[1] Lectures on Ancient History, vol. i. p. 131.
[2] Rawlinson's Herodotus, vol. ii. p. 594.
[3] "The debates of the conspirators," Mr. Grote remarks, "may be found recounted by Herodotus with his usual vivacity, but with no small addition of Hellenic ideas as well as of dramatic ornament."—*History of Greece*, vol. iv. p. 301. It is curious to note the firmness with which, in this instance, Herodotus insists on the truth of a tale which to Hellenic readers might appear incredible: ἐλέχθησαν λόγοι ἄπιστοι μὲν ἐνίοισι Ἑλλήνων, ἐλέχθησαν δ' ὦν (iii. 80).

becomes extravagantly absurd when put into the mouths of men whose sole idea of freedom lay in immunity from tribute and taxation.[1] The same vein of Greek idea, with its keenness and its beauty, runs through the exquisite tale of the council at Susa, and is seen most of all in the wise words of Artabanus.[2]

But if such a monument as the inscription at Behistun overthrows on such important points a series of narratives in the history of Herodotus, and if other large portions relating to the fortunes of the Persian kings are to be put aside as mere reflections of Hellenic feeling, alike absurd and impossible in the East, with what trust may we receive any story which paints the course of Eastern intrigue and illustrates the secret history of a Persian or Assyrian court? for, with the exception of the march of armies and tales of foreign conquests, the annals of these courts are only a secret history. Hints of execrable cruelties may force their way into the outer air; pictures of fancied luxury and generosity may light up the dim recesses of the hidden harem; but what reason have we to suppose that of any single motive we shall have a faithful description, of any single deed a true report? The answer to this doubt must seriously affect no small part of the tale of the great Persian war.

If such tales as those which describe the conspiracy of the Seven or the great council of Xerxes betray their

Difficulty of ascertaining facts in all Eastern history.

Plausible tales of Persian intrigue.

---

[1] Herodotus, i. 126.
[2] Ibid. vii. 10. Mr. Grote holds that "the speech which Herodotus puts into the mouth of Artabanus is that of a thoughtful and religious Greek."—*History of Greece*, vol. v. p. 10.

fictitious origin by their utter incongruity with Persian character, there are others so strictly Oriental in their colouring as to come before us with a specially deceptive force. Great enterprises, happy or ruinous in their issue, are made to spring from some passing whim or interested motive of a favourite wife or slave. The vexation of a moment is represented as giving birth to gigantic expeditions without a thought of their result. This eminently plausible form, assumed by the tales of Demokedes and Histiæus, tempts us almost to think that pictures so true to Persian character cannot be wholly destitute of historical value.

<small>Utter uncertainty in the details of Persian narratives.</small> It is a necessary evil of all traditionary history that it imposes on us the constant task of sifting evidence and balancing probabilities. The remark may appear almost absurd. Yet, if even contemporary records so frequently involve the same necessity, it must be the crowning difficulty of those times which with a mixture of undoubted historical facts mingle up the falsehood or fictions inseparable from any lengthened oral tradition. The different impressions which even eye-witnesses receive of the same events and the same scenes, the effect of time whether in enhancing or weakening those impressions in the same mind, the irresistible temptation or the unconscious tendency to vary the colouring of a story at each successive recital, must create a very strong reluctance to admit the truthfulness of vivid or minute detail in any but a written contemporary narrative. This reluctance must pass into positive unbelief, if the tradition involves an imputation of improbable or unaccountable motives or assigns some secondary and irrelevant causes where more simple

and forcible motives are not wanting. There is nothing to startle us when we meet with instances even of unbounded influence exercised by Oriental wives or slaves. There is nothing improbable in the tale that Darius was incited by his wife Atossa to an attack on Athens and Sparta.[1] Atossa, as Mr. Grote has remarked, is the Sultana Validi of the ancient Persian empire[2]; and we may well believe that (to use the expression of Herodotus) she had all the power.[3] But the admission of her influence need not of necessity lead us to admit motives which are improbable in the case of Demokedes, which are more unlikely still in the case of Histiæus, and almost pass the bounds of credibility in that of Themistocles. In this episode of Demokedes there is confessedly some mixture of legend; but, while admitting this, Mr. Grote regards it as "a history well deserving of attention, even looking only to the liveliness of the incidents, introducing us as they do into the full movements of the ancient world."[4] These incidents he sees no reason to doubt; but the very fulness of the revelation may lead us to question whether these are the genuine movements which stirred the ancient world. Polycrates is undoubtedly an historical person, but the tale of his life is in some part a romance to illustrate an ethical or theological theory; and the image of Demokedes already grows more indistinct, when we see that his career is altogether more legendary than that of his master. That he was carried to Susa, and that he there acquired influence

The story of Demokedes.

[1] Herodotus, iii. 134. [3] History of Greece, vol. iv. p. 341.
[2] Herodotus, vii. 3. [4] History of Greece, vol. iv. p. 349.

first over Darius, then over his wife, are statements fully probable, yet requiring some better confirmation before we can pronounce them to be absolutely certain. We need some surer evidence than that which we now possess, to justify the belief that Demokedes "cared not what amount of risk he brought upon his country in order to procure his own escape from a splendid detention at Susa."[1] If the facts could be proved, Demokedes stands convicted of a sufficiently dark treachery; but it is easier to prove his guilt than to show the necessity of the motive. In spite of the legend, Mr. Grote believes that Polycrates and not Amasis broke off the friendship which existed between them.[2] The aggressive necessities of all Eastern empires in their growth explain adequately the collision of the Lydian and Persian kings. The fall of Crœsus had brought the Persians into direct conflict with the Asiatic Greeks, and through these a struggle was, from the first, inevitable with their kinsmen in the West. Atossa needed not the words of Demokedes to make her seek Hellenic maidens for her slaves.[3] For the rest we can say but little. The inscription at Behistun scarcely bears out the rebuke of Atossa for the unwarlike inactivity of Darius in the first or in any other part of his reign. Yet she may have urged him to undertake at once a task which he had desired to postpone till he

---

[1] Grote, History of Greece, vol. iv. p. 350.
[2] Ibid. p. 325. Cf. Sir G. C. Lewis, Credibility of Early Roman History, vol. ii. p. 519.
[3] Herodotus, iii. 134. For the strong sarcasm of these touches, see Grote, History of Greece, vol. iv. p. 346.

had reduced the wandering hordes of the Scythians. She may have persuaded him to send Demokedes; and the Periplus of the Ægæan and Adriatic coasts may have been made by the Persians who were charged to take him home. All these things are possible, some of them even probable; but we cannot safely affirm more, or impute to Demokedes an attempt to precipitate the power of Persia upon Greece, while the city, to which the subsequent repulse of Xerxes was almost wholly owing, still lay under the tyranny of the Peisistratidæ.[1]

Still more full of contradictions or impossibilities is the tale of the Scythian expedition. No light is thrown upon it by the inscriptions at Behistun: but Herodotus speaks of two pillars on which Darius engraved the names of those tribes and nations which formed his army[2]; and if, as seems likely, he speaks from personal knowledge, the fact of the expedition and of the passage of the Bosporus is established. But it may yet be doubted whether the sequel of the tale is reported with any degree of truth. The knowledge of the Greeks must undoubtedly have been bounded by the Danube; and all the incidents for which they were indebted to Persian or Scythian informants may at once be put aside. For those which are stated to have occurred whether on the banks of the Danube or at the Thracian Bosporus, we have to bear in mind the exaggeration or inconsistency of narratives handed down by word of mouth, even where the speakers have no intention to

The Scythian expedition of Darius.

[1] Grote, History of Greece, vol. iv. p. 350, &c.
[2] Herodotus, iv. 87.

deceive or mislead. Mr. Grote lays much stress "on the personal knowledge of the Milesian historian Hecatæus, who took an active part in the Ionic revolt a few years afterwards, and who may perhaps have been personally engaged in the expedition."[1] Even if the conjecture could be verified, Sir G. Lewis has remarked the absence of any proof that he included a narrative of the Scythian expedition in any of his writings.[2] But if the tale of the adventures in Scythia be "nothing better than a perplexing dream," what sufficient evidence is there that we re-enter "the world of reality" on the north bank of the Danube?[3] If the story of the disgraceful retreat carries with it a strong appearance of improbability, or at least of exaggeration, many of the incidents connected with the bridge across the Danube are deprived of all historical value. If there is no evidence that the Persians reached the river in utter defeat, with a merciless enemy close at their heels, there is no need to suppose a haste to cross the river so pressing as to make it impossible to wait till the day had dawned.[4] Still less is it necessary, with the noise of an army in disorderly retreat, to introduce the Egyptian herald with his stentorian voice to rouse the attention of Histiæus.[5] In the debates which the Scythians caused among the guardians of the bridge, we cannot decide what amount there may be of exaggeration, or possibly of wilful falsehood. If they occurred, the

[1] History of Greece, vol. iv. p. 368.
[2] Credibility of Early Roman History, vol. ii. p. 508.
[3] History of Greece, vol. iv. p. 361.
[4] Herodotus, iv. 140.   [5] Ibid. iv. 141.

Ionians undoubtedly lost, by their refusal to unloose the bridge, an opportunity of inflicting a signal blow on the Persian power; but it is not easy to see why the death of Darius should have emancipated them from Persian dominion, or more than temporarily deferred the invasion of Greece, when the death even of Cyrus himself, after humiliating defeat in an enemy's country, had no permanent influence on the aggressive designs of the Persian kings. But, apart from any refusal to leave Darius to his fate by abandoning the bridge, Histiæus may without difficulty have done such good service as well to deserve the grateful return which he is said to have received. And Miltiades may easily have given so much offence to the Persians as to render a retreat from the Chersonesus prudent or necessary, without being known as the giver of advice, a compliance with which must have consigned the whole Persian army to destruction.[1] And in such a case it is just possible that an incursion of the Scythians may have hastened a resolution which other circumstances rendered advisable.

[1] Mr. Grote seems to attribute to Dr. Thirlwall a stronger acquiescence than is warranted by his words, in the story that Miltiades left the Chersonesus to avoid the Scythians. History of Greece, vol. ii. p. 371. Dr. Thirlwall merely expresses his doubt that Miltiades could, after his alleged conduct at the bridge, have any cause to fear the Scythians. But he also draws from the narrative of the conquest of Lemnos reasons for thinking that he might have given offence to the Persian government quite unconnected with his proposal to unloose and destroy the bridge, and that on this account only he abandoned the Chersonesus. History of Greece, vol. ii. Appendix 2, on the conduct ascribed to Miltiades in the Scythian campaign of Darius.

The removal of the Pæonians.

The forcible transportation of a people from one land to another is in full accordance with the character of Eastern governments. But if there is nothing in itself improbable in the removal of many of the Pæonians by Megabazus, can it safely be stated as an historical fact that Darius had been induced to give the order by seeing at Sardes a Pæonian maiden who, with a vessel on her head, led a horse to water and spun flax all at the same time?[1]

The story of Histiæus.

Nor is any surer ground furnished by the strange tale of Histiæus. The gratitude of Darius, it is said, gave him the territory of the Edonian Myrkinus for the purpose of founding a city.[2] Such an undertaking, in such a country, implied of necessity the erection of strong walls as a mere measure of self-defence. Nor is it easy to see how, if left to himself in his Thracian home, Histiæus could ever have become really formidable to the Persian king. Still, for the offence of doing that which the gift of Darius wholly authorised him to do, he is, at the instigation of Megabazus, enticed away to Susa, and there made an unwilling partaker of royal magnificence and luxury. By night and by day the thought of the freedom which he had lost oppressed him. Scheme after scheme for escape from thraldom passed through his mind, but the fear of detection made him abandon all. Like Demokedes, he remained in misery at Susa until he was cheered by the happy thought that he might perhaps secure his freedom merely by the ruin of his country. By a chance still more happy, his message,

---

[1] Herodotus, v. 13. Grote, History of Greece, vol. iv. p. 372.
[2] Herodotus, v. 11: πόλιν κτίσαι.

written on the head of his slave, reached his kinsman on the sea-coast just when other forcible reasons had decided him to take the step which Histiæus in pure selfishness urged upon him.[1] But the intrigues of the Naxian exiles with Aristagoras[2], while they furnish an occasion for Persian intervention, do not in reality explain its cause. Their influence with the tyrant of Miletus would have availed them little with the Persian satrap, apart from other reasons which determined him to take an active part against the Western Greeks. But that which Artaphernes must at once have refused to the mere prayer of some homeless oligarchs, he grants without hesitation to the exiles of the house of Peisistratus.[3] The counsels of Hippias had long since filled him with the hope of bringing Athens itself under Persian rule; and his restoration to the power which he had lost was welcomed as the means not so much of subverting a free constitution as of extending the dominion of the great king. Henceforth the idea of Hellenic conquest became a religious passion, not less than a political purpose. It led Artaphernes to insist on the reinstatement of Hippias, when the Athenian ambassadors came to plead the cause of their city against him.[4] It moved Darius not less than his satrap to embrace eagerly the proposals of Aristagoras for an expedition nominally against Naxos, really against the European Greeks.

In the expulsion of Hippias and his abode at Sigeium,

---

[1] Herodotus, v. 35.   [2] Ibid. v. 30.
[3] Ibid. v. 96. Grote, History of Greece, vol. iv. p. 379.
[4] Herodotus, v. 96. Grote, ibid.

Hippias in the schemes of Aristagoras.

we have the determining cause of all the efforts whether of Darius or of Xerxes. It is a cause which renders the selfish treachery of Histiæus utterly unnecessary, even if it cannot be urged with equal force against the legend of Demokêdês. The recesses of a Persian palace are not less an unknown land than the vast Scythian deserts beyond the Danube. From them issue the dark waters of legend and fiction, mingling themselves with the stream of genuine history or flowing by its side. But we may hold ourselves, with greater truth, to enter on the world of reality in the traditional history of the Asiatic Greeks, than when Darius returned from the Scythian wilderness to the bridge which the Ionians were guarding. We may believe that Histiæus was carried by Darius to Susa; we may believe that he was sent down to the coast when the failure of the Naxian scheme seemed likely to drive Aristagoras to revolt. But the whole intervening narrative must come from a Persian source; and it may be hard to show why such testimony should be admitted, when other calculations might justify the resolution of Darius. It is unnecessary to impute any pure patriotism to a tyrant; it may be impossible to know whether Histiæus had resolved on his future course before he reached Ionia. But Darius had no reason to suspect active resistance from the man who had rendered him such signal service on the banks of the Danube; and a natural impulse to employ Histiæus to check disaffection could scarcely be charged with folly. His subsequent conduct is easily explained without any reference to premeditated rebellion. The suspicions of Artaphernes would naturally lead him to connect the acts of Aristagoras with the counsels of his kinsman, while the expression of his doubts might determine him to take part in a rebellion which he found himself unable to repress.[1] The tale of his home-sickness and his selfish stratagem introduce a superfluous machinery into the narrative: the authority for these incidents is worth nothing, and it is not professed that Darius himself gave credit to the idea of such overstrained and needless cunning.

If, again, the fact of the Naxian expedition may be accepted as historical, less reliance can be placed on the circumstantial narrative which explains its failure. The details are suspiciously minute, and Megabates is represented as acting on motives scarcely less perplexing than those of Histiæus. The report of a spy or a deserter is not incredible even under the conditions of scanty intercourse which kept asunder the islanders from the Asiatic Greeks. But whether here or in the subsequent and more authentic narrative of the Persian struggle, from the tale of Marathon downwards, legendary details and episodes are mingled with genuine history. The task of separating the one from the other may not always be easy; but the process of sifting the grain from the chaff need not leave us with the worthless possibilities which may lie at the bottom of the tale of Troy or of such legends as those of Histiæus and Demokêdês. Some suspicion may attach to highly wrought detail in a narrative which for many years must have been preserved by mere oral tradition; but even the statements which maintain that the Athenians were the first who

The expedition to Naxos.

---

[1] Herodotus, vi. 1, &c.

were not dismayed at the sight of the Persian dress, or that Samos and the Pillars of Heracles were held to be equally distant from Attica or Salamis, show less of exaggeration than may at first sight appear.[1] Incidents become less trustworthy in the measure in which an epical handling of the tale becomes prominent. The efforts of Hippias had probably excited in the mind of Darius a greater hatred of the Athenians than can have been produced by the scanty aid which they afforded to the Ionians, the special objects of his anger. But the first open conflict of Athenians with Persians was an occasion which could not be lightly passed by; and the accidental burning of Sardes is connected directly

[1] With Colonel Mure, in his Critical History of the Literature of Ancient Greece, vol. iv. pp. 405-6, Mr. Rawlinson thinks that these expressions are rhetorical exaggerations and may be deservedly reprehended. (Herodotus, vol. i. p. 103.) The former appears indeed a strange phrase after the history of the Ionic revolt: yet the account seems to show little for the courage of the Greeks when face to face in the field with the Persians; and the Athenians, the representatives of the Western Greeks, won no laurels in the ill-advised expedition to Sardes. The second Mr. Grote (History of Greece, vol. v. p. 201) does not consider as a proof either of exaggeration or of geographical ignorance: he thinks that "no inferences of this kind ought to be founded upon it," but that "it marks fear of an enemy's country which they had not been accustomed to visit, and where they could not calculate the risk beforehand, rather than any serious comparison between one distance and another. Speaking of our forefathers, such of them as were little used to the sea, we might say, 'A voyage to Bordeaux or Lisbon seemed to them as distant as a voyage to the Indies,'—by which we should merely affirm something as to their state of feeling, not as to their geographical knowledge."

with the fight at Marathon and at Salamis. On the Ionians Darius bestows no thought; but before every meal the voice of his slave bids him remember the wrongs which he has suffered at the hands of the Athenians.[1]

Still against these distant foes his vengeance is allowed to slumber. In spite of the angry outburst which made the reduction of Ionia of less moment than the punishment of the Athenians, the efforts of Darius are confined to the former. The details of the history are not free from the special difficulties which are found in the chronicles of a people so destitute of historical sense as the Persians, as well as from other difficulties which the historian Hecataeus probably never attempted to remove. Not only do the numbers of the Phœnician fleet express, as do all Oriental figures, the idea of absolute completeness and irresistible force[2], but the men of towns so important as Ephesus, Colophon, Lebedus, and Eræ, take no part, apparently, in the common efforts of their kinsmen.[3] The Ephesians even cut off the Chians who fled from Ladé, as thieves who had entered their land to carry off women in the time of their solemn festival. The brief splendour of the Ionic revolt was closing in darkness and disaster. The Phokæan Dionysius flies in utter despair to Sicily.[4] The cities of the islands and on the mainland are pillaged and destroyed; and the future victor of Marathon escapes hardly with his

The Ionian revolt.

---

[1] Herodotus, v. 105.   [2] Ibid. vi. 9.
[3] Thucydides, viii. 14.   Grote, History of Greece, vol. iv. p. 412.
[4] Herodotus, vi. 17.

own life, and leaves his son in the enemy's hand to become a father of Persian slaves.[1]

The taking of Miletus.
The lost drama of Phrynichus might possibly have explained the reason for that abandonment of the Ionic cause by the Athenians which Mr. Grote attributes to the desertion of their Asiatic allies, and which certainly sealed the fate of the Ionic rebellion.[2] It might also have taught us the nature of those evils or misfortunes the remembrance of which induced the Athenians to punish the poet with a heavy fine. But although the subjects of tragedy had hitherto been chosen mainly, if not altogether, from the old legends or theogonies, it may be doubted whether their resentment was caused by any effort on the part of the poet to interest his audience in Persian success and Grecian suffering[3], or by any dread of similar disasters for themselves, so much as by the intimation that the fall of Miletus was in reality chargeable to them. Apart from this consciousness of guilt or weakness, the picture of Hellenic misfortunes could have roused them only to more determined resistance, and stirred them under disappointment or defeat with an enthusiasm not less deep and keen than that with which, after the victory at Salamis, they drank in the words of Æschylus.

The treatment of the Persian envoys at Athens and Sparta.
The knowledge that we are not reading a strictly contemporary narrative may reasonably lead us to question even trivial points of detail, as we remember the almost irresistible temptation under which all labour to vary such details in successive narrations of the

[1] Herodotus, vi. 41.
[2] History of Greece, vol. iv. p. 392.
[3] Ibid. p. 419.

same story. Among the many perplexing statements in the history of the Persian war, not the least remarkable is the occasional vehemence displayed by men who for the most part were little chargeable with any furious and unreasoning valour. The subsequent conduct of the Athenians exhibits nothing inconsistent with the tale that they threw into a pit the heralds who came to ask earth for King Darius.[1] But neither their pride as the acknowledged heads of the Hellenic world, nor their security against Persian invasion, can wholly explain the strange agreement of the Spartans in a retaliation which it is unlikely that they would have devised for themselves, and which, while inconsistent with their subsequent conduct, was by no means justified by the submission of their near neighbours of Argos and Ægina.

In the tale of Marathon we have a history of which it would be a sacrilege to diminish the splendour. But such an attempt is unnecessary even after the application of the most exact and searching criticism. That the great question of Hellenic freedom or barbaric tyranny was settled on this memorable field, that this battle decided the issue of the subsequent invasion of Xerxes, and that the glory of this victory belonged altogether to the men of Athens and Platæa, are facts which can be disputed by none. The numbers engaged on either side, the precise position of the Athenians and the barbarians, the exact tactics of the battle, are points of little moment in comparison; and the decision of the historical critic can in no way affect the glory of

The battle of Marathon.

[1] Herodotus vii. 133.

the struggle and its issue. The tale is manifestly one of which we have no narrative written at the time; and it would appear useless to resort to later writers for information upon points on which Herodotus has kept silence and with which he was perhaps unacquainted. The number engaged on the side of the Greeks may have been more or less than twenty thousand; but neither Pausanias nor Plutarch, Trogus or Cornelius Nepos, had any means for ascertaining the fact which were not accessible to Herodotus, and their computations furnish but slender footing for the conjecture that the light-armed troops are omitted in their lists. The battle has its full tale of marvels. The old heroes of the land rise to mingle in the fight, while living men do battle with superhuman strength and courage.[1] With these wonders and with perplexities of a less extraordinary kind, any elaborate description of the battle and its military incidents appears at best a superfluous labour. If we are told that Hippias guided the Persians to Marathon as being the best Attic ground for the action of horsemen, still in the battle no cavalry are mentioned; and it would seem to be immaterial whether the conjectures which explain their absence should be formed by writers of the times of Pausanias or Plutarch or of our own day. Colonel Leake supposes that narrowness of space induced the Persian general to send away his cavalry to a neighbouring plain with orders to remain " motionless in its cantonments ;"[2]

[1] Herodotus, vii. 114. In the later account of Justin, the courage is exaggerated into ferocity. Grote, History of Greece, vol. iv. p. 474.
[2] Rawlinson's Herodotus, vol. iii. p. 533.

while Mr. Rawlinson thinks that their absence was accidental and caused by the conviction of Datis that the Athenians purposed only to stand on the defensive.[1] Mr. Grote notices the statement of Nepos (which Mr. Rawlinson, who adopts his lists of numbers, seems to have passed over) that Miltiades " protected his position from the attacks of the Persian cavalry by felled trees obstructing the approach,"[2] while Dr. Thirlwall believes this fact to be one on which Herodotus could not have kept silence if it had been known to him, but which may have been the foundation of an obscure account by another writer to explain a common proverb.[3] If again it seems clear that Miltiades was as anxious to hasten as the Persians were to put off the battle, and that Hippias relied rather on the efforts of his partisans to produce disunion in Athens, it seems impracticable to analyse the movements of the engagement itself. The event of the battle is made to turn on the rapid charge of the Athenians, and on the success gained by their two wings while their weaker centre was broken by the barbarians. The ill success of the centre, and its cause, have been both debated by recent historians. Mr. Rawlinson believes Mr. Grote to be mistaken in attributing it to the disorder produced by the rapid

[1] Rawlinson's Herodotus, vol. iii. p. 534.
[2] History of Greece, vol. iv. p. 470.
[3] χωρὶς ἱππεῖς. Thirlwall, History of Greece, vol. ii. ch. xiv. p. 240. The popular Roman sayings may be compared, with their many explanations. "Talassio ferri."—*Livy*, i. 9. Sir G. C. Lewis, Credibility of Early Roman History, vol. i. p. 421. "Væ victis."—*Livy*, v. 48. Sir G. Lewis, ibid. vol. ii. p. 333, 356.

advance, and thinks it unlikely that, if this had been so, Herodotus would have failed to notice it.[1] It can scarcely be said that he has failed to do so. He states that the wings were strong and the centre the weakest part of the army,—that they advanced at a running step for about a mile of ground,—and that after great efforts the Persians broke this weak centre and drove it back.[2] The inference is that their haste had something to do with their repulse, unless the force opposed to them was stronger than that which encountered the wings, which we are not told. There would seem to be little use, then, in the attempt to determine the extent of ground over which the Greek centre was driven back; and, whatever may be the exaggeration of Herodotus[3], it is not easy to see how the narrative of Plutarch can possess a greater intrinsic authority.

The motives of the Athenian generals in bringing on the battle.

The motives of the Athenian generals have been analysed with equal minuteness. In Mr. Rawlinson's opinion their desire to await the coming of the Spartans kept them at first inactive; but the fear of conspiracy at home, and the discovery that the Persian general had sent away his cavalry to forage in the plain of Tricorythus or the valleys opening out of it, suddenly determined Miltiades to take advantage of this fatal error and lead his people to an assured victory.[4] The tale in Herodotus puts a passing reference to disunion at home into a speech of Miltiades to the polemarch Callimachus, and states that, when the latter had given his casting

---

[1] Rawlinson's Herodotus, vol. iii. p. 501.
[2] Herodotus, vi. 111.
[3] Rawlinson's Herodotus, vol. iii. p. 539.
[4] Ibid. p. 537.

vote for battle, Miltiades still refused to fight until his own day of command came round.[1] But when Mr. Rawlinson insists that, unless we are to set aside altogether the narrative of Herodotus, the Greeks must have been encamped for several days opposite to the Persians[2], he is not more in accordance with that narrative, as a whole, than Mr. Grote, who thinks that Miltiades would not have postponed the battle for such a reason as the one here assigned to him.[3] The tale may not improbably have been framed to heighten the glory of the great Athenian general; but in the story of Herodotus it is as prominent as any of the incidents and arrangements of the battle. If we may reject the former, we give up at the same time our title to retain the latter.

But the tale of Marathon is connected with dark and mysterious plots in Athens. It would seem clear that Hippias was not without partisans still, and probably we may admit with Mr. Grote that his march from Marathon would have been not less easy than that of his father, if the character of the great mass of the citizens had not since their expulsion been altogether changed.[4] The commonly believed story was that the signal agreed on between the party of Hippias and the Persians was the raising of a white shield on Mount Pentelicus.[5] The time and the motives for so doing

Charge of treachery against the Alcmaeonidae.

---

[1] Herodotus, vi. 110.
[2] Rawlinson's Herodotus, vol. iii. p. 500.
[3] Ibid. p. 500; Grote, History of Greece, vol. iv. p. 465.
[4] History of Greece, vol. iv. p. 450.
[5] Herodotus, vi. 115, 124.

seem to be as suspicious as the charge brought against the Alcmæonidæ of having thus designed to betray their country. Mr. Grote believes that "the bright shield uplifted on Mount Pentelicus, apprising the Persians that matters were prepared for them at Athens, was intended to have come to their view before any action had taken place at Marathon, so that Datis might have sent a portion of his fleet round to Phalerum, retaining the rest for combat with the enemy before him."[1] But according to the narrative of Herodotus the armies faced each other for several days before the battle was fought; and we may well be at a loss to see why the shield was not raised before the Athenians had reached the field of Marathon, or why after that time they should still have insisted on giving so unnecessary a signal. With the Athenians drawn up before their eyes, there was little need of any sign to tell them that "the Marathonian army was absent"[2] from Athens, while this very absence would be a better surety to Hippias for the success of his schemes than any signal which might have been exhibited by his friends. There is probably little doubt that the shield was raised; there is, it would seem, none that the Alcmæonidæ were charged with having raised it: but beyond this everything appears to be hopelessly uncertain.

Change in the character of the narrative after the battle of Marathon.

From the battle-field at Marathon we are carried back to the palace at Susa and the closing days of King Darius, — from a land imperfectly known to one of

---

[1] History of Greece, vol. iv. p. 477.
[2] Grote, History of Greece, vol. iv. p. 475.

which we can scarcely with truth be said to know anything. In the long interval which preceded the march of Xerxes, the character of the drama is changed. Thus far the contest between Greece and Persia exhibits something like a connection of political causes. The tales of Demokêdês and Histiæus, whether true or false, exhibit the working of human influence and supply motives not different in kind from the expulsion and intrigues of the Peisistratidæ, the attack on Sardes by the Athenians and Ionians, or the schemes and revolt of Aristagoras. But from the return of Datis to Susa the machinery of the tale becomes strictly ethical and religious. The victory of Miltiades is received with a fierce outburst of rage; and the mind of the Persian king is henceforth concentrated on the one desire of revenge.[1] All the might of his empire must be put forth for the destruction of the city which has dared to withstand his will. It is the crowning effort of human pride; and the gods come forth at once to curb and repress it. The impulse of conquest has carried the Persian power to a height not safe for men, and the great king must be driven by supernatural forces to take up a ruinous scheme against the warnings of his better mind. In the exquisite tale which relates the death of Darius and the council and visions of his son, it is difficult to separate the contributions of Persian or Greek informants. That the story of the dream was as familiar to the Persians as to himself, we are expressly told by Herodotus[2]; but although the form into which the incidents are cast reflects the inspiration of the old

[1] Herodotus, vii. 1.   [2] Ibid. vii. 12.

Homeric legend, it seems impossible to determine how much of the beautiful imagery was grouped around them by the genius of the historian himself. To seek for the historical facts which may lie beneath this magnificent epical narrative, is labour thrown away. The death of Darius, the suppression of the Egyptian revolt, and the march of Xerxes to the Hellespont, are historical facts; but to trace out the secret influences of the court of Susa is beyond our power, while no advantage is gained by "explaining the visions of Xerxes and Artabanus by a plot in the palace."[1] The evil influences of Mardonius,—the blind obstinacy of thwarted passion, —the conquering impulse of Oriental empires,—the desire to surpass the achievements of his ancestors,—all these are motives which, whether single or combined, appear equally probable, and equally impossible to prove. Whatever may have been the truth of the facts, we can only believe with Mr. Grote that the common belief of the Persians must have attributed the expedition to the interested counsels of Mardonius, or of some other adviser to whom the blame of its failure might be transferred from the king.[2] And to Herodotus himself (although the marvellous beauty of the tale is due to his fulness of Homeric inspiration) it is no less certain that we cannot impute the invention of the religious sentiment which pervades it. That sentiment was shared in common with him by most if not all of his contemporaries. The provocation of divine jealousy by Persian presumption, the irresistible impulse which

---

[1] Rawlinson's Herodotus, vol. i. p. 92.
[2] History of Greece, vol. v. p. 9.

drove Xerxes to his ruin by dreams and omens, were accepted as facts by all his informants[1]; and it remained for him only to fill up the outlines of the mythical picture, while he yet was careful to omit none of the human and political motives by which the Persian king and his counsellors might at any time have been influenced.

But if,turned in the narrative of this crisis, Persian speakers give utterance to distinctively Hellenic sentiments and a philosophy which was never known in the East, the tale is not without touches which are eminently true to the Persian character. If the story of Atossa and Demokedes harmonises wonderfully with all that we can be said to know of Oriental intrigue, the same natural air is impressed upon almost every incident which reveals to us the personal character and disposition of Xerxes. But the reasons for distrusting or rejecting the episode of Demokedes apply with less force to the history of Xerxes, in proportion as we approach the borders of the Asiatic Greeks. The scourging of the Hellespont is not more true to Eastern instinct than the influence of Atossa; but the punishment of the rebellious sea must have been inflicted in the sight of European witnesses, if it was ever inflicted at all. There is scarcely the same amount of corroboration for the murder of the son of Pythius; and the fact that a similar tale is told of Darius may either serve to give credit to the story or to involve it in greater suspicion.[2]

[margin: The march of Xerxes to the Hellespont.]

---

[1] See Mr. Grote's remarks on Hoffmeister (Lebensansicht des Herodotos), History of Greece, vol. v. p. 15.

[2] Herodotus, vii. 27, &c. Mr. Grote (History of Greece,

If, again, the immense preparations of Xerxes for this decisive effort, and the course of his march from Susa, may fairly be accepted as historical, no trust can be placed, it would seem, on the numbers, the quality, or the organisation of his forces. All historical critics acknowledge an indefinite amount of exaggeration: most of them believe that some groundwork is left by which we may obtain a reckoning approximately true. The uncertainty and constant change in oral tradition is in nothing more conspicuous than in lists of names or numbers. The abundance of witnesses is no guarantee for the truthful preservation of such details, in the absence of written documents drawn up at the time. The lapse even of a few years will leave nothing but vague impressions, whose inaccuracy must be candidly acknowledged or whose defects must be supplied by unconscious variations or wilful falsehoods. On such points as these no man would trust his own memory at a distance of half a century; and a tradition spread over more than a single generation must, on such subjects, lose all positive value. It can therefore be of little use to examine the lists given by Herodotus, or to correct them by the statements of later writers. No written lists are known to have been drawn up at the time, and if drawn up they would not pass into the hands of those from whom Herodotus would derive his knowledge; nor was there any fresh source of information which could impart a greater worth to the statements of Diodorus and Pausanias. We need

vol. v. p. 39) admits the fact of the murder, but puts no confidence in the estimate of the wealth of Pythius.

not question the overwhelming magnitude of the Persian army, and we cannot doubt that it produced everywhere an impression of irresistible force. The fact of this impression is unaffected, whether the hosts of Xerxes are to be numbered by tens of thousands or by millions; but it seems rash to go beyond the assertion of this general impression, on the ground urged by Mr. Grote, that Herodotus must have conversed with persons who had witnessed the review at Doriscus "and had learnt the separate totals promulgated by the enumerators."[1] Thucydides confesses that he could not learn the exact number of those who were engaged in the battle of Mantineia; and Mr. Grote remarks that we need not therefore "be ashamed to avow an inability to count the Asiatic multitudes at Doriscus."[2] But not only is the enumeration undeserving of credit. No greater faith can be put even in the statements of time; and no aid is given towards estimating the amount of the Persian army when we are told that seven days and seven nights, without intermission, were taken up with the passage of the host over the bridge across the Hellespont.[3] And, however probable may be the numbers of the ships at Salamis as given by Æschylus[4], yet even his contemporary witness cannot be taken as altogether conclusive on a subject of which he could have had no written information. All that can be said is, that the tragedian cast his own version into a form which would not be affected by the variations in the common rumours of the people. His enumeration both of the Greek

[1] History of Greece, vol. v. p. 49.
[2] Ibid. p. 52.
[3] Herodotus, vii. 56.
[4] Persæ, 340—343.

and Persian ships is comprised in five short lines, while the Homeric catalogue of the combatants at Troy extends over more than four hundred. But the epic poet confesses instinctively the great difficulty of his effort to perpetuate this unwritten tradition even with all the artificial aid of metre and rhythm. If the catalogue of the Persian forces had been cast into a similar form, the numbers there assigned would have been preserved, with little if any change, to a much later day than that of Herodotus; but the adoption of this form was not more necessary than the solemn prayer for aid, in a matter where human memory was especially weak and deceptive. Four elaborate similes, with an invocation to the heavenly Muses, precede the recitation of the Homeric catalogue, which, as in the play of Æschylus, would have formed the easiest and the shortest portion of a written poem.[1] There is no evidence that the men from whom Herodotus gained his information had access from the first to any written catalogue of the land or sea forces of Xerxes.

The bridge of the Hellespont, and the canal of Mount Athos.

Of the bridge across the Hellespont we cannot be said to know much more than the fact of its existence. The account given by Herodotus is singularly obscure; and it is not easy to determine how much of its difficulty may be owing to the want of a contemporary written narrative.[2] The existence of a canal across Mount

---

[1] These considerations leave it absolutely certain that the Homeric catalogue was never composed for a written poem. The subject is fully worked out by Mr. Gladstone, Homer and the Homeric Age, vol. i. p. 246, &c.

[2] Mr. Grote has examined the subject at length, and with as

Athos, executed at the command of Xerxes, is attested by evident traces of the work at the present day; but Mr. Grote has remarked that the fact would be sufficiently proved by the testimony of Herodotus, when compared with the words of Thucydides.[1] But here also the attestation extends only to the naked fact, not to the time over which the work is said to have been extended or to the method of its accomplishment.

The tale of the unbroken good fortune which is said to have attended both his land and sea forces until they reached the Magnesian coast and the passes of Thermopylæ, is not without its difficulties. The epical method of Herodotus represents Xerxes as connecting his own expedition with the fallen kingdom of Priam, and as sacrificing a thousand oxen to Athena on the Ilian hill, thereby to win her favour in his efforts to avenge the invasion of Agamemnon.[2] But his ignorance of the name and fate of Protesilaus would indicate a very imperfect acquaintance with the poem which told the story of Hector and Achilles. More strange, however, is the uninterrupted pomp and splendour of his march through the rough lands and the barbarous tribes of Thrace and Macedonia. Lions and wild bulls are said to have caused some hurt to his baggage camels[3]; but from the inhabitants of each town he experienced nothing but the most unbounded servility and the most lavish hospitality. A few months later his army, in its retreat, followed once again the same track.

The march of the Persians through Thrace and Macedonia.

much success perhaps as its nature admits, in a note to p. 24, vol. v. of his History.

[1] Grote, History of Greece, vol. v. p. 33.
[2] Herodotus, vii. 43.   [3] Ibid. vii. 125.

He had some little cause for fear and more for selfish anxiety; but the army which attended him had not caused or shared the disasters of the fleet at Salamis[1], while they could boast of something like victory in their single encounter with the Spartans of Leonidas at Thermopylæ. He had left behind him thirty myriads to carry out the scheme which he had only delegated to another; and there was nothing in the circumstances of his retreat to justify any marked change in the policy of the cities and tribes who had welcomed and aided him before. But in that retreat no mention is made of banquets and entertainments, or even of requests for such kindly deeds. The forcible plunder of stored grain takes the place of willing contributions; and where this is not forthcoming, the army are left to appease their hunger as best they may, while the diseases which follow on famine so thin his hosts that, in the phrase of Herodotus, he reaches Sardes with the merest fraction of his once overwhelming force.[2] Yet, unlike Artabazus in his flight from Platæa, he has not, it would seem, to resist any attacks from the Thracian mountaineers; the disasters which befall his army lie at his own door. He is robbed and cheated by the Pæonians[3], but of open violence there is no sign. The mysterious change in the circumstances of his homeward journey may justify a doubt in the uniform prosperity which is said to have characterised his march from Susa to Thermopylæ.[4]

The counsels of Demaratus.

In this westward journey the religious sentiment of

[1] Herodotus, viii. 100.   [2] Ibid. viii. 115.
[3] Ibid. viii. 115.   [4] Ibid. vii. 184.

the time could not dispense with the usual ethical machinery. The part of Crœsus with Cyrus and Cambyses, and of Amasis with Polycrates, is here filled towards Xerxes by the banished Spartan king Demaratus. If his existence is historical (and this it is impossible to question), his story is full of mystery from its commencement to its close. There may be nothing strange in his flight to Susa, or wonderful in the favour shown to him by the Persian king; but it is perplexing that so little should follow from his deep resentment against his countrymen. To Xerxes he acts the part not only of a wise counsellor and a fearless friend, but his wisdom is set forth as a foil to the obstinate imbecility of the Persian. In him is the foresight which suggests, and the judgment which dictates, the right measures to be taken at every step and under all circumstances; but his counsels are never followed, and his rivals for the royal favour see treachery in the advice which, if followed, must inevitably have involved the ruin of his country. Still his friendly feeling receives ample acknowledgment, while it is from him (by a device which bears a suspicious resemblance to that of Histiæus) that the Spartans receive the first intimation of the dangers impending over them.[1] In the conflicts at Thermopylæ he prepares the mind of Xerxes for a determined resistance from his own countrymen, while, with characteristic Spartan pride, he takes no count of the noble courage of the Athenians.[2] And when the rejection of his advice to occupy the island of Kythêra has sealed the doom of the Persian expedition[3], his name no longer

[1] Herodotus, vii. 239. [2] Ibid. vii. 102. [3] Ibid. vii. 234.

occurs in a story which has no further room for his moral and religious functions.

The motives and conduct of the Greek states and their leaders.

But the difficulties of the history are not confined to the fortunes of Xerxes and his army. The utterly perplexing accounts of the movements and motives of the several Greek states still show that we are within the limits of oral tradition. Nor are these difficulties caused solely by what Mr. Grote speaks of as the inter-political conditions of Hellenic life. The impracticability of establishing a real Panhellenic confederacy fettered the inherent powers of the several independent states, and insured the final overthrow of all; but throughout the Persian war we are perplexed not so much at the reluctance to coalesce, which is the chief characteristic of the Greeks in every stage of their history, as by the fluctuations in the conduct of the several states from motives which very inadequately explain them.[1] From the time when the Greek commanders fell back from

---

[1] The neutrality of Argos, or rather her obstructive aid, is said to have been acquired by an assertion of ethnical affinity between the Argives and the Persians. Herodotus, vii. 150. On equally mythical grounds the men of Tegea claim the post of honour in the battle of Plataea. Herodotus, ix. 26. It is curious that Argos should have been regarded as connected with the royal house of Macedonia. But this connection seems to have arisen from the equivocal use of the word Argos. See Niebuhr, Lectures on Ancient History, vol. ii. p. 254. But the negative aid of Argos furnishes no real explanation for the vehement Medism of the Thebans. It is clear that the Boeotian cities were, with the exception of Thespiae and Plataea, passive instruments in the hands of their chief men; but the intensely anti-Hellenic feeling of these rulers is very surprising. Defeat and disaster has little power to repress or even to check it.

the gates of Thessaly, down to the capture of Athens and the battle of Salamis, their movements and their plans are such as almost to baffle every effort to understand them. It is strange enough that they should be ignorant of the existence of other passes, while they occupied those of Tempe[1]; but still more strange that not even a thought should be given to the possibility of guarding the pass through the land of the Perrhæbians near Gonnus, as soon as they were made aware of its existence. These difficulties, however, appear slight indeed, when compared with those of the story of Thermopylæ. There is a natural reluctance to touch with the rude hand of criticism this beautiful legend, which vindicates for the Spartans something like an equal glory with that of the Athenians in their resistance to the barbarian; but when once the narrative is convicted of inconsistency or contradiction, the extent of the contradiction becomes a matter of little practical moment. From the Isthmus of Corinth Leonidas is stated to have led to Thermopylæ 300 Spartans (with a force of helots of whose numbers we are not informed), 500 hoplites from Tegea, with the same number from Mantineia, 120 from the Arcadian Orchomenus and 1000 from other Arcadian cities, 400 Corinthians, with 280 men from Phlius and Mykenæ.[2] What light troops may have attended them we are not told; but the presence of some may be reasonably assumed. In Bœotia they were joined by 400 Thebans and 700 hoplites from Thespiæ, while jealousy and hatred of the Thessalians brought 1000 Phokians to guard the heights of Anopæa above

The story of Thermopylæ.

[1] Herodotus, vii. 173.   [2] Ibid. vii. 202.

the pass of Thermopylæ.[1] If we allow to each Spartan citizen the same number of helots as those which accompanied the force sent afterwards to Platæa[2], and take 1000 as the lowest number of light-armed troops[3], there was assembled under the command of Leonidas a force of not less than 8300 men. The religious infatuation of the Spartans may explain adequately the small number of their citizens present at Thermopylæ. We know that the keeping of Carneian and Hyakinthian festivals was urged as a plea for disregarding the most pressing duty in times of strictly contemporary history; but the absence of the Athenians presents a more serious difficulty, on which Niebuhr lays much stress.[4] Yet, while noticing this point, he has curiously exaggerated or misrepresented inaccuracies for which it is very difficult to account, if with him we assume the existence of authentic contemporary chronicles now lost. He is mistaken in supposing that no Arcadian force was present; and he appears to make no allowance for light-armed troops and helots. The Ætolian roads seem, as he remarks, to have been left open; but, if we may assume the truth of the legend, an attempt was made on the passes at Delphi and failed. But it is perhaps more important to notice that with these forces Leonidas succeeded for ten or twelve days in checking the advance of the whole Persian army and inflicting on them very serious loss. Nothing could have proved more clearly the practicability of the posi-

---

[1] Herodotus, vii. 203. [2] Ibid. ix. 10.
[3] This number would seem to be altogether below the mark.
[4] Lectures on Ancient History, vol. i. p. 336.

tion, and the probability of success if he kept his ground without diminishing his forces. But the treachery of Ephialtes betrayed the secret of the mountain path which was intrusted to the Phokians, and a discharge of arrows from the soldiers of Hydarnes caused these at once to abandon their trust and seek the summit of the hill whereon to make their final stand. The loss of this pathway cut off, we are told, all chance of ultimate success; but retreat was still possible. The men of Corinth, of Phlius, and Mykênæ, with all the Arcadian forces (including, as it would appear, their light-armed troops), were at once dismissed by Leonidas, who, having thus sent away scarcely less than 4000 men, retained along with his helots the troops furnished by Thespiæ and Thebes. The Thebans in the ensuing conflict did as little as they could; but, even without their aid, 20,000 Persians are stated to have been slain by the 300 Spartans and the 700 Thespians. If to each of the former we allow, as before, seven helots as attendants, we have a number which seems to fall short by five hundred of the four thousand whose bodies Xerxes is said to have displayed to his army on the battle-ground of Thermopylæ.[1] If a loss so enormous was caused to the Persians by so scanty a band of antagonists, it is difficult to calculate the probable result, if Leonidas had kept his four thousand allies to share the danger and the glory of the struggle. Of the personal motives of Leonidas it would be rash to advance any positive opinion. If the Spartan military code forbade flight from a battle-field, it had no precept to sanction the

[1] Herodotus, viii. 25.

abandonment or even the wilful weakening of a perfectly tenable post; and the imputation of bad generalship is the price which Leonidas must pay for the glory of his self-devotion. Nor does Mr. Grote seem to be justified in reckoning amongst his possible motives the declaration of the Delphian oracle " that either Sparta itself or a king of Sparta must fall a victim to the Persian arms."[1] He has already expressed his doubt of the existence of this response before the battle of Thermopylæ.[2]

The conduct of the Thebans at Thermopylæ.

Nor is it altogether easy to understand the facts related of the Thebans whom Leonidas retained by his side against their will. Their presence can scarcely be explained by the admission that the Thebans and Bœotians, feeling little sympathy for either side, were passive instruments in the hands of their leaders, who judged it imprudent in this instance to refuse the request of Leonidas.[3] Still less safely may we adopt the conclusion of later writers, that they were citizens of the anti-Persian party and so remained of their own free will, but, after the fight, took credit for a Medism which they did not feel, by the pretence that they had been detained in the Spartan camp by force.[4] We do not know that Diodorus or Pausanias had access to any information of which Herodotus was ignorant; and the latter distinctly contradicts any such supposition. He maintains that their profession of Medism was the truest of all pleas[5]; nor is it likely that the Thessalians would

---

[1] History of Greece, vol. v. p. 124.
[2] Ibid. p. 84.   [3] Ibid. p. 104.   [4] Ibid. p. 126.
[5] λέγοντες τὸν ἀληθέστατον τῶν λόγων.—*Herodotus*, vii. 233.

have upheld the credit of men of whose Hellenic sympathies they must have been aware.

The personal anecdotes which enliven the story of the battle furnish us with matter not less questionable. The wit of Dienekes[1] may have been invented to explain a popular saying, while the desperate form assumed by Spartan resistance in the pass[2] points to the source which has produced the anecdotes of the Athenian Kynegeirus[3] and the Æginetan Pytheas.[4] The tales of Eurytus and Aristodemus serve at least to illustrate the ferocious military spirit of Sparta, whether the story be true or false, and whether Herodotus intends to impute to the latter any faintness of heart by the word which Thucydides employs when speaking of the swoon of Brasidas.[5] The story of Partites[6] is scarcely less characteristic, and can scarcely be rejected on the mere ground that there was no one with whom his own return placed him in prominent contrast. The strange tale of the diver Skyllias[7] is stripped of its wonder by Herodotus himself, but it serves to illustrate the method by which fictitious details were grouped round real events. The legend of Arion was questioned in succeeding generations; but in the story of Skyllias we see the working of contemporary criticism on popular versions of historical facts.

Personal anecdotes connected with the battle.

---

[1] Herodotus, vii. 226. [2] Ibid. vii. 225.
[3] Ibid. vi. 114. [4] Ibid. vii. 181.
[5] Ibid. vii. 229: λειποψυχέοντα. The same expression, as applied to Brasidas at Sphacteria, fully warrants Mr. Grote's conclusion that Herodotus does not imply by it anything more than the effect of extreme physical suffering. History of Greece, vol. v. p. 129. [6] Herodotus, vii. 232. [7] Ibid. viii. 8.

It would be an assumption to say that the tidings which Skyllias conveyed to the leaders at Artemisium did not in all points agree with the narrative which has come down to us. Yet even the account of Herodotus would justify the inference that Leonidas was culpably careless of a defensible position, or else that other events occurred with which we are not acquainted. The impression at Sparta and throughout the Peloponnesus was that the pass of Thermopylæ and the Artemisian shore of Eubœa were both tenable, and it cannot be said that, with regard to the former at least, the impression was unjustifiable. With our uncertain knowledge it is impossible to determine whether the defeat of the Greeks may not have been much greater than the account of Herodotus would lead us to suppose.

Whatever may be the difficulties involved in the tale of the abandonment of Athens and Attica, they appear to have been unnecessarily exaggerated by Niebuhr[1], whose scepticism in the early portions of Greek history is more rigorous than that which he exhibits in his reconstruction of the early history of Rome. The rapidity with which the proclamation of Themistocles was acted on, and the extent to which it was carried out, are sufficiently surprising. In six days all the inhabitants of the city and country, except the few who remained in the Acropolis, were transported to Trœzen, Ægina, or Salamis.[2] But the method of their conveyance and their means of subsistence in exile are questions which

---

[1] Lectures on Ancient History, vol. i. p. 339.
[2] Herodotus, viii. 60; Grote, History of Greece, vol. v. p. 148.

there is no need to discuss. It was but the first of
many similar incidents in Athenian history from the
days of Themistocles to our own; and the miseries
which they endured in Ægina or Trœzen may have
been not less overwhelming than those which they
underwent during the War of Liberation in the present
century.[1] The readiness with which they obeyed the
command to dismantle their homes at the approach of
the Persian is less credible. There had been nothing in
their past history to account for such general and hasty
compliance; and we might have looked for some signs
of that reluctance which the Athenians of a later day
opposed to a similar order from Königsmark and
Morosini.[2]

The inroad of the Persians on Delphi is the climax *The attack on Delphi.*
of the great epic of Herodotus. It is the most daring
provocation of divine jealousy and wrath by the barbarian despot; and while it precedes immediately his
own humiliation, it insures also the final destruction of
his army. But the poetical handling of the tale has
shrouded it with an uncertainty beyond that of most
other incidents of the war. The words of Mardonius
before the battle of Platææ would lead us to think that
the expedition never took place at all[3]: but there
also we are reading only another part of the great
heroic legend, how the gods made the prime mover of
all the evil believe a lie and utter words of more than

---

[1] See Grote, History of Greece, vol. v. p. 149.

[2] Laborde, Athènes aux xve, xvie, xviie Siècles, tome ii. p. 178.

[3] Herodotus, ix. 42.

mortal pride in the hour of his doom. It was not the
first time that the majesty of Zeus had come between
the spoiler and his temple; but it would be the absurdity of rationalism to explain the rending of the
crags of Parnassus as an accident of nature, like that
which destroyed the army of Cambyses on their way
to the shrine of Ammôn.[1] The fall of the rocks at
Delphi cannot be separated from the other miraculous
details,—from the unseen arm which laid the sacred weapons before the temple doors, and the visible aid of the
deified heroes of the place. The same supernatural intervention recurs in the story of the later attack on
Delphi by Brennus and the Gauls.[2] In the narrative
of Plutarch the Delphian temple was not only taken
by the Persians, but underwent the lot which certainly
befell the kindred oracle of Abæ. On that point, however, the authority of Plutarch has little more weight
than that of Ctesias. The splendid offerings of an earlier age, the magnificent gifts, bearing the names of
Gyges and Crœsus, which were seen in the Delphic
treasury by Herodotus himself[3], seem sufficiently to
prove that the temple was not plundered, and far less
burnt by the Persians. But how the expedition came
thus to fail, and why its failure was not followed up by
an attack with forces far more overwhelming, are questions to which no answer can be given. The epical conception of history made it indispensable that Xerxes
should insult the majesty of Apollo; and the contradic-

[1] Herodotus, ii. 26.
[2] Pausanias, x. 23; Grote, History of Greece, vol. v. p. 158.
[3] Herodotus, i. 50.

tions of the tale may almost warrant the conclusion that Mardonius spoke truly when he denied that any attack had been made on the sanctuary of Delphi.

The battle of Salamis showed the way in which Apollo took his vengeance. It was the complete confirmation of the truth that pride must have its fall; and the fall of the mightiest of all earthly kings must be ushered in by ominous sights and sounds on the earth and in the heavens. Each day, and almost every incident, has its own peculiar marvels. The island of Salamis was shaken by an earthquake which upheaved the waters of the sea.[1] The cloud of dust showed the march of a mysterious host moving from Eleusis to avenge the wrongs of Athena.[2] The car of Dikæus comprehended sounds which bore no meaning to the uninitiated Demaratus; and he knew that the Mighty Mother was going with her Child to execute justice upon her enemies.[3] He saw the throng as of three myriads of men move slowly towards the sea, and in that sign he read the coming ruin of the fleet whose overwhelming force the gods had, of wise purpose, beaten down on the rock-bound shores of Thessaly. Yet once the historian forgets the steady course of his great epical tale, when he says that the Greeks encountered at Salamis a fleet not less in numbers than that which had reached, uninjured, the shore of Sepias and Thermopylæ.[4] The toil of the

The battle of Salamis.

---

[1] Herodotus, viii. 64.   [2] Ibid. viii. 65.
[3] Niebuhr (Lectures on Ancient History, vol. i. p. 339) asserts, apparently without authority, that this incident occurs in two separate traditions, the latter making it happen on the day of the battle of Salamis.   [4] Herodotus, viii. 66.

gods had for once been thrown away; but it was only to add to the pure glory of Athens and Themistocles.

<small>Ethical and poetical features of the narrative.</small> The day of disaster was at hand for Xerxes; but no link must be wanting in the great preparation. If we are reading a tale much of which is undoubted history, it is not the less true that mythical incidents are inextricably interwoven with the most authentic facts, or else that many of the facts are so handled as to deprive them of all historical value. We do not question the truth of the Persian expedition; we do not doubt the design of the barbarian king or the accomplishment of his purpose. He had taken Athens, he had seized the Acropolis; but what amount of resistance he had to overcome, or how its defenders were overpowered, we cannot tell. Here also we are moving in a land of prodigies and wonders. The departure of the sacred serpent had foreshadowed the capture of the Athenian citadel [1]; the mysterious sprouting of the sacred olive-tree announced the coming retribution.[2] And when the temples had been burnt and the messengers of Xerxes had departed with the tale of his glory to Sardes and to Susa, not one thing must be passed by which might show how the lightning strikes ever the tallest tree.[3] The great king must be made to choose his own destruction. He must hear from the wise what he ought to do, and he must deliberately reject the counsel whose adoption would have brought all Hellas under his dominion. As, after the fight at Thermopylæ, he had neglected the advice of Demaratus to occupy the island of Kythêra[4], so now he must despise the warning

[1] Herodotus, viii. 41.
[2] Ibid. viii. 55.
[3] Ibid. vii. 10, 5.
[4] Ibid. vii. 234.

which sought to convince him of the weakness of his fleet.[1] But in neither case can we say with any certainty that the counsel was ever given. The words of Artemisia, like those of the Spartan king, seem rather the expression of a subsequent feeling among the Greeks than of convictions which, even if entertained, could with any safety have been revealed to Xerxes. In the case of Artemisia an easier faith may seem to be justified by the knowledge which Herodotus must have had of the life and actions of one who had ruled in his own city; but we can scarcely accept the fact that she advised Xerxes by every means to avoid a sea-fight, if, with Mr. Grote, we reject altogether the grounds of her opinion.[2] It is difficult to suppose that the reasons which she gave could have been so utterly lost or misrepresented, while the nature of the counsel was so distinctly remembered. If we cannot believe that she "delivered an estimate not merely insulting to all who heard it, but at the time not just," we may with equal fairness question the fact that she gave advice for which, on this hypothesis, she had no adequate grounds. According to the story, the opinion of Xerxes was not unjustifiable, and he had further convinced himself that his own presence was alone needed to make his seamen invincible.[3] The counsel of Artemisia expressed well what the Greeks of a later day felt that Xerxes ought to have done; but its entire agreement with this sense of fitness is perhaps the strongest reason for calling the tale into question.

[1] Herodotus, viii. 68. [2] History of Greece, vol. v. p. 163.
[3] Herodotus, viii. 69.

The history of Artemisia.

But, in truth, the whole story of Artemisia is full of difficulty. Although the historian undoubtedly represents her bravery or her good faith as by no means equal to her wisdom and foresight, it is almost incredible that such shallow selfishness could have been so successful. If we may not accept the grounds on which she is said to have urged her former advice to Xerxes, and if his remarks on her collision with the Calyndian ship "read like nothing but romance," there is little to be gained by asserting that the story of her exploit "has the air of truth."[1] And if we reject the other parts of the tale, it seems impossible to believe that even the total destruction of the ship and crew could have saved her from detection. We are expressly told that other friendly ships[2] checked her flight no less than that of the Calyndian king; they were present to see what was done, and we cannot suppose that all were unconscious of the selfish device of Artemisia, and that none would have had the courage or the indignation to denounce it. But if her first advice to Xerxes betrays a freedom and boldness of speech which well became one who bore rule over a Greek city, her subsequent counsel after the battle of Salamis exhibits a servility not less excessive[3]; and the reward which she received appears a strange recompense for one who had boasted of special bravery in the battles at Artemisium.[4]

The counsel of Mnesiphilus.

From this region of mere romance or distorted history

---

[1] Grote, History of Greece, vol. v. p. 186.
[2] Herodotus, viii. 87: ἔμπροσθε γὰρ αὐτῆς ἦσαν ἄλλαι νῆες φίλιαι.
[3] Herodotus, viii. 102.   [4] Ibid. viii. 68, 1.

we pass with a curious suddenness to a relation of motives and actions which seems to be but little embellished by a lofty or exuberant imagination. There is little appearance of romance in the conduct of men whose fear and cowardice overpower every feeling of duty or of shame. Yet in this strange narrative of selfishness, jealousy, and disunion, something of that uncertainty may be traced which is inseparable from all oral tradition; and even in some trivial details we may detect the foundation on which was raised a more formidable structure of calumny and injustice. The interval which separates the policy of Themistocles and the obstinate folly of his opponents from the romance of the march of Xerxes or the mysterious signs which cheered the Greeks at Delphi, or Athens, or Salamis, seems not less wide than that which distinguishes the dreams of Arabian tale-tellers from the sober narratives of our own age and country. Yet it is not easy to believe that the wavering resolution of Themistocles was fixed by the vehement remonstrance of Mnesiphilus; that the failing firmness of the man who had marked out a definite line of action and adhered to it with singular pertinacity, needed the support of one who suggests nothing with which he had not been long familiar.[1] It would almost seem as though there were an epical necessity for the counsel of Mnesiphilus, as for that of Demaratus and Artemisia. The one determines the resolution of the future conqueror, as the other convicts his enemy of a blind infatuation. But Themistocles hears from his friend nothing but what he knew and

---

[1] Herodotus, viii. 57.

what he had urged already; and Mnesiphilus appears only as the personified opinion of the great Athenian leader.[1]

The mention of Keos and Kynosûra. To the changing details of oral tradition are owing also the words which speak of a part of the Persian fleet as stationed at Keos and Kynosûra.[2] Both positions are improbable; one is impossible. But it seems unnecessary to confine to Herodotus himself the desire to find the oracles of Bakis truly fulfilled. His verses were not less familiar to many of his informants who may have produced or strengthened his error.

The defeat and flight of Xerxes. The general movements of the Persian fleet form a part of that narrative which passed under the personal observation of the Greeks. We are carried again into the land of fiction, as we read of the complaint which the Phœnicians urged against the Ionians for a wanton destruction of their ships.[3] In this instance the eyes of Xerxes are quick to discern a wonderful exploit which furnished an immediate contradiction to their charge of treachery. The punishment which he immediately inflicts on the accusers is not placed beyond the bounds of credibility by its madness; but it needs better testimony than that of Persians to prove the truth of a vengeance so suicidal against the only men in his fleet who deserved the name of seamen. The

---

[1] Mr. Grote (History of Greece, vol. v. p. 167) speaks of Mnesiphilus as the "inspiring genius" of Themistocles. He has applied expressions not very different to the counsels of Artabanus, which he is not altogether disposed to regard as historical.

[2] Herodotus, viii. 76; Grote, History of Greece, vol. v. p. 176.

[3] Herodotus, viii. 90.

Phœnicians, according to a statement of Diodorus[1] which we may well believe, made their escape in indignation during the following night; but the mind of Xerxes was made up to risk no new turn of fortune. He left Mardonius to carry on the war; but as we do not know how far Mardonius had been his evil genius in the great council at Susa, or whether he simply applauded a determination not growing out of his own suggestions, so also we cannot tell whether he thought that to remain behind was his only chance of escaping the wrath of Xerxes.[2] Of the council which preceded his flight we have no certain knowledge, while in the speech of Artemisia[3] we simply notice its inconsistency with the tone of her language before the battle of Salamis. The sudden departure of the fleet may perhaps be assumed as true, while in the terror with which the rocks of Cape Zôstêr are said to have filled them, we may fairly see something more than "silly exaggeration" on the part of the informants of Herodotus.[4] The incident harmonises strictly with the epical handling of the history; while there is no improbability in the tale that the seamen, in their abject fear, should take the small and slender rocks which jutted out beyond the promontory to be ships belonging to the enemy. We need only better witnesses to believe an incident less marvellous than many of its kind which we know to be true.

[1] Diodorus, xi. 19; Grote, History of Greece, vol. v. p. 188.
[2] Herodotus, viii. 100. [3] Ibid. viii. 102.
[4] Grote, History of Greece, vol. v. p. 188. Dr. Thirlwall (History of Greece, vol. ii. p. 313) states it historically.

The story of his retreat.

Historical criticism has dealt roughly with the story of the flight of Xerxes, and the only remaining doubt relates to the amount of detail which must be rejected. If the account given by Æschylus is obviously impossible[1], there are difficulties almost as great in following the narrative of Herodotus. If we take his numbers as furnishing even a relative proportion, Xerxes must have led back from Athens a larger army than that which he left behind him with Mardonius. Yet his numbers were so far lessened as to throw great suspicion on the tale of utter starvation and misery from the time that he entered Macedonia. On his former march from Doriscus westward, his men are said to have been fed from the accumulated stores of three years[2], as well as from the forced or voluntary contributions of the inhabitants. Of these magazines the narrative of the retreat in Herodotus says nothing, and it is scarcely more safe to infer from his silence that they had been emptied by the dishonesty of their guardians, than to fill up his narrative with such incidents as the marvellous freezing of the river Strymon.[3] Yet Xerxes unquestionably contemplated a speedy return to his own land, and had his dreams of leading back a long line of Athenian and Spartan slaves in addition to the hosts which he was leading on to conquest. His need of food would be increased by the measure of his success, and his care to preserve and

---

[1] Persæ, 494, &c.   [2] Herodotus, vii. 25, &c.
[3] Contrast the criticism of Mr. Grote (History of Greece, vol. v. p. 193) with that of Dr. Thirlwall (History of Greece, vol. ii. p. 316).

extend these stores would be stimulated by his hopes of immediate victory. Yet, as though submitting to an ordinary necessity, he leaves his army to subsist by plunder or die by famine, in a land where, as it would seem, not a single arm was raised against him, and where we are told that he left his sick in the cities through which he passed[1], not without good confidence in the kindly feelings of their inhabitants. Still, with this friendliness or at least neutrality of the people, his passage is more disastrous than that of Artabazus who, after the day of Platæa, fought his way through the wild tribes of Thrace.[2] The story of Herodotus would give some countenance to the Macedonian boast that they had slaughtered and almost cut off the whole army in its flight[3]; and unless we assume some great hostility, whether of Macedonians or Thracians, we are tempted to infer with Niebuhr that "Xerxes had not brought many more troops with him into Greece than those who afterwards fought under Mardonius at Platæa."[4] But the change which comes over the spirit of the narrative as soon as Xerxes is safely restored to the luxurious tyranny of his own land, tends more than anything else to call into question the tale of misery and ruin which precedes it. From the moment that Artabazus has dismissed his master, he appears as a man well able to hold his ground against all efforts of his enemies. We hear no more of famine or disease, of men plucking grass and roots and then lying down to die. Instead of this, we find him deliberately resolving to remain in Macedonia until the

[1] Herodotus, viii. 115.   [2] Ibid. ix. 89.
[3] Niebuhr, Lectures on Ancient History, vol. i. p. 340.
[4] Ibid. p. 342.

return of spring allowed Mardonius to move his army in Bœotia.[1] So completely is he master of his position and his movements, that he determines to attack the Greek colonies who had dared to revolt against the king.[2] Olynthus is taken and its citizens slain, and a blockade of three months is kept up against Potidæa. Of the extent of his loss in the disastrous close of this siege we are not informed; but as we find him at Platæa with forty thousand men still under his command[3], we may fairly suppose that these were a portion of the sixty thousand who escorted Xerxes to the Hellespont. The loss, therefore, does not appear disproportioned to the greatness of his efforts and his failures. We are, however, told that Mardonius retained the flower of the Persian army in Bœotia; and some allowance may be made for the fact that Xerxes took with him men who would have been of little use under any circumstances. But if these men were even as worthless and as helpless as they are represented to have been, they cannot well have been more helpless on the march to the Hellespont than they were in the barren lands of Attica, unless we assume a constant hostility from the cities and tribes through which they had to pass. Nearly three months had elapsed between his victory of Thermopylæ and his defeat at Salamis. During that time his whole army had lived in a land where he had no long-established magazines and where the resolution of the people had greatly lessened the profits of plunder. Whatever, then, may have been the sufferings of the march, they could have differed nothing in kind and perhaps not

[1] Herodotus, viii. 126. [2] Ibid. viii. 127. [3] Ibid. ix. 66.

greatly in degree from the hardships which they had to undergo during their sojourn at Athens.

A strange picture of fickleness and uncertainty of purpose, of utter prostration alternating with momentary outbursts of vehemence, comes before us in the history of the Greek states after the battle of Salamis. It is impossible to question its general truthfulness; impossible to doubt the firm courage and Panhellenic feelings of the Athenians, or the selfish procrastination shown by all the men of the Peloponnesus. There can be no motive to deny the statements made by Herodotus through the mere force of conviction[1] and against his clear interest,—statements which prove that the final salvation of Hellas was mainly due to the fearless determination of that people who continued to keep the Persian power at bay for the space of three generations. Yet we cannot as readily accept the literal truth of the details which go to make up this picture of calm and fixed energy on the one side, and of a selfish vacillation on the other. It is not likely that the mere departure of the Persian fleet should have caused such extreme confidence as that which is said to have followed the victory of Salamis. It can scarcely be said that the "terrific cloud impending over Greece was dispersed,"[2] while Mardonius remained close at hand with the real strength of the whole Persian army. And if there is any reason for thinking that this exultation is exaggerated, we may make the same allowance for the alleged selfishness and backwardness of the Spartans and their

[1] Herodotus, vii. 139.
[2] Grote, History of Greece, vol. v. p. 196.

Peloponnesian allies.[1] The warning given to the Spartan ephors by Chileus of Tegea[2] appears almost as superfluous as the advice of Mnesiphilus to Themistocles. It is said to have produced a complete and sudden change in the policy and plans of the ephors; but it is entirely uncalled for, unless we assume that such a change really did take place. Mr. Grote questions not so much the fact of the change as the correctness of the narrative in Herodotus. He thinks that the helots must have followed Pausanias, because it is difficult to see "how so great a number could have been all suddenly collected and marched off in one night, no preparations having been made beforehand."[3] But if we reject the sudden change and the want of preparation as alike incredible, the whole story is, at the least, placed on a consistent and plausible basis. Secresy in counsel and execution was undoubtedly a prominent feature in Spartan government; but although Mr. Grote refuses to admit, with Dr. Thirlwall[4], that the conduct of the ephors in the story of Herodotus is adopted only to give point to a "paltry and most unreasonable jest," still the historian must, it would seem, have discerned in it a desire to surprise the Athenian ambassadors, and to startle them into admiration for efforts which, without forethought or preparation, would equal or surpass their own. Such conduct, although perhaps not childish, is yet, even from a Spartan view, unaccountable, if the only motive was supplied by Chileus, who told them simply what

---

[1] Herodotus, ix. 8, &c.   [2] Ibid. ix. 9.
[3] Grote, History of Greece, vol. v. p. 213.
[4] Thirlwall, History of Greece, vol. ii. p. 329.

they knew before and what the Athenians had already impressed upon them far more forcibly and solemnly.[1] But the hostile designs of the Argives fully explain the policy of the ephors, if they were known at Sparta; and we can scarcely suppose that they could long remain unknown. If the Argives had already made a compact with Mardonius and boasted that they would keep the Spartans at home by force[2], there was every reason to make their preparations in secret, and to withhold all knowledge, even from the Athenian envoys, until the army was actually on its march. If, with Dr. Thirlwall, we suppose that the return and death of Cleombrotus took place during the detention of the Athenians at Sparta, it may serve to account still more for the delay in setting out; but such a statement can in no way affect the other incidents of the story. The mere assertion that in a single day they sent out of the country a force of fifty thousand men, tends not only to prove that so vast an effort was not made without full preparations, but to acquit the Spartans in some measure of the vacillation with which they were charged, as well as of an utter unconcern for the interests and welfare of every other state but their own.

The epical method of the historian is again disclosed as he approaches the great battle in which, according to the promise of Xerxes, Mardonius was to give the Spartans satisfaction for the death of Leonidas.[3] The pride and arrogance of the Persian leader is strengthened, while the hopes of his followers are dying away. A blindness sent by the gods is on his eyes, while others

---
[1] Herodotus, ix. 7.   [2] Ibid. ix. 12.   [3] Ibid. viii. 114.

foresee the ruin, of which they dare not speak to their
commander. The tale of the Orchomenian Thersander,
which Dr. Thirlwall refuses to receive unreservedly,
Mr. Grote admits to be " one of the most curious reve-
lations in the whole history; not merely as it brings
forward the historian in his own personality, communi-
cating with a personal friend of the Theban leaders
and thus provided with good means of information as
to the general events of the campaign, but also as it dis-
closes to us, on testimony not to be suspected, the real
temper of the native Persians, and even of the chief
men among them."[1] That Herodotus heard the story
from Thersander; that he received it substantially in
that shape in which he has given it to us; and that
Thersander, while relating it to Herodotus, fully believed
in the truth of the tale and the accuracy of his own
memory, it is impossible to question. But when we
remember that probably more than a quarter of a century may have passed away after the battle of Platæa
before their acquaintance began, we may not unreasonably doubt the fidelity of an impression of the truth of
which he may nevertheless have been sincerely convinced. But the anecdote is of special value as showing
the extent to which the ethical and poetical sentiment of
the historian was shared by many of his countrymen.
The tendency to look at historical facts through the
medium of philosophy or religion is sufficiently shown
throughout the whole work of Herodotus; but this is
perhaps the only instance in which we have his own
assurance that this tendency was not confined to himself.
And unless we admit without reserve the truth of the

[1] History of Greece, vol. v. p. 217.

story, its exquisite beauty, not less than its touching
simplicity and truthfulness of feeling, shows further that
this method of interpretation was carried by others to a
perfection scarcely inferior to his own. What the facts
may have been which it professes to relate, or whether
they may not have occurred precisely as they are said
to have occurred, we are unable to determine, not so
much in this case from the circumstance that it was not
immediately committed to writing, as because we cannot
trust, even for a few days or months, the memory of a
man who lives under the influence of a system so hostile
to the growth of the historical faculty. The sentiment
put into the mouth of the Persian at the banquet of
Attaginus seems to be not less distinctively Greek than
those which are uttered by the seven conspirators
against the usurpation of the Magians. The expression of any foreboding however slight, of any remark
on the uncertainty of life, as vague and general as that
of Xerxes when he surveyed his fleet in its glory[1],
would unconsciously shape itself in the mind of Thersander into that philosophical form which imparts to
the tale its exquisite and perpetual freshness. But if
we cannot, on such testimony, assume that such utter
anticipation of ruin was present to the mind of the Persian leaders (and that it oppressed the Persians generally
we have no evidence), the anecdote, from every other
view, becomes superfluous. In the ethical conception
of the history, Mardonius was already doomed from the
day when Artabanus warned him that from his westward journey there would for him be no return[2]; and

[1] Herodotus, vii. 46.   [2] Ibid. vii. 10.

the parting words of Xerxes consecrated him as the victim which was destined to expiate the slaughter of Leonidas.

The battle of Plataea. If there are any uncertainties in the story of the battle at Plataeae, they are chiefly confined to the words and the actions of Mardonius. There is no reason to question the answers given to the Greek and Persian leaders by their respective soothsayers. They may be classed in the number of safe statements which include the warnings given to Croesus or Maxentius[1]; and the disobedience of Mardonius not only accords with the epical method of the history but also comes not unnaturally from a man who, if numbers were to decide the conflict, was conscious of possessing an immeasurable advantage. A greater difficulty is presented by his last speech to his officers[2], when he had determined to begin the engagement. If we receive the story, his words must either bring the Delphian expedition altogether into doubt or prove that he was uttering a conscious lie on a matter with which his officers could have been scarcely less acquainted than himself. On this supposition his implied scepticism would belong rather to a later day and to such men as Appius Claudius Pulcher, or Lucius Saturninus.[3] The contrast between Persian bravery and Spartan cowardice, which the military changes of

---

[1] See p. 302.   [2] Herodotus, ix. 42.
[3] Cicero, De Nat. Deor. ii. 3; Arnold, History of Rome, vol. ii. p. 607, and Later Roman Commonwealth, vol. i. p. 124. The sentiment which Cicero (De Senectute, iv.) puts into the mouth of Fabius, is only an expansion, and therefore a weakening, of the words of Hector which cheered on Epaminondas in the day of his victory and his death.

Pausanias suggested to Mardonius, and the contemptuous challenge to decide the issue by an equal number of Lacedæmonians and Persians[1], spring from the same poetical sentiment which recognised everywhere the proofs that the greatest height of insolence is then only reached when the offender stands on the very verge of the abyss.[2]

But the narrative of this battle serves, by this same sentiment, to prepare us for the subsequent fortunes of the Spartan Pausanias[3], as that of Salamis seems in one or two incidents framed to meet the after fate of Themistocles.[4] The image of Pausanias, standing between the meagre fare of Sparta and the sumptuous Persian feast, at once connects the hour of his triumph with the tale of his pride, his treachery, and his death, and suggests a comparison with the warning given by Sandanis to Crœsus. His reply to the advice of Lampôn, that he should crucify and mutilate the body of Mardonius[5], is, as Mr. Grote has remarked, rather "a poetical contrivance for bringing out an honourable sentiment, than a real incident."[6]

Anecdotes of Pausanias.

The historical method of Herodotus fails to justify a belief in the wonderful coincidence by which the battles of Platæa and Mycalê are said to have been fought on

Coincident battles of Platæa and Mycalê.

---

[1] Herodotus, ix. 48.

[2] ὕβρις, εἰ πολλῶν ὑπερπλησθῇ μάταν,
ἃ μὴ 'πίκαιρα μηδὲ συμφέροντα,
ἀκρότατον εἰσαναβᾶσ'
... ἀπότομον ὤρουσεν εἰς ἀνάγκαν.
Soph. Œd. Tyr. 877.

[3] Herodotus, ix. 82. [4] Ibid. viii. 109, 110.
[5] Ibid. ix. 78. [6] History of Greece, vol. v. p. 250.

the same day. It would need the written contemporary evidence of more than ordinarily accurate writers to believe that these battles, as well as those of Salamis and Himera[1], with all their detailed coincidences, took place as they are related.[2] Events which occur at very short intervals naturally cause in the mind a close association, which would be expressed by assigning them to the same day or the same hour.

The Phêmê or Rumour at Mycalê.
Much stress has been laid on the Phêmê, or Rumour[3], which is said to have run through the Greek army before the fight at Mycalê. If this rumour was held to be a divine voice or vocal goddess[4] (and this cannot be questioned), we may yet notice the differences in its operation. When the horsemen of Mardonius surrounded the men of Phokis[5], the Phêmê, or "sudden and simultaneous impression," was communicated to all, that the hour of their death was come. At Mycalê it is not easy to determine from the words of Herodotus[6] whether the Phêmê preceded the coming of the herald's staff, or whether the sight of the staff conveyed to all an instantaneous knowledge of the victory at Platææ. The two instances suffice to show that its evidence was not always conclusive. If the impression at Mycalê was afterwards proved to be correct, the anticipation of the Phokians was not realised; and Herodotus confesses

[1] Herodotus, vii. 166.
[2] Diodorus (xiii. 62) makes the battle of Himera fall on the same day with that of Thermopylæ. Mr. Grote is inclined to reject both accounts. History of Greece, vol. v. p. 301.
[3] Herodotus, ix. 100.
[4] Grote, History of Greece, vol. v. p. 263.
[5] Herodotus, ix. 17.   [6] Ibid. ix. 100, 101.

his ignorance of the motive which prompted a demonstration familiar to all modern Oriental horsemen. But it argues, perhaps, some rashness to connect this Phêmê of the old Greek world with that spontaneous impulse of an ordinary multitude which seems for the time to efface each man's individuality.[1] The vehement language in which French writers not unfrequently give utterance to excited thought, results in an exaggerated impression which imparts some appearance of personality to the common impulse of a crowd. The account which Mr. Grote cites of the destruction of the Bastile, is only an instance of a narrative which desires a human originating cause, because we cannot ascertain the man who set it in motion. The crowd which attacked the Bastile may have been an extraordinarily large or powerful crowd; it may be more or less difficult to trace to its source the influence which drove it on; the impression may have become universal with a rapidity unknown before; and the separate wills of the men who composed it may have been merged to a pre-eminent degree in the execution of the purpose. But, with the features modified, this is only the history of all crowds; and it holds good of the Porteous mob only to a less extent than of the one to which M. Michelet boldly avers that no man gave the first impulse.

To the Phêmê at Mycalê these remarks apply with less force, if we reject the tale of the herald's staff. On this point Mr. Grote has not expressed himself very decidedly; but he connects the common impression of

The incident of the herald's staff.

---

[1] See the comparison as drawn out by Mr. Grote. History Greece, vol. v. pp. 264, 265.

the army with the previous sight of the cheering sign. If, however, we put aside the marvel which is the essential feature of the story, it must require some stronger evidence than that which we possess to prove that this coming of the Phêmê was not the unconscious invention of a later day.

The story of Xerxes and Amestris.

The battles of Plataeæ and Mycalê closed for ever the dream of European supremacy which had cheated the wiser mind of Darius not less than his pampered and headstrong son. With the final fortunes of the Persian generals the history of Herodotus draws towards its close. His means of information furnish the only difficulty in a narrative for the most part clear and intelligible. If there is something inscrutable in his sudden desertion of Mardonius without striking a single blow, yet Artabazus displays, in his rapid march through Thessaly and Thrace, a readiness of wit and firmness of will which raise him far above the level of Eastern generals.[1] Of his adventures, as well as of the conduct of Xerxes at Sardes, Herodotus might have had fairly trustworthy information. But this remark will scarcely apply to the highly characteristic tale which reveals to us the miserable weakness of Xerxes and the loathsome brutality of Amestris.[2] We can but say that such a scene was well worthy to close the chronicle of a man who had sought to repress in the deadly bonds of Persian despotism the intellect and freedom of the world. And the contrast must likewise have presented itself to the mind of the historian, unless, on little evidence or none, we assume that he did not intend

[1] Herodotus, ix. 89.   [2] Ibid. ix. 112.

here to close his narrative. If we cannot so believe, then we may think that Herodotus did well to portray, in his last picture, the physical and moral degradation of a line of kings who had sought to close the long quarrel which began with the wrongs of Io and Medeia, of Europa and of Helen.

Thus, then, in this history of the Persian war we have the narrative of a struggle of which we cannot doubt the reality and whose general features we need not question. But it is a tale in which every incident must be submitted to a searching test before we can admit it without reserve, and in which the most plausible statements will be found sometimes the most questionable. From the beginning to the end, we find an ethical or religious purpose overlaying or putting out of sight all political causes and motives, and substituting appeals to exploits done in the mythical ages for less fictitious but more substantial services. Throughout we find narratives constructed to meet a popular saying [1] or illustrate a popular belief.[2] We find national struggles which are unquestionably historical, illustrated by imaginary combats of well-chosen champions[3], and momen-

[1] The history of Syloson was connected with two popular sayings, ἡ Συλοσῶντος χλαμύς, and ἴητι Συλοσῶντος εὐρυχωρίη. Sir G. Lewis (Credibility of Early Roman History, vol. ii. p. 520) believes the incidents to which they relate to be well authenticated history. See also Grote, History of Greece, vol. iv. p. 339.

[2] It is needless to multiply instances: the most prominent example is that of Crœsus.

[3] Sir G. C. Lewis thinks that the recognition of the battle of Othryades by both Argos and Sparta in the Peloponnesian war, must be considered as removing all reasonable doubt as to its

tous national changes in which a contradiction runs through the most important features.[1] We find a sequence of events in which every step and every turn is ushered in by tokens and wonders or the visible intervention of gods and heroes. We find legend and fable interwoven with the unadorned details of political intercourse and the movements of fleets and armies. But we find also, in the great men of that city on which was centred the hope and the salvation of the Hellenic

---

historical character. (Credibility of Early Roman History, vol. ii. p. 515.) The battle is said to have been fought a little while before the overthrow of Crœsus, which is assigned to the year 546 B.C. The national recognition of it belongs to 420 B.C. (Thucydides, v. 41.) Mr. Grote accepts the duel as historical, but remarks that it was represented by the men of Argos in a manner totally different from the version of the Lacedæmonians. (History of Greece, vol. ii. p. 606.) Mr. Grote and Sir G. C. Lewis both notice the objections of Niebuhr (Lectures on Ancient History, vol. i. p. 268). They appear to me more forcible than the arguments for the authenticity of the story. It is much to expect that oral tradition should for nearly one hundred years have preserved without exaggeration the details of such an encounter. At the utmost, we can hardly admit more than the bare statement that some sort of battle took place; the details of number, place, and issue seem to be wholly uncertain.

[1] The variations in the tale of Harmodius and Aristogeiton have been already referred to (p. 283). A more remarkable instance is furnished by the narrative of the attempt of Kylôn to seize the Athenian Acropolis. According to Herodotus it was unsuccessful (v. 71), while Thucydides (i. 126) says that he did seize it, and underwent a siege in it along with the other conspirators. The two narratives differ also as to the personal fate of Kylôn. See Sir G. C. Lewis, Credibility, &c. vol. ii. p. 532.

world, a distinct and deliberate policy which neither sign nor portent, seer or soothsayer, dream or marvel, can avail to crush or even to turn aside,—a foresight which took the true measure of their enemy's power and their own,—a character as real and as tangible as that of the great men who have done good service to our own country or to any other land in Christendom.

CHAP. VI.

ON THE CHARACTER OF THE GREAT ATHENIAN LEADERS IN THE PERSIAN WAR.

Nature of the difficulties involved in the history of Miltiades and Themistocles.

If the history of the Persian war involves (especially in all that relates to the barbarian world) the task of sifting truth from fiction, difficulties of a very different kind present themselves in the lives and fortunes of the most eminent of the Hellenic leaders. They are difficulties caused not by any commingling of legend with reality, not by any substitution of superhuman or accidental causes in place of human and political motives, but by the misrepresentations or misconceptions which ensue from the changes of public feeling, and which must be especially powerful in an age which can make no appeal to contemporary history. By a singular fortune the names of the two foremost Athenian leaders have come down under an obloquy which more than balances their former glory; and if in the conqueror of Marathon our perplexity arises chiefly from a notion of popular fickleness, we are bidden to see in the victor of Salamis one of the worst and most selfish of traitors,—to discern in the man whose wisdom and indomitable firmness carried his country triumphantly through a struggle for life and death, a schemer who designed the ruin of that country even before he had finished the task of her salvation. It would be presumptuous to maintain that any new evidence is forthcoming to determine the measure of their guilt or innocence. But although the verdict of their countrymen has never been reversed by the historian, it may yet be possible to show that the evidence brought forward against them will warrant at least a suspense of judgment; and the life of Themistocles was such as we would not willingly see clouded by an accusation which is not perhaps deserved.

In the case of Miltiades, the charge of fraud and deception has been almost merged in that of fickleness and levity against the people which condemned him. Such an accusation, it must be admitted, is eagerly welcomed by all to whom any form of democratical government appears repulsive. Our natural tendency to sympathise with the individual against an aggregate of citizens is so strong that we are disposed to forget that the most distinguished services can confer no title to violate the law. At once, therefore, it must be acknowledged that the general " who has earned applause by eminent skill and important victories " is not to be " recompensed by being allowed the liberty of breaking his trust afterwards, and exposing his country to peril without censure or penalty."[1] And as little can it be questioned that fickleness and ingratitude, in the meaning commonly attached to those words, are not to be reckoned among the special sins of a democracy, and, least of all, of such a democracy as that of Athens. A democratical society is, as Mr. Grote has forcibly urged, precisely that in which personal influence, when once

The Athenians charged with ingratitude towards Miltiades.

[1] Grote, History of Greece, vol. iv. p. 500.

acquired, is least easily shaken, and where confidence, once bestowed, is continued even in the teeth of evidence which proves incapacity or demerit.[1] Had it not been so at Athens, the overwhelming ruin of the Sicilian expedition would have been avoided; but the respectability of Nikias first won and then retained for him an uncriticising confidence, to which nothing but the general correctness of his conduct in any way entitled him. The same confidence, accorded on the same inadequate grounds, continued to Phokion the office of general, until the opportunity of resisting the growing power of the Macedonian king was lost for ever.[2] And it was precisely this feeling of gratitude for real or supposed benefits received, or an esteem for strict morality which would seem entitled to still more gentle treatment, that prompted the people to retain in office men whom it was at once their interest and their duty peremptorily to dismiss. But because in a democracy a change of opinion, when once admitted, must be expressed freely and candidly, the expression of that change is apt to become vehement and angry; and the language of indignation, when it comes to be felt, may be interpreted as a feeling of ingratitude when the offender happens to be a man eminent for former services. Yet more it must be admitted that the ingratitude and injustice of democracies (whatever it may be) is neither more frequent nor more severe than that of any other form of government. When the Spartans of a later generation con-

The charge of ingratitude untenable.

---

[1] Grote, History of Greece, vol. iv. p. 502.
[2] Ibid. vol. xii. p. 482, &c.

demned to death their king Pausanias for an issue over which he had no control, but really for a charge on which he had been tried and acquitted eight years before[1], they exhibited an injustice and ingratitude fully equal to any of which Athenians were ever guilty. And further, although the custom of modern society permits the initiation of new laws without attaching to the proposer either a legal or moral responsibility, yet, to use Mr. Grote's words, it cannot be considered unreasonable that before proposing a new decree or law the mover "should take care that there was nothing in it inconsistent with existing laws, or, if there were, that he should first formally bring forward a direct proposition for the repeal of such pre-existent law."[2] Such a rule, although it may sometimes appear a hard condition, might, when once recognised, be enforced without injustice; and it must certainly have the effect of keeping down the body of statutes into something like a reasonable compass, as well as of rendering impossible the nominal retention of a mass of obsolete and contradictory legislation. And further, it is true that the dangerous tendency at Athens was rather to an excessive submission to the mere will of popular leaders, and that it was of paramount importance to take all practicable securities against this besetting weakness.[3]

Still, with all these dangers and all these duties, it may perhaps be doubted whether there was not in the Athenian people a disposition to shrink from respon- *Their fault lay in a disposition to shrink from public responsibility.*

[1] Grote, History of Greece, vol. ix. p. 416.
[2] Ibid. vol. v. p. 510.
[3] Ibid. vol. iv. p. 506.

sibility not altogether to their honour, and a reluctance to take to themselves any blame for results to which they had deliberately contributed. When the Syracusan expedition had ended in utter ruin, they accused the orators who had urged them to undertake it.[1] When they had condemned to death by a single vote the six generals who had just returned from their victory at Arginusæ, they decreed that the men who had entrapped them into the sentence should be brought to trial.[2] Yet in both these instances they were finding fault for the result of their own verdict or of undertakings to which they had given their solemn sanction. In the former case, the remembrance of his original advice prevented them from uttering a word of blame against Nikias himself, although the extent of the disaster was due in great measure to his own exacting timidity.[3] Yet the citizens, who had been brought up in the daily exercise of a judicial and critical power, were scarcely justified in throwing upon others the blame of their own inconsiderate vehemence. Here, however, they knew what they were about to undertake; they gave their full consent to more than all that Nikias had ventured to ask, well knowing the object for which their preparation was to be made. But the case is altered when a

---

[1] Thucydides, viii. 1.

[2] Xenophon, Hellen. I. vii. 39; Grote, History of Greece, vol. viii. p. 278.

[3] The magnitude of the effort was due almost wholly to Nikias, who staked the whole power of Athens on the hazard of this single die. A more wonderful instance has perhaps been never known in which mere caution has infinitely increased the evil which it dreaded. Thucydides, vi. 20—26.

leader, however illustrious, comes forward with enthusiastic hopes and seeks to lead his countrymen blindfold into some scheme, of which he will not reveal the nature, and of which he would be more than mortal if he could guarantee the issue. It matters not what benefits his wisdom or his patriotism may have conferred; it matters not what surety his previous moderation may have given for his future success. No state or people can, under any circumstances, be justified in engaging the strength of the country in any enterprise with the details of which they have not been made acquainted. And if their admiration for lofty sentiment or heroic courage tempts them to give their sanction to such a scheme, the responsibility is shifted from him who gives to those who adopt the counsel,—to this extent at least, that they cannot, in the event of failure, visit him in any fairness with penal consequences. Dismissal from all civil posts, and the humiliation which must follow the resentment or the contempt of his countrymen, are not for such a man too severe a punishment. But a more rigorous sentence clearly requires purer hands on the part of the men who must be his judges. Nor can we allow much force to the plea that Athenian polity was then only in the days of its infancy, and that peculiar caution was necessary to guard against a disposition too favourable to the re-establishment of a tyranny. Such a sentiment could not be felt or expressed at the time; and the imputation is not flattering to men who had lived for twenty years under the constitution of Solon, as extended and reformed by Cleisthenes. The grounds on which they condemned Miltiades would have amply justified any sentence in such a case as that of Alkibiades; but they are scarcely becoming towards a man of whose folly or guilt they had deliberately made themselves partakers.[1] It may be true that "a leading Greek could not bear" prosperity "without mental depravation," and that, owing to this tendency, "the successful leader" became "one of the most dangerous men in the community;"[2] but this fact cannot divest a people of all responsibility for their own resolutions. Miltiades may have been utterly corrupted by his glory; but very shame should have

[1] Mr. Grote (History of Greece, vol. iv. p. 499) charges Miltiades with employing "his prodigious ascendency" over the minds of the Athenians "to induce them to follow him without knowing whither, in the confidence of an unknown booty." It is a humiliating admission for a free people even in the very infancy of their freedom. Comparisons are often dangerous; and the condition of the English people after Waterloo was not in all respects similar to that of the Athenians after Marathon. Yet we might not unreasonably have expected that the answer of the Athenians to Miltiades might have resembled somewhat more nearly the reply which any similar proposal would certainly have brought down from the English people on the Duke of Wellington. In following Miltiades blindfold, they went against the first principle of their political life, and abandoned that birthright of Athenian citizens which enabled them to say: μόνοι γὰρ ... αὐτοὶ ἤτοι κρίνομέν γε ἢ ἐνθυμούμεθα ὀρθῶς τὰ πράγματα, οὐ τοὺς λόγους τοῖς ἔργοις βλάβην ἡγούμενοι, ἀλλὰ μὴ προδιδαχθῆναι μᾶλλον λόγῳ πρότερον ἢ ἐπὶ ἃ δεῖ ἔργῳ ἐλθεῖν.—*Thucydides*, ii. 40.

[2] Grote, History of Greece, vol. iv. p. 505. The silence of Herodotus, as Mr. Grote observes (History, &c. vol. iv. p. 496), is a strong argument against the statements of Cornelius Nepos, Diodorus, and Plutarch, that Miltiades was put into prison and died there.

withheld the hands of the Athenians from one whose folly they had not checked and whose honesty they had not paused to question.

The life of Themistocles was closed under a yet darker cloud of shame and infamy. But whatever may have been the faults of the Athenian people with regard to him, we cannot reckon among them a blind participation in schemes of whose nature and object they were utterly ignorant. His character is one which has little to do with the mythical feelings and religious system of the age; and in the story of his life and policy we trace little or nothing of that kind of fiction which is busy with the history of Crœsus or Cyrus, of Xerxes or Polycrates. But it does not follow from this that the narrative of his actions is free from fiction of another kind. In the period which passed between the close of the Persian and the commencement of the Peloponnesian war, the spirit of the people began to exhibit that change which was consummated in the age of Pericles. During that time the mythical form of thought, which made historical truth altogether subordinate to the illustration of a religious belief or the establishment of an ethical principle, was displaced by that keen analysis of human motives and that singular insight into social and political causes, which seem almost to identify the age of Thucydides with our own. But this very process gave a new force to many sentiments whose action, unless controlled by a strictly contemporary history, must prove not less fertile in fiction than the religious sentiment of the age which was passing away. It was the fiction which springs from personal or poli-

Element of fiction in the history of Themistocles.

tical jealousy, — the exaggeration which assumes the certainty of guilt where, at the worst, there is ground simply for suspicion.

Exaggeration in the contrast between the character of Themistocles and that of Aristeides.

Themistocles died in the same year in which Thucydides was born. From the time, therefore, of his ostracism, at least, if not earlier, to the time when the great historian had grown up to manhood, the reaction, which accompanied the ascendency of Aristeides, had strengthened the prejudice which delights in exaggerated contrast. Themistocles began life in poverty; he closed it in wealth and dishonour. Aristeides was pre-eminent for the purity of his motives; and his justice was proved by the absolute want which left his family dependent on the public bounty. A bribe had for him no temptation; but the lust of gold served to account in Themistocles for a simultaneous action of contradictory motives, such as no other man ever exhibited. This feeling had received its direction while the rivalry between these two great men was not a thing of the past; it had grown into a deeply rooted conviction, before they had learnt to submit to a careful and impartial criticism the evidence on which it rested.

Uniform policy of Themistocles.

The result produced by the working of this prejudice is not disproportioned to the vehemence of the sentiment. The absence of a pure and lofty unselfishness, to which perhaps he never laid a claim, made the Athenian people ready to believe of him any degree of political corruption; and the charge of such corruption was taken, without evidence, as proof that he was prepared to undo the work of his whole life for the sake of that of which he had already an abundance. Yet nothing less than this are we called upon to believe with regard to a man who exhibited a fixity of purpose and a concentration of will, which a few perhaps may have equalled but none certainly have surpassed, and whose schemes assuredly served the good of his country, although they may also have advanced his own. From the time when the victory of Marathon had driven back the first wave of Persian conquest, Themistocles began to carry out that one object in which, with an astonishing foresight, he discerned the coming greatness of imperial Athens, and which he never ceased to further until the vote of ostracism sent him into banishment at Argos. From him came the impulse which concentrated the efforts of the Athenians on their navy, and which availed itself of the struggle with Ægina to lay the foundation of their future empire.[1] With him originated the determination to transfer the war from the land to the sea, when perhaps the words of the Delphian priestess pointed to the stronghold of the Acropolis.[2] To him it was owing that the allies fought at Salamis instead of throwing up their cause by a childish flight to the Isthmian wall, and to him was owing not merely the victory which sent Xerxes in haste and terror to the Hellespont, but the formation of that confederacy which identified the power of Athens with the true interests of her allies, and which checked during three generations the fatal tendency of the Hellenic world to an isolated independence.[3] And if we cannot say with certainty that he actually proposed the abandonment of the old

---

[1] Herodotus, vii. 144.   [2] Ibid. vii. 143.
[3] τὴν ἀρχὴν εὐθὺς συγκατεσκεύαζε.—*Thucydides*, i. 93. Grote, History of Greece, vol. v. p. 398.

city[1], we may yet be sure that no religious prepossessions would have withheld him from urging a plan which, in great part, he carried out by the only means left open to him. If chiefly by his strenuous efforts and ready wisdom the old city was surrounded by a wall strong enough to defy all assaults, he also called into being a new city at the great Athenian harbour. And all this he accomplished with some opposition of political jealousy in his own city and in spite of all the efforts of Sparta.[2] So mighty had been the impulse which he gave to Athenian enterprise, so completely had it moulded their character, that his great and uncorrupt rival gave his aid in the working of that maritime policy whose introduction he had opposed.[3] In this business of his life he had displayed wonderful powers,— a rapidity of perception which gave to his maturest judgment the appearance of intuition, — a fertility of resource and a readiness in action which were more than equal to every emergency. He had shown a courage rising in proportion to the dangers which he had to face,— a calmness of spirit which turned to his own purpose the weakness and selfish fears of other men. He had kept others in some degree true to the common cause, when a blind and stupid terror seemed to make all possibility of union hopeless. These

---

[1] This is the conclusion of Niebuhr (Lectures on Ancient History, vol. i. p. 349). Mr. Grote (History, &c. vol. v. p. 340) does not admit it, and the words of Thucydides (i. 93) do not imply it.

[2] Thucydides, i. 90, &c.

[3] Grote, History of Greece, vol. v. pp. 371, 372, &c.

were great qualities and great deeds; they argued much love of his country and more appreciation of her real interests. They were the virtues and exploits of a man who discerned all the strength and flexibility of her political constitution, and the mission which his city was charged to fulfil. They are virtues which show a devotion to his country not inconsistent with a regard to his own fortunes,—an indomitable energy in her service which need not imply a fastidious integrity of character. His patriotism was not hostile to his self-love; his political morality made use of the fears or the hopes of others to increase his own wealth, while they furthered the interests of his countrymen. He was a great leader, but not the most uncorrupt citizen; a wise counsellor, but no rigid and impartial judge,—a statesman formidable to the enemies of his country, yet not altogether scrupulous in the choice of the weapons which he employed against them.

It is a mixture of lofty purpose and selfish calculation, of heroism and meanness, which has been seen in many of the greatest men of any age and any country. It is a character not wholly unlike that of Warren Hastings or of the illustrious statesman who has just finished the work of Themistocles for the Italian kingdom. And yet we are asked to believe, not that this man yielded to some mean temptation,—not that he began his career in poverty and closed it in riches,—not that he made use of his power sometimes to advance his own temporal interests and sometimes to thwart or oppress others; but that from the beginning he distinctly contemplated the prospect of destroying the house which he was building up, and of seeking a home in the

Mixed character of Themistocles.

palace of the king on whose power and hopes he was first to inflict a deadly blow. We are told that at the very time when, by an unparalleled energy of character and singleness of purpose, he was driving the allies into a battle which they dreaded, he was sending to the Persian king a message which might stand him in good stead when he came as an exile to the court of Susa. We are told that he deceived his enemy by a lie in order to win his favour against the time of trouble which he knew was coming,—that he looked indulgently on the guilt of Pausanias, although he despised the weakness of his intellect,—and that, on the death of the Spartan regent, he took up the work of treachery which in his hands had come to nothing. And yet further we are asked to believe that in the Persian palace he actually found the refuge which he had contemplated,—that his claim to favour was admitted with unquestioning submission,—that he pledged himself to destroy his country and received the revenues of large towns to enable him to fulfil his word. We are told that years passed away in preparation for his journey to Susa, in familiar sojourn with the Persian king, in almost regal luxury on the Asiatic coast; and yet that he died, not having made a single effort to fulfil even a part of the promise which he had made to the Persian king. It is a conclusion which we may hesitate to receive for a time which has no strictly contemporary history, and when every motive existed to heighten a contrast and exaggerate a failing or a vice.

Prejudice of Herodotus in

To the fortunes of Themistocles subsequent to the period of his history, Herodotus makes but one passing reference[1]; but his expressions appear to show that, in common with the popular feeling of the day, he had prejudged his character. It must have been no faint prepossession which led him to discern a deliberate piece of double-dealing, not in the second message which Themistocles sent to Xerxes by Sikinnus, but in his advice to the Athenians after the flight of the king, that they should postpone further efforts against the barbarians to the more necessary work of restoration at home. It is a rare instance of partiality in a writer who is singularly strict in acknowledging the merits even of those men and states to whom he might be least attracted either by their general character or by his own personal sympathies.[2]

the case of Themistocles.

From Thucydides we have received a sketch of the public life and policy of Themistocles after the flight of Xerxes and the defeat of Mardonius. It is a sequel strictly in accordance with all that we read of him in the pages of Herodotus, showing the same almost intuitive foresight, the same wisdom in planning, the same firmness in execution. In a few sentences also he has summed up his own estimate of his character and genius; and his judgment, with all its terseness and brevity, brings before us a clearer and more real image of the man than even that which is presented in the more detailed and pictorial narrative of Herodotus. But his words furnish no unquestionable evidence of the extent or the nature of his guilt. The first charge of treachery,

Judgment of Thucydides on the guilt of Themistocles and Pausanias.

[1] Herodotus, viii. 109.
[2] See especially his lenient criticism of the conduct of the men of Argos throughout the war (vii. 152).

made during the lifetime of Pausanias, was successfully repelled; and before his second accusation by the Spartans he was already in exile at Argos. The Lacedæmonians referred to proofs of his complicity with Pausanias; but Thucydides does not say that these proofs were exhibited to the Athenians[1], or that they were of such a nature as that they could be exhibited. By the peculiarity of the Spartan system, documentary evidence was held to be inconclusive without oral testimony; and the guilt of Pausanias was determined not by the discovery of his correspondence but by the conversation which the ephors overheard between himself and his slave Argilius.[2] His last letters to Xerxes were laid before the ephors by this slave, who discovered in them his own death-warrant. What the remaining contents of these letters were, and whether or how far they implicated Themistocles, we are not told; and the expression of Thucydides seems unduly strained if we gather from it that either he or the Spartans had ever seen any other portions of his correspondence.[3] The answers of the Persian king might have fallen into their hands; but it

[1] He merely says that the Spartans accused Themistocles from evidence which had come before *them* in the time of Pausanias: ὡς εὕρισκον ἐκ τῶν περὶ Παυσανίου ἐλέγχων.—i. 135.

[2] See the excellent appendix of Mr. Grote on Spartan education. History of Greece, vol. ii. pp. 639, &c. 657.

[3] Speaking of the letter conveyed by Gongylus for Pausanias, Thucydides says: ἐνεγέγραπτο τάδε ἐν αὐτῇ, ὡς ὕστερον ἀνευρέθη. It would not appear to be a necessary inference that he had himself seen them (i. 128). Grote, History of Greece, vol. v. p. 363.

is not likely that such a document as that which was intrusted to Gongylus of Eretria would ever return from the archives of Susa. There is something suspicious in the style and still more in the length of this letter. There is no reason to suppose that Pausanias was able to write himself, and it is strange that his scribe should exhibit a power of writing altogether beyond that of the secretary of Mindarus who, seventy years afterwards, announced in eleven words the death of his master and the destruction of the fleet at Kyzicus.[1] Still less easy is it to understand how the Athenians could be made acquainted with the letter of Themistocles to Artaxerxes.[2] The letter is stated not only to have been received but to have procured for him a hearty welcome at the Persian court; and further, in his case, we read of no intercepted documents, and he died in high esteem and favour with the Persian king. The subjugation of his country is mentioned by Thucydides under an expression which leaves it uncertain whether the historian construed it as intended treachery or as a wilful deception of the sovereign whose bounty had loaded him with princely riches.[3] Of the secret burial of his bones in Attic ground he speaks as a popular report[4], which must to himself have furnished anything but a proof of lifelong double-dealing.

[1] Xenophon, Hellen. L. i. 19. Grote, History of Greece, vol. ii. p. 661.
[2] Thucydides, i. 137.
[3] διὰ τὴν ... τοῦ Ἑλληνικοῦ ἐλπίδα, ἣν ὑπετίθει αὐτῷ βουλήσεων.—*Thucydides*, i. 138. At most, Thucydides could have no more than hearsay evidence for the compact.
[4] τὰ ὀστᾶ φασὶ κομισθῆναι.—i. 138.

Statements of later writers. The statements of such a writer as Diodorus or even of Plutarch are of little value where they contradict, either expressly or by implication, the assertions of Thucydides. They are also frequently inconsistent or contradictory in themselves, and spring sometimes from a total misconception of historical facts, sometimes from the mere love of producing a highly coloured picture. The tale of Plutarch, that Themistocles designed to burn the allied fleet at Pagasæ, is absurdly opposed to the whole line of policy which he is known to have been carrying out at the time.[1] His mysterious secrecy with regard to this design is transferred by Diodorus, with an extravagance of absurdity, to the building of the walls of Athens.[2] From the many personal anecdotes which illustrate his arrogance before his exile or serve to establish his treachery after it, we cannot with safety draw any positive conclusions. Some are utterly incredible; others, if true, prove very little. To discern an intolerable pride in his dedication of an altar to Artemis Aristoboulê was a hard interpretation[3]; but the wise Themistocles must have fallen into a second childhood before he could have even thought of comparing himself to a plane tree which the men, who had sought its shelter during the storm, were now cutting down.[4] The whole story of his adventures after his

[1] Plutarch: Themistocles, 20; Aristeides, 22. Grote, History of Greece, vol. v. pp. 275, 276.

[2] See the appendix (V.) of Dr. Thirlwall on a stratagem ascribed to Themistocles by Diodorus (xi. 41—43). Vol. ii. p. 398.

[3] Grote, History of Greece, vol. v. p. 378.

[4] Thirlwall, History of Greece, vol. ii. p. 380 (ch. xvi.).

departure from the Asiatic coast must be not less cautiously received than the Herodotean narratives which reveal the secret life of Persian palaces. We leave the known Hellenic world and enter a land of romantic or malicious fiction. And if it is not easy to realise the feeling which loved to represent the victor of Salamis as painfully learning the intricate ceremonies of Oriental servility, it is still more difficult to believe that the memory of his ancient greatness could suggest to him nothing better than a loathsome satisfaction in his present incredible degradation.[1]

If, after sweeping away the tales which fall before the ordinary tests of historical criticism, a scanty foundation seems to be left for so great a charge of long-planned yet ineffectual treachery, it has nevertheless sufficed to establish a general conviction of his guilt. In Mr. Grote's mind this conviction is heightened by a remembrance of the tendency of Greek leaders and statesmen to yield to temptations of wealth and power. So strong and so common was this miserable tendency that a reputation for personal integrity served to keep up public confidence in men who were in every other respect utterly undeserving of it. And in Themistocles there was unquestionably a self-consciousness and an eager love of money, perhaps also of ostentation, which it is unnecessary to palliate, and which makes it ridiculous to speak of him as a man of strict and discriminating equity. But, after every allowance has been

General assumption of his guilt.

[1] Dr. Thirlwall utterly rejects the anecdote of Plutarch which makes Themistocles rejoice in his shame. History of Greece, vol. ii. ch. xvi. p. 389.

made for his faults and his vices, and while we bear in mind the extent to which these vices prevailed in the greatest statesmen or generals of the Hellenic world, the evidence before us seems scarcely to warrant the sweeping judgment that though "he was in the early part of his life sincerely bent upon the upholding and aggrandisement of his country and was on some most critical occasions of unspeakable value to it, yet, on the whole, his morality was as reckless as his intelligence was eminent;"[1] and that he ended his life "a traitor and a pensioner to the great king, pledged to undo his own previous work of liberation accomplished at the victory of Salamis."[2] This conclusion has led Mr. Grote to believe that Thucydides was satisfied with the evidence of his guilt[3],—to put the darkest interpretation on his withholding from his countrymen the knowledge which he may have possessed of the designs of Pausanias, —to assert that after his exile he probably took a more decided share in them than before,—and, finally, that, after taking refuge in Persian ground, he promised to King Artaxerxes a long series of "victorious campaigns"[4] against the country which had cast him out. One part, at least, in this judgment seems unnecessarily harsh, if not actually unjust. His motives may not have been as pure as those of Aristeides; he may not even have pretended to the personal incorruptibility of Pericles: but there is no evidence that his love for his country was confined to his earlier years. No one has shown with more vigour and ability than Mr. Grote the para-

[1] Grote, History of Greece, vol. iv. p. 457. [2] Ibid. p. 458.
[3] Ibid. vol. v. p. 383. [4] Ibid. p. 390.

mount greatness of the change which Themistocles introduced into the policy of Athens; no one has more clearly traced out the enormous influence which he exercised in directing all her energy to naval enterprise, and the effectual aid which he gave to the establishment of her maritime supremacy. That influence and that aid was continued by an unbroken and uniform line of conduct to the time of his expulsion by the vote of ostracism. In spite of the wealth which he amassed and the acts of personal injustice which are laid to his charge, there is no proof that he had abandoned the policy of his past career, not a shade of evidence that he had given to his countrymen any counsel which he believed likely to do them injury. There can be little doubt of the consistency of his public conduct from the commencement of his career as a statesman till (in the true interests, perhaps, of his country) he was banished from the city which owed to him her very existence; and the problem which remains to be solved is not that such a man, thus driven into banishment, should resort to mean and unworthy schemes in his own self-interest or fall indefinitely lower in his personal morality, but that, without an effort to resist it, he should yield to the temptation to undo that which had been thus far the aim and the passion of his life.

The treasonable intrigues of Pausanias furnish no real parallel to the treachery imputed to Themistocles. It is impossible to believe that any one who had really loved and served Athens could descend to a depth of double-dealing, which on due evidence we may be less reluctant to admit in a Spartan king or leader. It is hard to think that one who prized that magnificent polity which

The case of Pausanias furnishes no parallel to that of Themistocles.

grew with the growth of Athenian freedom, could forget his old devotion with the case of a man whose country was to him simply a school of military discipline.[1] The example of Alkibiades proves nothing. He had neither loved nor served his country, and he was conscious that the one enterprise which he had vehemently urged was precisely that one which the wise foresight of Pericles had utterly condemned.[2] But, apart from all such previous considerations, we have in Pausanias and Themistocles two men who stand in entirely different positions. Intrusted with the kingly power, owing to the minority of his nephew the son of Leonidas[3], Pausanias had to look forward to a possible future descent from his high authority; but even if we suppose him not to have been influenced by such a thought as this, he was yet only a man who had to carry out the traditional system of his country, and who, with whatever bravery and judgment, fought at Platææ as his ancestors had fought elsewhere. But Themistocles had given a new direction to Athenian energy[4], he had shaped the future fortunes of his country, and he lived to strengthen and secure the empire which his own wisdom and courage had called into being. The work of Pausanias was finished by the issue of a single battle; the mind of Themistocles, after he had won the

[1] See the contrast between Spartan and Athenian polity, and the moral and political result produced by both, drawn out at length in the funeral oration of Pericles. Thucydides, ii. 37—41.

[2] Thucydides, ii. 65. 7. [3] Herodotus, ix. 10.

[4] τῆς θαλάσσης πρῶτος ἐτόλμησεν εἰπεῖν ὡς ἀνθεκτέα ἐστί.—*Thucydides*, i. 93.

victory of Salamis, was turned to the harder task of building up the Athenian confederacy and of imparting something like a fixed principle of union to a mass of atoms which were ready at any time to part asunder. And throughout his whole course his work was such as to need the fullest concentration of mind and will; it was one which had to be carried on in the face of overpowering difficulties, and which a divided heart and wavering purpose could never have accomplished.

Yet the facts of his exile, of his flight into Asia, perhaps also of his sojourn at the Persian court, cannot be called into question. It is quite possible that his ready wit might devise some plan of winning the favour of Artaxerxes, and more than possible that even without such a plan the Persian despot would welcome the conqueror of Salamis, although he came with no other submission than his own. It is not improbable that princely revenues may have been continued to him on no other profession than that of a general desire to further the Persian interests. His voluntary submission might stand in the place of defeat in war; his very banishment from his country was something like a sign that the temporary union of Hellas would soon be broken up. For the rest, his mere presence at Susa was no slight honour to the Persian king, who might well suppose that the other leaders of Athens and Sparta might be driven to follow the footsteps of Pausanias and Themistocles. If this may be held sufficient to explain his welcome in Persia and the powers intrusted to him on his return to the coast, the idea of a deeper and more deliberate treachery must be modified or abandoned. The charge of mean and undignified selfishness, of unscrupulous

Reasons for the welcome given by Artaxerxes to Themistocles.

lying or equivocation, may yet remain; but there will be no necessity to suppose that, while he arranged the positions of the ships at Salamis, he looked forward to the day when he should befriend the barbarian king as earnestly as he was then aiding the free land of his birth.

Ostracism of Aristeides.

If the evidence before us will scarcely warrant a harsher judgment, it appears without difficulty to fall in with this one. His whole public life displays a long rivalry between himself and Aristeides, interrupted only by the greatness of the common danger. These two men seemed as though born to exhibit in the same age the strongest contrasts of political and personal character; and the success or failure of the one was sure to heighten the merits or exaggerate the defects of the other. It was perhaps during the banishment of Aristeides that the anecdote was circulated which represented some poor and ignorant citizen as voting for his ostracism "on the simple ground that he was tired of hearing him always called the Just." It was after the exile of Themistocles that a fresh impulse was given to invectives and accusations such as those of the Rhodian poet Timocreon.[1] All who, like Timocreon, had suffered from his personal injustice and want of faith, were ready to see in Aristeides an untainted integrity, while they discerned in his rival the very embodiment of a lying treachery. These feelings, not without a good foundation on either side, were heightened by each successive conflict of opinion, which threat-

---

[1] Plutarch: Themistocles, 21. Grote, History of Greece, vol. v. pp. 380, 381.

ened to involve the ruin of their common country. The growing wealth of Themistocles, the increasing poverty of Aristeides; the rigid integrity of the latter, the winning versatility of the former; the attachment of Aristeides to the old forms of Athenian life, the determination of Themistocles to make Athens pre-eminently a maritime power,—all presented a contrast full of danger to the state, and which called, if anything could call, for the expedient of ostracism. In Aristeides she lost a citizen incomparably superior to his rival in every private virtue and in general morality: in Themistocles she retained the only man who could have guided her, through hopeless difficulty, to victory and imperial power. In spite of all opposition, he turned the whole resources of his country to the strengthening of her power by sea; and when the attack for which he had long looked for at length came, he adhered to his resolution of encountering the enemy's fleet at the earliest available opportunity. If the decision could have rested with him, the battle of Salamis might have been preceded by a struggle not less glorious at Artemisium. But the disaster of Thermopylæ determined the allies to retreat; and it was at this juncture that the Eubœans made a compact with Themistocles[1] which gave a colour to the subsequent accusations of his public and private enemies. By a bribe of thirty talents, Herodotus states that they gained over Themistocles, and received his pledge that, by every means in his power, he would strive to bring on a battle at Artemisium. Of these thirty talents he gave five to the Spartan Eury-

<small>Compact of the Eubœans with Themistocles after the battle of Thermopylæ.</small>

[1] Herodotus, viii. 4.

bindes; with three more he silenced the opposition of the Corinthian leader Adeimantus.[1] The rest, without the knowledge of the other generals, he retained for himself. The gain was great, and Mr. Grote believes that his pecuniary corruption made the presents of the Eubœans "both admissible and welcome."[2] But in this instance it is hard to see how the charge of corruption, though it applies in all strictness to Eurybiades and Adeimantus, can be urged against Themistocles. A man cannot with truth be said to be either bribed or persuaded into doing that which he had resolved to do before; and it seems almost a contradiction in terms to assert that by this bribe Themistocles was *tempted* to do that which he had wished and had probably tried to accomplish without the money."[3] The corruption lay with the Spartan and Corinthian leaders; and if the lust of gain may be charged upon Themistocles, it is a charge which probably he would not have cared to disclaim. The talents were given with the full purpose that they should be employed, according to his judgment, as secret-service money; and probably not even the morality of Englishmen would be shocked if a general so worked on the feelings of men who were open to such underhand influence. The guilt of reserving some portion to himself is a sin which must be shared by many other great men with whom history has not dealt so harshly.

The efforts of Themistocles to further the wish of the

---

[1] Herodotus, viii. 5.
[2] History of Greece, vol. v. p. 134.
[3] Ibid.

Euboeans were unsuccessful; and it appeared as though his success would not be greater in keeping the allies at Salamis, where success was to him and to Athens a matter of life and death. In this great strait his ready wit and rapid decision devised a secret method for determining the action of the allies, when he found that warnings and prayers were alike thrown away. But it is strange that this device has nothing to do with bribery. From the narrative of Herodotus it would seem that two-and-twenty talents of the Euboean money still remained to him; and his fiercest opponent is that very Adeimantus[1] to whom at Artemisium three talents had furnished an effectual argument for submission. But the contradictory accounts of the council which preceded the battle tend to show how little reliance can be placed on the more minute details even in this part of the history.[2] It was certainly a time at which the inducements which prevailed on Adeimantus before, might have been tried again with fair justification; but Themistocles addressed his persuasion not to the Corinthian but to the Persian leaders[3]. By the announcement that the Greeks were intent on flight, they were led to obstruct the narrow outlets between Salamis and the mainland. The stratagem was successful, but the accounts given of it are by no means consistent. The contemporary poet Æschylus[4] represents Themistocles as sending his messenger not to the Persian leaders but to Xerxes himself, and speaks of Xerxes as charging

Themistocles to Xerxes.

---

[1] Herodotus, viii. 61, &c.
[2] Grote, History of Greece, vol. v. p. 169.
[3] Herodotus, viii. 75.   [4] Persæ, 356.

his generals on their lives to see that not one of the enemy escaped them. If the message was sent (and this we can hardly doubt), the statement of the poet in this instance exceeds that of Herodotus in probability as much as his story of the passage across the Strymon passes into the regions of fiction. But throughout the narrative we are constantly obliged to resort to a balance of probabilities. The orator Isocrates appears to know nothing of the stratagem of Themistocles; Herodotus seems as little to be aware of the fact which Plutarch states, that the ostracism of Aristeides and other exiles had been revoked before the fight at Salamis, at the urgent desire of Themistocles himself.[1] The language of Herodotus appears even to contradict the supposition. He speaks of Aristeides as a man still under the sentence of ostracism, and makes the offer for the suspension of personal enmity to originate with him and not with his more fortunate rival.[2]

Revocation of the ostracism of Aristeides.

The battle which followed destroyed all chance of Persian superiority by sea, and determined Xerxes at once to abandon his army. On the eve of his flight, the messenger of Themistocles, it is said, again appeared, and told him that he might journey at his ease to the Hellespont, since his master had dissuaded the allies from sailing thither and breaking up the bridge.[3] With regard to Xerxes, the several accounts assign different objects for this second message; all seem to agree that for himself Themistocles sought by means of it to win the gratitude of the king and a refuge in the time of trouble

The second message of Themistocles to Xerxes.

---

[1] Grote, History of Greece, vol. v. pp. 151, 174.
[2] Herodotus, viii. 79.   [3] Ibid. viii. 110.

which even then he anticipated. Assuredly such a fact, if proved, would be one of the most astonishing in all history; for we are asked to believe that a man, engaged in saving his country from dangers apparently overwhelming, and struggling with the jealousy, or selfishness, or disaffection of his confederates, was actuated at one and the same moment by two entirely distinct and conflicting motives. With his whole soul he was bent on setting his country free; and yet not less earnestly was he bent on securing a place of retreat among the very enemies whom he was driving out. Such a condition of mind, we may well suppose, could have produced nothing but distraction of purpose and utter weakness in action,—a turmoil of contrary desires with which the calm judgment and profound energy of the man stand out in incomprehensible contrast. The depth of such treachery it is perhaps beyond our power to realise; some notion of it may be formed if we should suppose that when Nelson, before the fight at Trafalgar, warned every man that England looked to him to do his duty, he had already done his best to secure the future good-will of the enemies whom he was advancing to encounter. But if Herodotus represents Themistocles as holding out to Xerxes the prospect of an unmolested march, there were other, and apparently more popular versions, which spoke of him as terrifying the king by a warning that he might be intercepted on the road.[1] With statements so inconsistent, Dr. Thirlwall very justly rejects the double meaning which is alleged to lie in the message, on the ground that "such a conjecture

---

[1] Thirlwall, History of Greece, vol. ii. p. 315.

might very naturally be formed after the event, but would scarcely have been thought probable before it."[1] The sending of the message may, he thinks, be easily accounted for by the love which a man like Themistocles would feel for the arts in which he excelled for their own sake, and that the delight of conducting an intrigue might often be in itself a sufficient motive of action. Yet such a supposition would impute to him a childishness scarcely less than that which he is said to have shown in his inordinate vanity, and would rank him with the sagacious schemers who cannot eat a meal except by stratagem. But a doubt may be fairly admitted of the reality of this second message. Like many other incidents in the narrative of Herodotus, it is quite superfluous. It moves Xerxes to a resolution which he had already formed; and it implies such an utter credulity of belief as even the most credulous of fools could scarcely exhibit. His compliance with the former message had brought about the destruction of his fleet; it is impossible that he could have failed to regard the second as intended to accomplish his own. To him Themistocles could have appeared nothing but a liar; and the second message could have left him only with an impression of yet more execrable falsehood, uttered to entrap him in a yet more deadly snare.

The ostracism of Themistocles.

The treachery of Pausanias brought about the downfal of the great Athenian statesman. In his conduct to the confederate allies of Athens, Themistocles had not acquired a reputation which would of itself suffice to repel the charge of complicity with the Spartan. Still,

[1] Thirlwall, History of Greece, vol. ii. p. 314.

in spite of the efforts of Aristeides, of Kimon and
Alcmæon, the first accusation was repelled with success,
and the influence of Themistocles was strengthened only
to embitter the animosity of his opponents and redouble
the energy of their resistance. Both he and his rivals
were probably not unwilling to resort to the test of
ostracism; and the remembrance of his ancient triumph,
as well as of his more recent acquittal, might inspire Themistocles with a natural confidence in its issue. But
the tide had turned against him; and he went into
banishment not unprepared to consult more exclusively
his own interest, since he was precluded from advancing
further the interests of his country. In the day of his
power he had made little profession of a scrupulous
integrity; it was not likely that his morality would
become more fastidious in exile. If there is little reason
to question his knowledge of the designs of Pausanias,
it is not easy to see how a man like Themistocles should
have felt himself bound to reveal them.[1] But there is
no evidence that he took any active part in them himself, or that any documents were discovered after the
death of Pausanias which established the guilt of Themistocles. Still, probably, neither the remembrance of
his own failings nor his consciousness of the present
temper of his countrymen would tempt him to await at
Argos the arrival of the men who had been sent to seize
him; and after a series of strange adventures and (as
it is said) of narrow escapes, he found a refuge in the
dominions of the great king. Yet from those dominions

[1] Thirlwall, History of Greece, vol. ii. p. 384. Mr. Grote is
less lenient. History of Greece, vol. v. p. 383.

the Spartan Pausanias had been compelled to return home by the threat that his refusal would be followed by a declaration of war against him and that he would be treated as a public enemy.[1] The fact that similar measures were not held out against Themistocles would seem to disprove the statement that he remained for a year near the coast, and so within the reach of his enemies, before he went to Artaxerxes at Susa.[2]

The compact between Themistocles and Artaxerxes.

But while yet living near the coast he is said to have sent to the despot of Persia a letter written in terms which Mr. Grote admits that no modern European king would tolerate except from a quaker.[3] Of the contents of this letter, as of those sent by Pausanias, we cannot tell how Thucydides obtained his knowledge. But if the letter which the Eretrian Gongylus conveyed from the Spartan regent was too presuming and boastful to be altogether palatable to an Eastern king, it was yet free from the falsehoods which formed the substance of this letter of Themistocles. The plea that self-defence alone had led him to resist and repel the invasion of Xerxes[4], must to his son have appeared not less ridiculous than false; the boast that, as soon as he could with safety do so, he had compensated his injuries by greater benefits, must have seemed an extravagant and shameless lie. But whether the letter was sent or not, and whether it was couched in these or in

---

[1] Thucydides, i. 131. Grote, History of Greece, vol. v. p. 365.

[2] Thucydides, i. 137, 138.

[3] Grote, History of Greece, vol. v. p. 388.

[4] Thucydides, i. 137.

CONTRADICTORY ACCOUNTS OF HIS DEATH.

other phrases, the details of his journey to Susa, as well as of his sojourn in the palace, are purely fictitious. As little can we venture to determine the motives which led Artaxerxes to befriend the Athenian exile, or the terms on which he extended to him his lavish bounty. The mere fact that, during his long residence at Magnesia, he made no effort to fulfil the promise which he is said to have given, must go far to prove that no direct enterprise against the freedom of the Hellenic world could have been involved in it. The supposition of such an engagement gave rise to the tale that his death was caused by taking poison; but the story obtained no credit with Thucydides, whose account would appear to justify the inference drawn from his inactivity at Magnesia. By a version scarcely less extravagant than his tale of the rebuilding of the Athenian walls, Diodorus represents his death as a crowning stratagem to preclude all further attacks from Persia on the liberty of his country.[1]

There can be no doubt that, if he had entered into any such compact with the Persian king with any intention of fulfilling it, he had it in his power to inflict enormous damage on the growing empire of Athens. That not a single injurious act can be laid to his charge would seem to prove not merely that he cheated the great king by a series of gratuitous falsehoods, but that Artaxerxes imposed no such obligation as the price of

Probable nature of his relations with the Persian king.

---

[1] xi. 358. Compare a stratagem, very similar in its spirit, though with a different object, by the Persian satrap Harmozan when brought before Omar. Gibbon, Roman Empire, ch. li. vol. v. p. 97.

his friendship and hospitality. His degradation was great enough already without adding to it a larger measure of infamy. Like the son of Miltiades[1], the victor of Salamis, the deliverer of Athens and of Hellas had stooped to receive a Persian wife. He had prostrated himself before the footstool of a despot, and received the wages of a slave. And, as he looked back on the days of Marathon, of Salamis and Plataea, as he thought of the new field which his own wisdom and strength of purpose had opened to his countrymen, as he dwelt on the image of Athenian freedom and of a supremacy exercised not without benefit to the most unwilling member of her great confederacy, he may have felt that his punishment was fully equal to his sin. And the thought may perhaps arise that his guilt would have been not so deep, and the issue of his rivalry not so disastrous, had there existed in his day the historical tribunal before which the life and acts of Pericles were passed in strict and impartial review. We may see that the absence of restraining influence may have added strength to party faction and bitterness to personal jealousy,— that the want of full available evidence may have encouraged the growth of slander and falsehood, while it indefinitely increased the difficulty of weakening or removing a popular impression. We may understand how, with the consciousness of much demerit and with a yet keener consciousness of his unparalleled greatness, he may not have cared to confront his accusers, or have felt that a second accusation was a virtual condemnation before his cause was heard. We may learn how

[1] Herodotus, vi. 41.

he might depart into exile with enough of indignation against his countrymen to make him careless of his own reputation and of their esteem, yet with not enough of hatred to tempt him to move hand or foot against that country which owed to him her very existence, her freedom, and her greatness.

He had saved Athens from dangers such as have rarely fallen to the lot of any people: but his hands were not clean, or his heart pure; and in his later years the dross had much hidden the fine gold. Yet his vices were perhaps not greatly darker than those of Francis Bacon or Warren Hastings; while for him the plea may be urged with more of force than for Bacon or for Hastings, that much of his mean and secret dealing was intended to carry his country through a struggle for life or death. Had he lived but one generation later, the issue of his career might have more resembled the fortunes of a better if not a greater man. Like the illustrious Athenian to whom, in readiness of plan and boldness in action, he presents so striking a likeness, Lord Dundonald suffered from calumny and falsehood; but he had better ground for the assurance that the cloud would not long rest upon his name.[1] Still the failings of the man must not unduly take from the glory

The guilt of Themistocles heightened by the want of strictly contemporary historians.

---

[1] Lord Dundonald has vindicated his own fame in his "Autobiography of a Seaman;" but Themistocles is not the only man of great name, whether for good or evil, of whose actions and motives we should wish to read their own account. Probably the worst of men and of nations may suffer for lack of a history of their own fortunes written from their own point of view; and their judges are left with hints and conjectures where they might have supplied them with knowledge.

of his work; and it is no light thing if we may be permitted to believe that Themistocles was not guilty of the unspeakable and inveterate treachery which has given to his life a character of inexplicable mystery. We are not unwilling to think that, with much to mar its ancient strength, he yet carried the love of his country to the grave; and that no pledge to work the ruin of that country laid on him the guilt of superfluous treachery towards the despot who gave him a home in his unworthy and dishonoured old age.

INDEX.

Abdéra, 162.
Abydos, review of the Persian army at, 75.
Achæmenes, 57, 114.
Acropolis of Athens taken by the Persians, 132.
Adeimantus, the Corinthian, bribed by Themistocles, 119, 408; opposes the counsels of Themistocles, 133; reviles Themistocles, 136; flies from the battle of Salamis, and is brought back, 150.
Adrastus, son of Crœsus, 6.
Æacus, 137, 146.
Ægina, war between Athens and, 90, 393; meeting of the Greek fleet at, 107.
Acimnêstus, 202.
Æschylus, accounts of the Persian war by, 317, 109.
Aglauros, chapel of, 132.
Alcmæonidæ, charge against the, 341.
Alexander, the Macedonian, 97, 168; visits the Athenian generals at Platæa, 198.
Alkibiades, 404.
Amasis, king of Egypt, 18, 72, 326.
Ameinias, 146, 149.
Amestris, barbarity of, 84, 232, 380.
Amompharetus, obstinacy of, 202; bravery of, 212.
Amphiaralis, oracle of, 2.
Amphictyons, 105.
Andros, siege of, 158.

Anopæa, heights of, 107.
Aphetæ, storm at, 121.
Apis, the calf-god, 19.
Argives, the, embassy to, from Xerxes, 92, 352; inform Mardonius of the march of the Spartans, 178.
Ariabignes, death of, 148.
Aristagoras, 38, 40, 45.
Aristeides at Salamis, 144; cuts off the Persians in Psyttaleia, 151; his rivalry with Themistocles, 392; ostracism of, 406, 410.
Aristodêmus, the Spartan, 111, 112, 213, 357.
Aristogeiton and Harmodius, 20.
Aristophilides, 32.
Artabanus, son of Hystaspes, 61, 67, 76, 78, 79, 378.
Artabazus takes Olynthus, 164; besieges Potidæa, 165; flight of, from Platæa, 210; his passage through Macedonia and Thrace, 221, 350, 369.
Artaphernes, 38, 46, 47.
Artaxerxes, hospitality of, to Themistocles, 405, 414.
Artayctes plunders the treasures of Protesilaüs, 233; crucified by the Athenians, 231.
Artaÿntes, 230.
Artemisia warns Xerxes against fighting by sea, 139, 363; sinks a Calyndian ship, 147, 149, 364; advises Xerxes to accept the offer of Mardonius, 151.

Artemisium, 98; gathering of the Greek fleet at, 117; first battle at, 120; second battle at, 122.
Athenian confederacy, beginning of, 229; its effect on the power of Persia, 240.
—— democracy, character of, 285.
Athenians, their treatment of Persian heralds, 85, 336; their patriotism, 86; migration to Salamis and Troezen, 130, 358; naval tactics of the, 135; they rebuke the Spartans, 175; answer the claims of the Tegeatans, 180.
Athens, debate at, on the oracle from Delphi, 89; capture of the Acropolis of, 133; second capture of, by Mardonius, 174.
Athos, Mount, 47; canal across the isthmus of, 70, 319.
Atossa, 30, 325.
Attaginus, feast of, 179, 373; escapes from Thebes, 220.
Autonoüs and Phylacus, 128, 266.

Bakis, prophecies of, 123, 143, 151.
Boreas, 101.

Cadmus, of Cos, 96.
Callatebus, plane-tree of, 72.
Calliades, archonship of, 132.
Callias, peace of, 240 note.
Callicrates, the Lacedæmonian, 213.
Callimachus, the polemarch, 50, 240.
Cambyses, son of Cyrus, 18, 321.
Catalogue, Homeric, 248.
Charles the Great, legends of, 272.
Charopinus, 41.
Chileus, of Tegea, 176, 372.
Chilon, 113.
Chronology, artificial, 260.
Cleombrotus, brother of Leonidas, 141, 373.
Cleomenes, king of Sparta, 40.
Coës, of Mitylêné, 34.
Coincidences in the history of the Persian war, 259, 377.
Confederacy, Athenian, beginning of, 229; its results, 240.
Critalla, 71.
Crœsus, 5, 8, 9, 12, 16, 290, 351.
Cyprus, revolt of, 42.

Cyrus, 8, 10, 320.

Darius, 20, 28, 34, 42, 54, 55, 293, 326.
Datis, 47, 49.
Deïphonus, the soothsayer, 223.
Delos, earthquake at, 48.
Delphi, oracle of, 6, 8, 87, 99, 108, 159; attack on, by the Persians, miraculously defeated, 127, 359; offerings of the Greeks at, 163, 288.
Demaratus, king of Sparta, 47, 81, 106, 113, 115, 187; credibility of his history, 251.
Democracies, character of, 285.
Demokêdes, 26, 29, 31, 83, 325.
Diêneckes, wit of, 110, 357.
Dikæus at Eleusis, 137, 361.
Dodôna, oracle of, 6, 7.
Doriscus, numbering of the Persian army at, 80, 247.
Dreams, personality of, 249.

Eclipse of the sun, 73.
Egypt, revolt of, against Darius, 55; suppressed by Xerxes, 67.
Eleusis, phantom hosts of Dêmêtêr at, 187.
Ephialtes, 108.
Epizêlus, 53.
Erectheus, chapel of, 132.
Eretria, 48.
Euripus, 119, 128.
Europa, legend of, 4, 255, 307.
Eurybiades, 118, 131, 137; opposes the counsel of Themistocles, 166.
Eurytus, 111, 357.

Gargaphia, fountain of, 182.
Gelon, tyrant of Syracuse, 93; his answer to the Athenian ambassadors, 96.
Genealogies, Greek, nature and value of, 286.
Gillus, 31.
Gobryas, 31.
Gorgô, daughter of Cleomenes, 41, 116.
Greek thought, influence of, 270, 322.
Greeks, the, council of, at the Isthmus, 98; terror of, at Salamis, 142; prepare for the fight at Salamis, 146; chase the Persian fleet as far as

INDEX. 421

Andros, 151; march to Platæa, 187; tombs of, at Platæa, 219; march against Thebes, 219; take counsel for the defence of Ionia, 229; distribution of merit amongst, in the war, 254; policy, conduct, and motives of, 371, &c.

Harmokydes, 182.
Harpagus, the Median, 11, 15, 48.
Hecatæus, the writings of, 282, 328.
Hégésistratus, the soothsayer, 195.
—————— Samian, 223.
Helen, legend of, 4, 276.
Hellespont, bridge across the, 72, 248; scourging of the, 73, 245.
Heralds, treatment of Persian, 55.
Hermolycus, 228.
Hermotimus, 155.
Herodotus, birth and lifetime of, 239, 281; historical method of, 243; compared with that of Thucydides, 257; digressions of, 244; epical method of, 245; connection of events in, 247—253; credulity of, 259; marvels in the narrative of, 260, 262; character of the age of, 263; general credibility of, 265, 269, 273, 283, 314; scepticism of, 268; impartiality of, 273; prejudice of, in the case of Themistocles, 298.
Hippias, 49, 50, 341.
Histiæa, Persian fleet at, 124.
Histiæus, 26, 37, 39, 43, 45, 46, 325, 326, 330, 332.
History, Eastern, difficulty of ascertaining facts in, 323.
Hydarnes, 106, 107, 161.
Hyroiades, 11.

Inscriptions, value of, 284, 290; Greek, 291; Egyptian, 290; Assyrian, 291, 316, 317; Persian, 292.
Io, legend of, 3, 267.
Ionia, first conquest of, 15; revolt of, against Cyrus, 15, 305 note; against Xerxes, 228; against Darius, 331.
Ionians, the, ask aid after the battle of Salamis, 167.
Isocrates, panegyric of, 249 note.
Isthmus, the Corinthian, wall across, 141.

Kelænæ, 71.
Keos, 143, 366.
Kerkyra, 95.
Kynégeirus, 53, 357.
Kynosarges, 52.
Kynosûra, 143, 366.
Kythéra, 112.

Labynétus, king of Babylon, 13.
Lampón, advice of, to Pausanias, 216, 377.
Leonidas, 103, 104, 355; sends away the allies from Thermopylæ, 109; death of, 110; his body crucified by Xerxes, 115; generalship of, 356, 358.
Leotychides, 167, 222, 225.
Lykidas stoned by the Athenians, 174.

Mæandrius, 26.
Magians, the, 84, 102, 292, 321.
Marathon, 49; battle of, 52, 53, 337.
Mardonius, 47, 56, 59, 140; offers to take the place of Xerxes in carrying on the war, 163, 367; selects thirty myriads from the army, 169; sends Alexander with an offer of peace to the Athenians, 168; advances against Athens, 173; sends a second message by Murychides, 174; takes Athens, 178; advances into Megaris and retreats into Bœotia, 179; rejects the advice of Artabazus, 197; determines to fight, 198, 376; reviles the Spartans, 201; is slain at Platæa, 209; his body stolen and buried, 218.
Masistes reviles Artayntes, 230; murdered by his brother Xerxes, 232.
Masistius harasses the Greek army, 184; his death, 186; mourning for, 186.
Massagetæ, 15.
Medism of the Thessalians, 97, 98; of the Argives, 92, 352; of the Thebans, 109, 112, 220, 356; of the Phokians, 183.
Megabates, 38, 39.
Megabazus, 37.
Megistias, the soothsayer, 108, 111.
Melanthius, 41.
Mélos, massacre at, 257, 258.
Milétus, taking of, 336.

Miltiades, 26, 50, 51, 329, 340; charges against, 385, &c.; treatment of, by the Athenians, 388.
Mitrobates, 21.
Mnésiphilus, counsel of, 134, 264.
Môs, 168.
Musæus, prophecies of, 151, 264.
Mycalè, the battle of, 223, 227; sign of the herald's staff at, 226, 279; Phêmê, or Rumour at, 226, 279; results of, 229—241.
Mygdonia, lions in, 84, 349.
Myrkinus, 57, 330.
Mythology, comparative, 318.

Naxos, expedition of Aristagoras to, 333.
Nineveh, conquest of, by Kyaxares, 5.

Œobazus, 232; is sacrificed to the god of the Apsinthians, 234.
Œroè, island of, 212.
Olive tree, sign of the, in the chapel of Erectheus, 138, 362.
Olynthus, capture of, by Artabazus, 165.
Onomacritus, the soothsayer, 87, 303.
Oracles, 87, 94, 99, 108, 168, 158, 205; evidence for, 296, 303; classification of, 300—305; historical value of, 306.
Oreithyia, 101.
Orestes, 24, 77.
Œbryades, legend of, 291.

Pæonians, the, cheat Xerxes, 160; transportation of, 330.
Parûtes, 557.
Patizeithes, 19.
Pausanias, the Spartan regent, sent with the army from Sparta, 177; alters the disposition of the army at Platæa, 200; protects the daughter of Hegetoridas, 214; rejects the advice of Lampôn, 215; compares Spartan with Persian fare, 216, 377; charges against, 399, 403, 414.
Peisistratidæ, the, expulsion of, 20; aid in the siege of the Acropolis, 132; intrigues of, 331.
Peisistratus, 9.
Persian fleet damaged by storms, 101;

defeated at Salamis, 146; and at Mycalè, 224.
Persian war, the, legendary causes of, 2, 5, 266, 267; character of, 242, 321; connection of events in, 247—253; coincidences in the history of, 253; religious causation of events in, 253, 256.
Phalêrum, the Persian fleet at, 138.
Pheidippides, the runner, 49.
Phêmê, or Rumour, before the battle of Mycalè, 278.
Phœnicians, punishment of the, by Xerxes, 149, 206.
Phoklans on Anopæa, 108; in the Persian camp, 182.
Phokis, invasion of, by the Persians, 126.
Phrynichus, tragedy of, 336.
Phylacus and Autonoüs, 128, 266.
Platæa, 50, 51; the Greek army at, 187; battle of, 205—209.
Polycrates, 21—27, 315, 326.
Polycritus, 149.
Poseidon, 102.
Potidæa, siege of, by Artabazus, 165.
Prôtesíláüs, the hero, 234.
Psammenitus, 18.
Psyttaleia, 143, 151.
Pylagoræ, 106.
Pythagoras, of Miletus, 45.
Pytheas, of Ægina, 99, 357.
Pythius, story of, 71, 74, 345.

Sacrifices, human, 84.
Salamis, Greek fleet at, 129; council on the shore of, 135; preparations for the fight at, 146; victory of the Greeks at, 147—150; examination of the narrative of the battle at, 361.
Samians, the, deprived of their arms by the Persians, 225.
Sandanis, the counsel of, 9, 320.
Sardes, capture of, by Cyrus, 11; by the Ionians, 42.
Scythia, expedition of Darius into, 34; its credibility, 327.
Sestos, siege of, by the Athenians, 234.
Sikinnus, first embassy of, to Xerxes, 142, 408; second embassy of, 157, 410.
Skyllias, the diver, 119, 357.

INDEX. 423

Smerdis, brother of Cambyses, 19.
———, the Magian, 19, 292, 321.
Sôphanes, of Dekeleia, 212.
Spartans, the, epitaphs of, at Thermopylæ, 111; claim recompense for the murder of Leonidas, 160; embassy of, to Athens, 170; send out an army under Pausanias, 176, 372.
Stesichorus, version of the Trojan legend by, 276.
Strymon, bridge across the, 71.
Syagrus, the Spartan, 95.

Tegeatans, rivalry between the, and the Athenians, 188.
Thales, of Miletos, 2.
Thebans, the, 109, 112, 220; motives of, in the war, 356.
Themistocles receives thirty talents from the Eubœans, 118, 407; device of, to detach the Ionians from Xerxes, 123; threatens Eurybiades with the desertion of the Athenians, 137; sends Sikinnus to Xerxes, 142, 408; sends Aristeides into the council of the Greeks, 145; urges the Greeks to sail to the Hellespont and destroy the bridge, 155; sends a second message by Sikinnus to Xerxes, 157, 410; is received with honour at Sparta, 164; definite policy of, 311, 392; character of the age of, 391; contrast between, and Aristeides, 392; mixed character of, 393; charges against, 400, 403; comparison of, with Pausanias and Alkibiades, 404; ostracism of, 412; nature of his relations with Artaxerxes, 416.
Thermopylæ, 98; gathering of the Greek army at, 103; last battle in, 109; sight-seeing of the Persians in, 124; difficulties in the narrative of the battles in, 353.
Thersander, tale of, 180, 375.
Thespians, 109.
Thessalians, the, request of, for aid from the Greeks, 97; demand fifty talents from the Phokians, 126.
Thorax, of Larissa, 173, 205.
Thucydides, treatment of myths by, 246 note; climax in the history of, 257; his judgment of Themistocles, 397, 413.

Tigranes, 224, 228.
Timagenidas, 196, 220.
Timocreon, the Rhodian, 406.
Timodêmus, 165.
Timon, of Delphi, 88.
Timoxenus, 165.
Tisamenus, the soothsayer, 194.
Tomyris, queen of the Massagetæ, 15, 320.
Tradition, oral, character of, 274; vehicles of, 275; conditions favourable to, 283.
———, Vedic, 277; Mahometan, 279; Mediæval, 280.
Tritantæchmes, saying of, 125.

War of Athens with Ægina, 90, 391.
———, Persian, the, legendary causes of, 3, 5, 266, 267; character of, 242, 281; connection of events in, 247—253; coincidences in the history of, 253; religious causation of events in, 256.

Xanthippus, 167, 232, 214.
Xeinagoras, 230.
Xerxes succeeds his father Darius, 56, 56; council of, 58—65, 342; visions of, 65—70; converses with Demaratus, 81, 105, 113; dismisses the Greek spies unhurt, 91; sends an embassy to Argos, 92; numbers of the army of, 100, 246; crucifies the body of Leonidas, 116; sends the news of his good fortune to Susa, 133; inspects the fleet at Phalêrum, 138; consults Artemisia before fighting by sea, 139, 363; praises Artemisia for sinking the Calyndian ship, 148; punishes the Phœnicians, 149; determines on flight, 151; sends news of his defeat to Susa, 152; consults Artemisia respecting the offer of Mardonius, 154, 367; retreats through Bœotia, 159, 368; leaves Mardonius to atone for the death of Leonidas, 160, 373; is cheated by the Pæonians, 161, 349; reaches Sardes, 161; abandons the wife of Masistes to Amestris, 231, 380; murders Masistes, 232.

Zôstêr, rocks at Cape, 135, 267.

LONDON
PRINTED BY SPOTTISWOODE AND CO.
NEW-STREET SQUARE

www.ingramcontent.com/pod-product-compliance
Lightning Source LLC
Chambersburg PA
CBHW022059300426
44117CB00007B/516